TEACHING
⧮ AFRICAN AMERICAN ⧮
LITERATURE

Transforming
Teaching
Series

Series Editor: James W. Fraser
Director of the Center for Innovation in
Urban Education Northeastern University

Routledge's Transforming Teaching Series represents a commitment to support teachers in the practice of their profession. Each volume in this series will link clritical educational theory to very specific examples of successful classroom practice and detailed descriptions of the kinds of curricular materials which are most useful in implementing theory in practice. Each volume will explroe the political barriers and intellectual issues involved in implementing new forms of practice. While each volume and each editor will take a different approach, all of the volumes will be united in addressing primarily the concerns of teachers—and students in teacher education programs—and in combining the voices of thoughtful theorists and currently practicing classroom teachers.

Also published in the series:

Assessment for Equity and Inclusion: Embracing All Our Children
A. Lin Goodwin, editor

Real Learning, Real Work: School-to-Work as High School Reform
Adria Steinberg

Unauthorized Methods: Strategies for Critical Teaching
Joe L. Kincheloe and Shirley R. Steinberg

TEACHING
₿₿ AFRICAN AMERICAN ₿₿
LITERATURE

Theory and Practice

edited by
Maryemma Graham,
Sharon Pineault-Burke,
and Marianna White Davis

Routledge
New York and London

Published in 1998 by
Routledge
29 West 35th Street
New York, NY 10001

Published in Great Britain by
Routledge
11 New Fetter Lane
London EC4P 4EE

Library of Congress Cataloging-in-Publication Data

Teaching African American literature : theory and practice / edited by
    Maryemma Graham, Sharon Pineault-Burke, Marianna White Davis.
        p. cm.
    Includes bibliographical references and index.
    ISBN 0-415-91695-X   0-415-91696-8 (pbk.)
    1. American literature—Afro-American authors—Study and teaching.
    2. American literature—Afro-American authors—Study and teaching—
    Theory, etc.   3. Afro-Americans—Intellectual life—Study and teaching.
    4. Afro-Americans in literature—Study and teaching.
    I. Graham, Maryemma.   II. Pineault-Burke, Sharon
    III. Davis, Marianna White   .
    PS153.N5T4   1997
810.9'8986073'07—dc21   97-19580
                                                                    CIP

☐: CONTENTS :☐

To teachers everywhere

ⵀ: ACKNOWLEDGMENTS :ⵀ

Our first and most important acknowledgment is to our chapter authors who have worked with us through this process of writing and editing. Beyond the chapter editors, we would like to thank Jennifer Novak, who provided excellent editorial assistance and bibliographic research. This volume would not have been possible without her diligence, hard work, and cool head, and her superb attention to detail. Thanks also to Ronald Bailey, James Fraser, and Stuart Peterfreund (Northeastern University) and Daniel F. Burke and Paul Sheppard for their encouragement and support, as well as to Carol Doherty, Angela Irving, Leslye Smith, Ralou Athas, Jean Duddy, and Elizabeth Wallace of Northeastern University, to Amy Kautzman of Harvard University, and Leslie Sanders of York University, who gave generously of their time on the bibliography. Thanks also to Patricia O'Neil of Northeastern University, H. Tiajuana Malone, and James Coffey. The entire staff wishes to thank Kelley Norman, superior researcher, writer, and editor, whose dedication to the Project on the History of Black Writing since 1991 makes her always available to do next-to-impossible texts.

We especially want to acknowledge the dedication of all of the teacher scholars who participated in the NEH Summer Institutes during 1993 and 1994, and particularly Roberta Hoke and Carole LaBonte of South Boston High School, Carol Leonard of Plymouth South High School, and Eileen Sadof of the Broad Meadows Middle School in Quincy. We are grateful to Annette Palmer and the National Endowment for the Humanities for continuing to fund important projects in humanities education.

WHEN TEACHING MATTERS

Maryemma Graham
Northeastern University

It has become commonplace lately to castigate that most honorable of professions—teaching. This is especially the case when we need to explain why our schools are in crisis and why our children are failing. We seem to want and need to make teachers bear far too much if not all of the responsibility for a society that cannot produce productive citizens united around a vibrant national vision or competent enough to meet the demands of an increasingly globalized economy. All of this seems to justify additional budget cuts and downsizing, making a most unlikely marriage with politically charged debates over multiculturalism and democratic values. Teachers are often defenseless against their attackers, powerless to act out their own sense of worth, their silence born of the fear that they cannot keep the promises they made to themselves when they began their careers.

I long ago made my peace with this debate. Teachers are, quite simply, a quick and easy target. Whether in the trenches of inner-city schools or tucked away in more elite suburbs, parochial or private schools, which bring an entirely different set of problems, most teachers are on the margins of contemporary discussions of education theory and practice or have limited access to the weighty discourses of race and ethnicity, deconstruction, postmodernism, feminism, ethnic

1

and cultural studies. The irony is these debates keep raging while teachers keep doing more with less. Nowhere was this more apparent than at the two NEH-sponsored institutes on the teaching of African American literature in the summers of 1993 and '94. It was here that their silence was broken, and we heard voices that we wanted to share with others.

There is, of course, a much longer story behind this collection of essays. Part of that story involves the recognition that we needed to provide a more public forum where the teachers could tell their own stories. In so doing, we could help bridge the widening gap between content and pedagogy. But we all agreed that these stories could not stand alone. The teaching of literature is a process whereby we are constantly making meaning from texts that imply a wide range of questions about life and living in realistic, speculative, and dramatic ways. As we observed the unfolding of African American literature from Phillis Wheatley to Toni Morrison, it was clear that teachers have a critical need to be part of an ongoing intellectual community that allows them to rebuild and reinforce their knowledge base through open exchange, dialogue, and debate. In other words, teachers do not want to be handed down judgments about any literature, and especially not about African American literature. They do want to be assisted with the process of engaging new literatures critically and holistically.

Day after day for a total of nine weeks spread over the two summers, we read, discussed, reacted, and questioned, burying myths and challenging our own as well as others' preconceptions about African American literature and culture. We were mostly women, and because we fully acknowledged the differences among us—racial, national, religious, and political—we grew stronger in our commitment to forge a community of teacher scholars. I take this to mean the process whereby an individual can effectively combine analysis and criticism with teaching/learning strategies. This book continues this process of community building. It recognizes that the most desirable community is made up of many different people, not all of whom will contribute in the same way, but who share a vision and a language for articulating that vision. Some have argued that such a language in literary studies is nonexistent for today's typical teacher, who is prevented scholarly access by the very nature of academic discourse. On the other hand, the intellectual rigor and excitement generated in our sessions were contagious, and I believe the sessions signaled the birth of a new dialogue in which university scholars and teachers could both participate.

We were fortunate in that all of us who embrace the label "teacher," regardless of the level, would not and could not sit passively but longed to experience what we wanted our students to experience. We are the models of our own goals in this sense. These models and this dialogue is what this volume is about.

If I had my way, this book would be a two-volume work. One volume would display the richness of our conversations as teachers came to terms with what was presented to them by leading scholars in the field of African American literature and cultural studies. The work of these scholars would comprise a second volume. Given the highly charged debates over multiculturalism, teachers naturally brought with them a wide range of conceptions and a burning desire to know more than they had been given an opportunity to learn. I think what they found was that the learning process for them, just as for their students, is being constantly challenged. Over the past twenty-five years, as conceptual and methodological innovations have affected the study and teaching of literature, including transformations of literary canons, we have seen our teaching practices expand in new and exciting directions. The debates about literature are contentious, and teachers are at best cautious about entering these debates. Our assignment was to complete a fairly comprehensive syllabus containing African American texts that are only rarely included in the traditional canon, few of which any teacher there had ever read.

My assumption, one shared by many who teach and write about African American literature, was that we come to know traditional canons shaped by exclusions of varying degrees based on race, gender, class, ethnicity, nationality, region, and sexuality. These exclusions become the codes through which we legitimize, interpret, and value experience and make meaning in our daily lives. The teachers' response was guided by an overwhelming desire to better instruct their students and hence bring more knowledge into the classroom. I found

3

them more open than most of my own colleagues, less polemical, more willing to suspend judgment, but always forcing intelligibility to the forefront. When they are able to transfer these qualities to the classroom, the results are astounding.

Marianna Davis began her teaching career in 1949 when racial segregation was the official mandate rather than the current de facto one. She used what she had learned and what she was born into to create an interdisciplinary learning environment for her students. For her, African American literature became an enabling site where the affective and the cognitive could merge. Her strategies worked because she and her students had a common history and because she could inspire in them a strong desire to excel. Today nearly fifty years later, with her knowledge considerably expanded and a career of stellar achievements established, she uses the same strategy. Even when there is no shared history, she makes sure that her "students"—today, a host of teachers around the world— can extract certain meanings from the narrative of her own extraordinary life as a master teacher.

Davis's essay "Teaching Against the Odds" recalls the story of Selena, one of the first young women she encountered in her teaching career. We include it here to remind us that our social environment may shape who we are but does not dictate what we must become. This is the subtext in the essays by Jane Skelton, Connie Borab, and Kate Coon, all of whom have learned how to reshape their teaching experiences to respond positively and meaningfully to a classroom filled with intellectual, emotional, and sexual intensities. The youngest of our teachers, Beth Swanson Goldberg, admittedly traverses the theoretical terrain more than the others, and yet does so without doing a disservice to what is central to education: how students learn.

For William L. Andrews, Bernard Bell, Thadious Davis, Trudier Harris, Leslie Sanders, and Jerry W. Ward, scholars who do primary research on African American autobiography, fiction, poetry, and drama, the institute fostered an awareness that even the most sophisticated research, when made accessible, can be the basis for transforming the classroom curriculum and energizing both teacher and student. Too many teachers reported how bogged down they are with teaching seven or eight classes a day, every day, unable to keep up with the pace of scholarship and the often esoteric discourse it is embedded in. Teachers speak very articulately about their marginalization in an academic environment that fosters insularity.

We learned very early that this volume could not reproduce the intensity of those two summers. Nor could we expect to present the work of every teacher in a form ready for public consumption. Four essays by teacher scholars in our institute are included in this volume. Connie Borab, Kate Coon, Marianna Davis, and Jane Skelton met the challenge. I say challenge because this project involved numerous meetings, drafts, and rewrites, carving out almost nonexistent time from all-too-busy teacher schedules. The efforts of Sharon Pineault-Burke, who made herself available and worked untiringly as our teachers' editor reflects our commitment to writing as a collaborative process. And though these appear as single authored texts, they are often the result of extensive conversations and strong editorial intervention. A final "teacher" essay is by Elizabeth Swanson Goldberg, who was not an original member of our institute. She is one of my former graduate students for whom teacherly issues are of primary importance.

The absence of more essays by teachers themselves, while disappointing at first, has led us to consider making better use of another important "document" from our institutes: an extensive collection of video and audio tapes from almost every session. We hope that we can develop edited video and/or audio versions of key discussions to highlight our strong belief that the integrity of our teachers' experience is the final authority for the value of this volume. In fact, we are proposing this compilation to the National Endowment for the Humanities and would suggest to others who organize institutes that gathering such a record, done in a manner that does not intrude on the ongoing process, would be a valuable contribution from practicing teachers to our collective knowledge.

What our project for those two summers focused on mostly was canon revision, expanding what teachers and students see as their cultural legacies and possibilities. What is to be gained when students are taught to think critically about any subject or situation, especially when they can use their own experiences as a filter? Teachers count their success when their students can enter any discourse community,

5

take a stand, and be heard by others. These essays talk long and hard about how teachers must prepare students with language skills and must instill the courage to use them.

As the above suggests, this institute was not about taking a position on one or another side of the culture wars. We did no Hirsch-baiting, opposing his position on cultural literacy with our own positions on canonical revision. As a result, many of these essays are not committed to overhauling an educational system that demands that teachers transmit specific quantifiable knowledge. Rather they display a paradigm shift in education today: a shift from the privileging of master narratives—and not their elimination, as some would claim—to a more critical engagement with these narratives.

We would counter Hirsch's view, however, that studying minority literature denies us a proper dose of cultural literacy. Jerry W. Ward's essay "To Shatter Innocence: Teaching African American Poetry" makes a strong case for why culturally literate Americans need to know more than Robert Frost and Shelley. For our teachers, the issues were never abstract. What does one do with the prevailing representations of one-dimensional black characters in canonical literature? How does one address the silent questions and sullen faces of students when they are confronted with this literature? Toni Morrison's elaboration of this question is revealing. The question is not so much about the distortion of black culture and identity or the devaluing of African American literature, but about how we can create an entire national literature in which black forms and stories are curiously absent. Studying African American literature is more than just an effort to rescue the self-esteem of our youth; it allows a broader presentation of humanity as well.

The study of race, gender, and class as part of the context of literature leaves us open to the charge that education has become a political project rather than an ideal pursuit. But we must remember that this is a context we have inherited, not one we invented. And honoring a sense of the complexity of our history, this approach to the study of literature in context becomes one important task of education. The study of African American literature in particular highlights one of the central issues in teacher training in the last quarter century. The academic and professional experience of today's typical educator has yet to integrate fully the study of various literary traditions. Thus despite the social movements of the 1960s, which brought ethnic studies to colleges and universities throughout the nation, the multicultural education agenda of the 1990s says to us that these movements did not go nearly far or deep enough. Only the site has changed. The literary and cultural traditions made visible by those movements still must intertwine and engage each other for a deeper, broader, and more challenging view of humanity. This must necessarily be the next paradigm shift.

The slave narrative is America's only indigenous literary form. The irony is that this literature, produced by a community of people for whom it was illegal to read or write, is at the center of modern American fiction of black and white writers alike. William L. Andrews's essay "Narrating Slavery" delineates theoretical and discursive strategies that were in no way static for early writers such as Frederick Douglass or Booker T. Washington, just as they were not for Richard Wright, Zora Neale Hurston, James Baldwin, Malcolm X, or Maya Angelou, their twentieth-century counterparts. A similar history of white authorship treats the black experience from an autobiographical perspective, including, for example, works by Harriet Beecher Stowe and Mark Twain. That shifted with the controversy over William Styron's *Confessions of Nat Turner* (1967). According to Andrews, at that point white writers relinquished the slave narrative genre, a fact that dramatized its successful reemergence in the 1970s by black writers.

Kate Coon follows a similar logic in her discussion of the relevance of studying African American literature. A "rip in the tent," a metaphor borrowed from Toni Morrison, is Coon's way of framing the impact and meaning of African American literature: it provides access to the "soul" of our country and invites us to enter a broader discussion of American literature and public life. For Coon, African American literature belongs to everyone. Not simply adding traditionally muted voices to the canon, but recognizing and hearing them, is the point. Teacher educators must have a "respectful attentiveness," says Coon, and she urges teachers to do their homework. All teachers must challenge their own assumptions about race. And for those who are nonblack, this may remove any doubts about teaching the literature of

7

other races and cultures. Coon reminds us that to understand one of the most canonized and highly revered American texts, *The Adventures of Huckleberry Finn*, we must recognize Twain's debt to the slave narratives, which were popular at that time, and his associations with black contemporaries Charles Chesnutt and Frederick Douglass. This intertextuality is relevant to the often repeated question, "Is African American literature worth studying?" To question the legitimacy of African American literature is to continue to render African American people invisible in literature as well as in life.

Even when African American people have a visible presence in literature, there is no guarantee that the images projected are sufficiently complex. Jane Skelton, for example, in "Multiple Voices, Multiple Identities," offers her students a wide range of images to combat the limiting histories they have inherited and to get them to participate more actively in their own learning process. The emotional investment is reminiscent of black adolescents watching a movie with a predominantly black cast where the call-and-response mode operates between them and the screen characters. From her experience, Skelton notes that students do identify with literature and oral language so that they can make a personal connection with the decisions and discoveries implied. Skelton concludes that if students are able to reflect on diverse representations of the human experience, they are in the position to recognize many different voices and claim new identities for themselves. Skelton's preference for and use of dramatic literature such as Alice Childress's *Trouble in Mind* to engage her students more interactively compares with Lesley Sanders's careful explication of *Little Ham*, a play that allowed Langston Hughes to make some breakthroughs in the black comic tradition. The performance of this play by institute teachers allowed Sanders to focus on the way that performance of black theater links itself to self-invention and representation as critical modes for understanding African American history and culture.

These voices and identities are not always without conflict, however. Constance Borab offers a psychological reading of the ways girls are silenced in the classroom. Supported by the work of Carol Gilligan (*In a Different Voice*), Borab shares her experiences with "Freeing the Female Voice," which made her rethink black women's voices as contrasted with male voices in African American literature. Borab discerns that her students enter texts through personal query rather than objective knowledge, an understanding that evolved out of her teaching experiences in an all-girls school. When we ask female students to start out analyzing objectively, separating from the emotional, spiritual, and psychological truths of their lives, we are asking them, in Gilligan's words, to "go underground." Borab also had to reframe her understanding of resistance, coming to see it as characteristic of African American core values essential in a race-conscious society.

Thadious Davis frames her discussions of voice within the broader context of black male subjectivity. While representations of the female are ever present in African American literature in the work of male and female authors, Davis details an evolving masculinity that reaches its height with Richard Wright in the 1940s. This masculine project is complicated by various racialized notions of manhood, double consciousness, and consistent efforts to contextualize and combat essentialized notions of black selfhood derived from the literary marketplace. Bernard Bell and Jerry W. Ward take up double consciousness as a theme in shaping either the hybrid tradition on the African American novel (Bell) or the oral traditions in African American poetry and vernacular literature (Ward).

In a final teacher essay, "The Way We Do the Things We Do: Enunciation and Effect in the Multicultural Classroom," Elizabeth Swanson Goldberg makes some startling revelations in a college composition classroom. Incorporating a film by a white author into a syllabus where African American literature is the focus highlights the racialized nature of all American literature, both popular and formal. Goldberg concludes that teachers must become conscious of displacement. Our students have absorbed some dangerous tendencies in a society that organizes identity characteristics in an unwritten hierarchy ranging from acceptable to intolerable. She believes that our primary task must be the undoing of these hierarchical categories, especially those that reinforce prevailing stereotypes of blackness, gayness, and poorness.

AnnLouise Keating is the second contributor who was not a participant in the summers' institutes. She is included here because of the clarity with which she addresses a central concern of all our participants. She explores one of the most fundamental ways in which hierarchies are ascribed in literature—that which surrounds the category of "race"—and she points to the difficulties in analyzing "white as a racialized category." Drawing on Toni Morrison's *Playing in the Dark* and other texts, she shows how rare discussions of "whiteness" as a racial category are, and how "this invisible omnipresence gives 'whiteness' a rarely acknowledged position of dominance and power." In "interrogating whiteness," however, Keating arrives at a second pivotal insight: "the way theorists who attempt to deconstruct 'race' often inadvertently reconstruct it by reinforcing the belief in permanent, separate racial categories." Important to her analysis is her actual classroom practice with her students as she seeks to present to them the theoretical debates over analyzing "raceness" in literature, and to encourage them to think critically about how these categories influence the making of literature and the making of literary canons.

"Lying Through our Teeth? The Quagmire of Cultural Diversity," by Trudier Harris, brings together many of the goals and hopes expressed in other essays. Put simply, we want our students to apply what they learn to their everyday lives. By questioning some of our current practices, Harris challenges us to further the project of education reform. How can diversity be real when our institutions are still racially separated? Urban schools in many cities are more segregated than ever before. For Harris, studying African American literature isn't enough to achieve diversity. Willful engagement is the only means of acquiring meaningful vested relationships between colored and noncolored peoples, for without it, there is only polite conversation, polemic prattle, or warfare. If the first step to cultural diversity is to transform our perceptions of the world we live in and the people we share it with, literature may be the most effective vehicle for transformation. Education is truly transformative, argues Harris, when it allows us to move across the barriers that history and custom have put in our way.

I do not believe that we can accomplish the formidable task of "reconstructing instruction" without a reconceptualization of literary history and the canon. We must make our students and ourselves more cognizant of the dynamics of value coding, and encourage them and ourselves to question structures of intelligibility and legitimacy based

INTRODUCTION: WHEN TEACHING MATTERS

on exclusionary practices. We need sustained partnerships and dialogues between our teachers in our schools and scholars in higher education. Teaching African American literature presents a particular challenge because its texts keep their literariness at the same time they position readers to consider new ways of seeing the world and the self. These insights undergird this volume as part of an ongoing process of educational revitalization. Success for us will ultimately be determined by the extent to which our students think critically, read with understanding, and develop and sustain democratic values as they meet the demands of an increasingly complex society and economy. These "habits of the mind" must be inculcated whether students go from high school into the work force immediately or on to higher education.

As teachers break the silence about what they do in our nation's schools, we will come to value their contributions to developing the kinds of students and citizens we need for the twenty-first century and the third millennium. We are also likely to gain more confidence in the ability of these teachers to direct the next paradigm shift in literature and, more broadly, in education.

11

▪ 1 ▪

NARRATING SLAVERY

William L. Andrews
The University of North Carolina at Chapel Hill

PART I
History of African American Autobiography

The autobiographical narratives of former slaves comprise one of the most extensive and influential traditions in African American literature and culture. The slave narrative is now probably the single most widely studied literary tradition in African American literature. Slave narratives are assuming increasing prominence in major anthologies of American literature, in reevaluations of the mid-nineteenth-century American literary renaissance, and in courses, both undergraduate and graduate, devoted to the history of American first-person narrative. Scholars now recognize the slave narrative's profound resonance in, and sometimes its direct influence on, classic white American fiction, as well as many modern African American novels, and some of the most popular black autobiographies of the post–World War II era.

The best-known slave narratives were written by fugitives from slavery who used their personal histories to illustrate its horrors. They probably did not think that their eyewitness reports of their experiences in slavery would lead to literary distinction in their own day—and certainly not in ours. Nevertheless, many of the most important figures in

African American literature before 1900, including Frederick Douglass, William Wells Brown, and Harriet Jacobs, launched their writing careers via the slave narrative. After the turn of the century, a single former slave's autobiography, Booker T. Washington's *Up from Slavery* (1901), overshadowed all other black narratives, fictional and nonfictional, for at least the first four decades of this century, until the publication of Richard Wright's *Native Son* (1940). The most celebrated post–World War II African American novel, Ralph Ellison's *Invisible Man* (1952), has often been associated with patterns and themes pioneered in the slave narrative. The great popularity of *The Autobiography of Malcolm X* (1965) in the 1960s, surely the most influential African American autobiography of our time, revived interest in and study of the slave narrative—mainly because Malcolm's autobiography revoices some of the most important patterns and themes of the slave narrative tradition. And the slave narrative continues to make its presence felt in recent fiction by African Americans, spawning the term "neoslave narrative" as a classification for some of the most powerful and influential novels of the last forty years, including Toni Morrison's *Beloved* (1987), winner of a Pulitzer Prize, and Charles Johnson's *Middle Passage* (1990), which won a National Book Award.

The slave narrative's impact on prominent works of fiction in white American literature has been considerable. For instance, the most widely read and hotly debated American novel of the nineteenth century, Harriet Beecher Stowe's *Uncle Tom's Cabin* (1852), was profoundly influenced by its author's reading of a number of slave narratives, especially *Narrative of the Life of Frederick Douglass* (1845) and *The Life of Josiah Henson . . . as Narrated by Himself* (1849). To these and other ex-slave autobiographies Stowe readily admitted she owed many graphic incidents and the models for some of the most memorable characters in her novel, including Uncle Tom himself and George Harris.

What is Mark Twain's classic *Adventures of Huckleberry Finn* (1884) if not the story of a runaway slave's search for freedom? Mark Twain's knowledge of and participation in the slave narrative tradition was not slight. I would argue that *Adventures of Huckleberry Finn* is his most notable contribution to the tradition, though in some ways that novel constitutes an unfortunate revision of some of the slave narrative's

classic themes. The key thing is to recognize that the two most important works of fiction created in the United States in the entire nineteenth century—*Uncle Tom's Cabin* and *Adventures of Huckleberry Finn*
—are both steeped in the slave narrative tradition and are themselves
contributions to it.

In the twentieth century, consider the fate of William Styron's *Confessions of Nat Turner*, which won a Pulitzer Prize in 1967. Styron's
novel is based on a slave narrative published in 1831 and widely read
in the North and South. Styron's novel was tremendously influential
and controversial, so much so that a weighty book, Albert Stone's *The
Return of Nat Turner* (1992), has been published recently on the novel
and its cultural impact in the 1960s. Styron's novel is the last of a
breed of fiction that goes back to the early nineteenth century, in
which a white author writes a slave narrative using the slave's point of
view (see also Richard Hildreth's *Archy Moore*, 1836; or Mattie Grif-
fiths's *The Autobiography of a Female Slave*, 1857). What does it mean
that whites stopped writing slave narratives after Styron's novel? And
indeed, that whites stopped writing novels through the point of view
of blacks after that book? Did the furor over Styron's appropriation of
Nat Turner signal a necessary stage in the twentieth-century liberation
of the slave narrative from the agenda of white literature, so that it
could reemerge in the 1970s and beyond as a key enabling tradition
for African American literature?

But perhaps in getting so far into recent literary history I have not
taken enough time to outline the history of the slave narrative proper
and its place in the history of African American autobiography.

More than any other literary form in African American letters, autobiography has been celebrated since its inception in the slave narrative
as a powerful means of addressing and altering sociopolitical as well as
cultural realities in the United States. Nineteenth-century abolitionists
sponsored the publication of the narratives of escaped slaves out of a
conviction that first-person accounts of those victimized by and yet
triumphant over slavery would mobilize white readers more profoundly than any other kind of antislavery discourse. A similar belief
in modern black American autobiography's potential to liberate white

14

readers from racial prejudice, ignorance, and fear has prompted an unusually large and generally supportive response on the part of publishers, reviewers, and critics to African American autobiographers of the twentieth century, particularly since the 1960s.

During the formative era of African American autobiography, from 1760 to the end of the Civil War in the United States, approximately seventy narratives of fugitive or former slaves were published as discrete entities, some in formats as brief as the broadside, others in bulky, sometimes multivolume texts. Slave narratives dominated the literary landscape of antebellum black America, far outnumbering the autobiographies of free people of color and the handful of novels published by American blacks during this time. After slavery was abolished in North America, ex-slaves continued to produce narratives of their bondage and freedom in substantial numbers. From 1865 to 1930, during which time at least fifty former slaves wrote or dictated book-length accounts of their lives, the ex-slave narrative remained the preponderant subgenre of African American autobiography. During the Depression of the 1930s, the Federal Writers' Project gathered oral personal histories and testimony about slavery from two thousand five hundred former slaves in seventeen states, generating roughly ten thousand pages of interviews that were eventually published by George P. Rawick in a "composite autobiography" of nineteen volumes. Marion Wilson Starling, one of the slave narratives' most reliable historians, has estimated that a grand total of all contributions to this genre, including separately published texts, materials that appeared in periodicals, and oral histories and interviews, numbers approximately six thousand.

The earliest slave narratives have strong affinities with popular white American accounts of Indian captivity and Christian conversion in the New World. But with the rise of the antislavery movement in the early nineteenth century came a new demand for slave narratives that would highlight the harsh realities of slavery itself. White abolitionists were convinced that the eyewitness testimony of former slaves would touch the hearts and change the minds of many in the northern United States who were either ignorant of or indifferent to the plight of African Americans in the South. In the late 1830s and early 1840s the first of this

15

new brand of outspokenly antislavery slave narratives found their way into print. These set the mold for what would become by midcentury a standardized form of autobiography and abolitionist propaganda.

Typically the antebellum slave narrative carries a black message inside a white envelope. Prefatory (and sometimes appended) matter by whites attests to the reliability and good character of the narrator and calls attention to what the narrative will reveal about the moral abominations of slavery. The former slave's contribution to the text centers on his or her rite of passage from slavery in the South to freedom in the North. Usually the antebellum slave narrator portrays slavery as a condition of extreme physical, intellectual, emotional, and spiritual deprivation, a kind of hell on earth. Precipitating the narrator's decision to escape is some sort of personal crisis, such as the sale of a loved one or a dark night of the soul in which hope contends with despair for the spirit of the slave. Impelled by faith in God and a commitment to liberty and human dignity comparable (the slave narrative often stresses) to that of America's Founding Fathers, the slave undertakes an arduous quest for freedom that climaxes in his or her arrival in the North. In many antebellum narratives, the attainment of freedom is signaled not simply by reaching the free states but by renaming oneself and dedicating one's future to antislavery activism.

Advertised in the abolitionist press and sold at antislavery meetings throughout the English-speaking world, a significant number of antebellum slave narratives went through multiple editions and sold in the tens of thousands. The first of the great slave narratives, Olaudah Equiano's *Interesting Narrative of the Life of Olaudah Equiano, or Gustavus Vassa, the African*, went through eight editions in Great Britain between 1789 and 1794, despite the fact that Equiano's was a two-volume autobiography and therefore not inexpensive to obtain. Moses Roper's fugitive slave narrative of 1838 went through ten editions in twenty years. Solomon Northup's story sold twenty-seven thousand copies in its first two years of publication. Numerous slave narratives were simultaneously published in England and the United States, and more than a handful were translated into such European languages as French, German, Dutch, even Celtic.

This popularity was not solely attributable to the publicity the narratives received from the antislavery movement. Readers could see that, as one reviewer put it, "the slave who endeavours to recover his freedom is associating with himself no small part of the romance of the time." To the noted transcendentalist clergyman Theodore Parker, slave narratives qualified as America's only indigenous literary form, for "all the original romance of Americans is in them, not in the white man's novel." White reviewers of fugitive slave narratives often compared these questing slaves with the heroes of European epic or with the ideals of the American "irrepressible desire to be free." Emerson foresaw and welcomed an increasingly democratic American literature in the 1850s, a literature that would replace "the sublime and beautiful" with "the near, the common, and the low." *The Dial,* launched in 1840, was determined to encourage work "not so much from the pens of practiced writers," as from "the discourse of the living." In other words, leading Romantic writers of the day were very much open to the experimental nature of slave narratives and indeed, almost certainly, read them.

In 1845 the antebellum slave narrative reached its epitome with the publication of the *Narrative of the Life of Frederick Douglass, An American Slave, Written by Himself.* Douglass's *Narrative* became an international bestseller, selling more than thirty thousand copies in its first five years, its contemporary readership far outstripping that of such classic white autobiographies as Henry David Thoreau's *Walden* (1854), Whitman's *Leaves of Grass* (1855), and *The Scarlet Letter* (1850) and *Moby-Dick* (1851) combined during their first five years of existence. The abolitionist leader William Lloyd Garrison introduced Douglass's *Narrative* by stressing how representative Douglass's experience of slavery had been. But Garrison could not help but note the extraordinary individuality of the black author's rendering of that experience. It is Douglass's style of self-presentation, through which he re-created the slave as an evolving self bound for mental as well as physical freedom, that makes his autobiography so important.

After Douglass's *Narrative,* the presence of the subtitle, *Written by Himself,* on a slave narrative bore increasing political and literary significance as an indicator of a narrator's self-determination independent of external expectations and conventions. In the late 1840s

17

well-known fugitive slaves such as William Wells Brown, Henry Bibb, and James W. C. Pennington reinforced the rhetorical self-consciousness of the slave narrative by incorporating into their stories trickster motifs from African American folk culture, extensive literary and biblical allusion, and a picaresque perspective on the meaning of the slave's flight from bondage to freedom.

As the slave narrative evolved in the crisis years of the 1850s and early 1860s, it addressed the problem of slavery with unprecedented candor, unmasking as never before the moral and social complexities of the American caste and class system in the North as well as the South. A heightening severity of subject matter and tone signaled the slave narrator's determination to break through the genteel proprieties of discourse that had previously inhibited the freedom of the genre to tell the whole truth. In *My Bondage and My Freedom* (1855), Douglass revised the triumphant ending of his *Narrative* of 1845 and revealed that his search for freedom had *not* reached its fulfillment among the abolitionists. Having discovered in Garrison and his cohorts some of the same paternalistic attitudes that had characterized his former masters in the South, Douglass could see in 1855 that the struggle for full liberation would be much more difficult and uncertain than he had previously imagined. Thus the slave narrative in the 1850s and 1860s asks increasingly searching questions about the meaning of freedom in a country as pervasively racist as fugitives found the northern United States to be.

Slave narratives also began to ask unprecedented questions about the relationship of slavery to the exploitation of women, white and black, in the United States. Harriet Jacobs, the first African American female slave to author her own narrative, challenged conventional ideas about true womanhood and freedom in her strikingly original *Incidents in the Life of a Slave Girl* (1861). Jacobs's autobiography shows how sexual exploitation made slavery especially oppressive for black women. But in demonstrating how she fought back and ultimately gained both her own freedom and that of her two children, Jacobs proved the inadequacy of the image of victim that had been pervasively applied to female slaves in the male-authored slave narrative.

In the immediate aftermath of the Civil War, Elizabeth Keckley's autobiography, *Behind the Scenes, or Thirty Years a Slave and Four Years in the White House* (1868), forecast new directions in which the slave narrative would go after the abolition of the institution of slavery itself. Though her experience in slavery was plainly parallel to that of Jacobs, Keckley would not discuss her sexuality or the moral implications of her having borne a child by a white man while she was a slave, preferring instead to stress how her energy and determination had propelled her out of the South and ultimately to economic success and intimacy within the inner circle of the Lincoln family. In most post-Emancipation slave narratives, slavery is depicted as Keckley represents it, as a kind of crucible in which the resilience, industry, and ingenuity of the slave was tested and ultimately validated. Thus the post-Emancipation slave narrative argued the readiness of the freedman and freedwoman for full participation in the post–Civil War social and economic order. Booker T. Washington's popular *Up from Slavery* was a classic American success story. Because *Up from Slavery* extolled black progress and interracial cooperation since emancipation, it won a much greater hearing from whites than was accorded those former slaves whose autobiographies detailed the legacy of injustices burdening blacks in the postwar South.

As African Americans learned the bitter lessons of the post-Reconstruction era, black autobiography became less focused on the individual's quest for personal power and more concerned with the realization of communal power and prestige in African American institutions, particularly the school and the church. Educators headed by Washington and his many protégés who wrote autobiographies and ministers whose influential memoirs range from Bishop Daniel Payne's *Recollections of Seventy Years* (1888) to Bishop Alexander Walters's *My Life and Work* (1917) argued that black survival and fulfillment depended largely on building institutional bulwarks against the divide-and-conquer strategy of American white supremacy. By sublimating his personal desires and ambitions in the work of an institution, the institutional man of African American autobiography asked the world to judge him primarily according to his usefulness, his ability to work within the existing socioeconomic order to accomplish good for his people.

19

Although the New Negro era was a time of comparatively few note-worthy autobiographies, William Pickens and Ida B. Wells, each of them Southern-born, middle-class, and dedicated to civil rights activ-ism, made signal contributions to African American autobiography in the 1920s. Pickens's *Bursting Bonds* (1923) chronicles the evolution of a latter-day Booker T. Washington into a militant proponent of the ideas of W.E.B. Du Bois. Wells's posthumously published *Crusade for Justice* (1970) tells an equally compelling story of its author's dauntless com-mitment to a life of agitation and protest on behalf of African Americans. The pioneering efforts of Pickens and Wells in the 1920s and James Weldon Johnson's *Along This Way* in 1933 helped to reori-ent African American autobiography to its roots in the slave narrative's ideal of the black leader as an articulate hero who uses words as weapons in the fight for individual and communal freedom.

The decade and a half after the New Negro Renaissance saw the pub-lication of several important autobiographies by literary figures, such as Claude McKay's *A Long Way from Home* (1937), Langston Hughes's *The Big Sea* (1940), Zora Neale Hurston's *Dust Tracks on a Road* (1942), and Richard Wright's *Black Boy/(American Hunger)* (1945). The unprecedent-ed emphasis in these texts on the search for an authentic selfhood, predicated on the autobiographers' skepticism about institutions and epitomized in their heightened sensitivity to literary style as self-pre-sentation, marks a turning point in the history of African American autobiography. *Black Boy* became the most widely read and discussed African American autobiography of the post–World War II period pri-marily because of its quintessentially modernist portrait of the black writer as alienated rebel, dedicated uncompromisingly to the expres-sion of truth as individually perceived.

This sense of the autobiographer's foremost responsibility to abso-lute authenticity of self-expression largely precluded Wright's partici-pation in what had become by the mid-twentieth century a traditional role for the African American autobiographer—that of representative of the African American community. To a new generation of self-styled "revolutionary" black autobiographers of the 1960s, however, Wright's ideal of personal authenticity could only be achieved by identifying with the oppressed masses of black America and then "telling it like it

is" to white America on their behalf. The exemplar of this mode of testimony, powerfully energized by the civil rights and Black Power
movements, was *The Autobiography of Malcolm X* (1965), which turned
a street-corner organizer for a splinter group of black separatists into a
cultural hero for young, disaffected middle-class whites and their black
counterparts in search of a standard-bearer for a new racial consciousness. Malcolm's successors produced a chorus of denunciation of
American racism and hypocrisy unmatched since the era of the fugitive slave narrative.

The appearance in 1970 of Maya Angelou's *I Know Why the Caged
Bird Sings* signaled one of the most remarkable developments in recent
African American autobiography—the unprecedented outpouring of
personal, sometimes very intimate, narratives by black women. Although longtime contributors to such bedrock traditions in African
American autobiography as the spiritual autobiography, recent women
autobiographers, led by Angelou, Audre Lorde, Marita Golden, and
Itabari Njeri, have reenvisioned the ideas of the spirit and salvation,
discovering them anew in the secular experience of black female artists
and activists. Through such reinvigorations of traditional forms and
themes, African American autobiography continues to bear profound
witness to its cultural heritage in the slave narrative and to its ongoing
responsibility to represent the personal and communal voices of black
Americans.

PART II
Constituent Elements of Slave Narratives

As a form of discourse, African American autobiography can best be
characterized in terms of the three elements of the word autobiography—*autos* (self), *bios* (life), and *graphe* (writing). Undoubtedly the
window that autobiography opens onto African American *bios*, life,
especially aspects of that life that have made black experience distinctive, has been crucial to the success of African American autobiography with the popular reader in the United States and abroad. But one
should not overlook the social import of the black autobiographer's

21

concern with claiming a psychological as well as an experiential distinctiveness for himself or herself. The black American autobiographer has traditionally felt an obligation to speak for and to people of color, rather than just on behalf of the individual self. Yet autobiographers from Frederick Douglass to Malcolm X have realized that by identifying the aspirations of a people with the ambitions of a self, genuine impetus to the cause of freedom could be generated.

A key manifestation of *autos* since the beginning of the African American autobiographical enterprise has been the struggle to attain the autonomy of authorship, the right to express oneself independent of the direction or approval of white sponsors and editors. Increasingly in the twentieth century, the act of writing, *graphe*, the representation of selfhood through a personalized storytelling style, has become the sign of the African American autobiographer's assertion of his or her independence of mind and individuality of vision.

It might be useful to chart the three-century history of the slave narrative by assigning each of these three elements—self, life, writing—to a century in which that element was most emphasized in the tradition.

In the eighteenth century, *bios* or life is the salient element of the slave narrative, as narrators and readers open up an intercourse about what life was like for Africans and slaves in the New World economy. The *Interesting Narrative of the Life of Olaudah Equiano, or Gustavus Vassa, the African* (1789) was the first great slave narrative in part because it gave a full chronological account of the life of an African who acclimates himself to the social and economic mainstream of English life. Equiano's massive two-volume autobiography centers on his life in Africa but also features his development and evolution from a terrified, confused slave to a successful seaman and merchant, and eventually a committed antislavery activist. Given the popular notion in eighteenth-century Europe that Africans were mired in a changeless condition of ignorance and superstition and incapable of developing the kind of civilization that Europeans admired, Equiano's rendition of his life as *dynamic* and *progressive* was a powerful instrument in combating fundamental European racism in the eighteenth century.

In the nineteenth century, *autos* or selfhood becomes the operative term, the *sine qua non,* for the slave narrator, as he or she works hard to assert autonomy of authorship and what I have called freedom of storytelling for the slave narrative. Douglass's 1845 *Narrative* bears the subtitle *Written by Himself* as a mark of its author's autonomy and as a signal that this is a departure from the dominant tradition of the slave narrative up to the 1840s. Before Douglass, the majority of slave narratives had been "dictated" to whites or "edited" by whites. While we have no reason to doubt the reliability of these narratives with regard to the life story they represent—the events of the life—we do have reason to question how much a dictated or edited narrative truly represents the thinking and individual style of self-representation of the former slave.

In our century, and particularly since the 1960s revival of the slave narrative in novel form, *graphe* or the style of representation, particularly the style of representing female subjectivity, has been the dominant issue in such texts as *The Autobiography of Miss Jane Pittman* (1971), *Dessa Rose* (1986), *Beloved* (1987), and J. California Cooper's *Family* (1991). Of course an interest in style in the slave narrative goes back well beyond the rise of the neoslave narrative. In Douglass's second autobiography, *My Bondage and My Freedom* (1855), he reveals the politics of style in a slave's narrative when he tells how the abolitionists tried to stage-manage the style of his narrations on the antislavery platform. "Tell your story, Frederick," said William Lloyd Garrison. "We will take care of the philosophy." "Be yourself," said another of Douglass's handlers. "Better have a *little* of the plantation manner of speech than not; 'tis not best that you seem too learned." Douglass goes on to stress that he understood the reasons his associates urged him to adopt the style of a plantation Negro—a lot of Northern whites would not believe he had ever been a slave if he sounded too sophisticated. But, as Douglass emphasizes, "I must speak just the word that seemed to *me* the word to be spoken *by* me."

One reason why *Incidents in the Life of a Slave Girl* was for so long regarded with suspicion is its style, which clearly exhibits the influence of domestic fiction and the novel of seduction. Until recently it was assumed that Jacobs's use of some of the conventions and style (particularly in the dialogues between Linda and Dr. Flint) was inauthentically "melodramatic." Of course most of the slave narratives have incidents in them that could be labeled "melodramatic"—consider the scene of the whipping of Douglass's aunt Harriet, surely a moment of intense emotionalism in that autobiography in which good and evil are portrayed in familiar melodramatic fashion. But for some reason Douglass's *Narrative* was never attacked for inauthenticity, despite its melodrama, while *Incidents in the Life of a Slave Girl* was long dismissed because of its melodrama. Much of the problem sprang from Jacobs's decision to use the style of women's fiction to talk about matters of sexual abuse in slavery. For most of the twentieth century, the style of nineteenth-century women's fiction has been regarded by male academic historians and literary critics as inherently excessive and unreliable, though the excesses and unreliability of male writers such as Cooper or Poe were routinely rationalized. But now, with the ascendancy of feminist criticism, we're beginning to read autobiographies like *Incidents*, based in the discourse of women's fiction, as specifically designed to evoke that discourse, so that *women* readers would respond appropriately to the cues that they knew to expect from their own reading experience.

In *Black Boy (American Hunger)*, Richard Wright constantly reminds his reader of the connection between true autobiographical authenticity and complete freedom to speak and write candidly and independently. This is partly why he makes much of his refusal to read the ninth-grade graduation speech that his principal wanted him to deliver as class valedictorian (although Wright did agree to cut certain passages from his own speech that his principal objected to, something he doesn't mention in *Black Boy*). In *I Know Why the Caged Bird Sings*, Angelou recounts the anticlimax of her high school education by emphasizing that the only way for her to achieve true independence and authenticity was to reject the kinds of writing she did in school and instead create a myth about herself that would enable her to get a job on the San Francisco streetcars. The myth of her identity that she creates in her application for that job is "a cat's ladder of near truths and total lies." But by this point in her life, Angelou is determined to take control of her life story and shape it to her own authentic needs, regardless of whether the content of that story is entirely factual. It is the *style* of her self-representation, the myth of herself, that she consciously fashions for the San Francisco Railway Commission that gets her the job she is after. Thus the *imaginative* manipulation of her identity in that job application actually enables Angelou to become the authentic person she wants to be. Hence the importance of writing, style, to the goal of self-realization in and through autobiography.

Here are a few key terms that can help students get a handle on the key concerns, the defining parameters, of any slave narrative.

First, what is a slave narrative? A slave narrative, in its earliest form, was simply an account of the life, or a major portion of the life, of a fugitive or former slave, either written or in some way orally related by the slave himself or herself.

The two themes that are most often identified with the slave narrative are *freedom* and *literacy*. Freedom, of course, is most simply the antithesis of slavery. In the nineteenth-century slave narrative freedom is understood

1. most naively as a place—the North.

2. most pragmatically as an economic condition, in which one can dispose of one's own labor according to one's own inclination.

3. most ideally as a state of the mind and spirit characterized by a sense of awareness of self and a sense of individual potential to affect the world and to effect one's own future.

Slavery is not only the absence of freedom. As Douglass was among the first of the slave narrators to demonstrate, slavery was designed to deny black people access to the *meaning and value* of freedom. It's not enough to place people in bondage; slavery must convince the slave that he or she is properly situated in bondage.

Thus in a classic slave narrative such as Douglass's, and in important successors such as Wright's *Black Boy*, slavery's physical cruelty is not stressed as much as its attack on the development of the slave's psychological, intellectual, and spiritual sense of self. Slavery's ultimate cruelty is its systematized denial of human attachments. Douglass describes his youth in slavery on the Lloyd plantation primarily in

25

terms of what he and other slaves were deprived of and the psychological effects of that denial. The greatest deprivation is that of knowledge. Slavery aims to keep the slave ignorant first and foremost, because the more the slave becomes self-conscious, the more trouble he is likely to be. Hence Douglass stresses early in life his desire for knowledge of himself, symbolized in the desire for knowledge of his birthday.

What is Douglass's definition of freedom? In part it's the North, a place, and especially a place where Douglass can get work and be a productive, self-supporting worker. But one of the key distinctions in Douglass's story is that he stresses he started becoming a free man *before* he ever got to the North. Freedom is a state of mind, not a place of residence. The high point of Douglass's life in the North as he portrays it in the *Narrative* is not economic success, but becoming a speaker for the abolitionist cause. To Douglass the power to use language to change the minds of others is the greatest power that an individual can exert. Ultimate power is the power of self-expression—to speak freely what is on one's mind and heart.

Other key terms to consider in reading slave narratives:

Manhood: Frequently cited in slave narratives by black men as that which a male slave is robbed of and must spend his greatest effort to regain. But what does manhood mean? Does it mean male honor? Does it mean humanity, humanhood, selfhood?

Womanhood: Frequently cited in slave narratives by black women as that which a female slave is denied and which she must claim for herself. But what does womanhood mean? Does it mean true womanhood à la the cult of female valorization in the nineteenth century? Do black women slave narratives create a new standard of womanhood? Does Maya Angelou change Jacobs's notion of what a woman should be and do, what a mother should be and do?

Self: A fundamental assumption of pro-slavery doctrine is that the dark-skinned Other is not a self, lacks selfhood, lacks the capacity to experience and express consciousness as whites. If black is the sign of darkness, of absence, it becomes easy to deduce that what is absent is the essence of human selfhood. How does a writer of autobiography claim the right to participate in this genre knowing that her or his reader doubts whether the black autobiographer has a self about which to write?

Community: Though the slave narrative arises out of an autobiographical tradition that celebrates individualism, the slave narrator usually has a larger purpose than self-celebration. But how to celebrate selfhood and one's communal identification at the same time? And what community does the narrator identify with? The community of slavery? The community of free people? The community of the reader? What sort of community is created by the narrative between the speaker and the reader?

Novelization: The process by which an autobiography becomes "literary," that is, influenced by the style and convention of the novel. Typically the slave narrative before Douglass and Jacobs is characterized by the former slave's monologue about his or her life, put in the simplest and most straightforward ways, with an emphasis on just the facts, with nothing "rhetorical" or re-created interposed to upset the reader's demand for strict factuality. A novelized autobiography such as Douglass's, and certainly Jacobs's, is no longer a monologue. In it appear many instances of reconstructed dialogues (of the sort the autobiographer could never transcribe from memory). More than one voice speaks in the text (Aunt Marthy's and Flint's in *Incidents*) and competes with that of the narrator. Instead of deadpan factual reporting, irony, parody, and rhetorical flourishes intervene (in Douglass's *Narrative*, for instance) to call attention not just to the facts but to the personality that is marshaling them through a distinctive style.

The novelization of Wright's autobiography is so pronounced that many critics do not speak of *Black Boy* so much as Wright's own personal narrative as a kind of representative or symbolic black youth's story, novelized to the point where it can speak for an entire genera-

27

tion of black southern boys in the early twentieth century. The same point about novelization could be made in connection with Angelou, especially when she gives us a comic, but poignant account of her youthful fantasies, such as the power fantasy she has involving her grandmother Henderson's intimidation of the white dentist in Stamps, Arkansas. Here the voice that reproduces the fantasy competes with grandmother Henderson's version of how she got the white dentist to pay for the tooth extraction—and the reader is left with a much richer sense of the multiple layers of comedy, irony, and pathos in the entire scene. Thus the emotional richness and sense of the narrator as a writer are enhanced by novelization.

I will conclude by offering one way to organize a discussion of four major African American autobiographies belonging to or arising from the slave narrative, using comparison and contrast in accordance with basic parameters of the slave narrative tradition, namely, 1) the concept of slavery, 2) the identity ideal, 3) the concept of freedom, 4) the role of literacy.

Incidents in the Life of a Slave Girl

1. Slavery is summed up in the dominance of men over women.

2. The identity ideal is the independent mother who holds her family together and creates a place of safety and sustenance, a home.

3. The concept of freedom is based in the idea of a home in the North (not marriage), a home as a place of economic independence and social respectability.

4. The role of literacy is to enable the "slave girl" to speak out about what had been secret—her sexuality and the abuses of it in the South, her dignity and the threats to it in the North.

Black Boy/(American Hunger)

1. Slavery is summed up in the demand for utter conformity and repression of individualism, by both blacks and whites in the South.

2. The identity ideal is the self-sufficient, uninhibited artist who allows nothing and no one to interfere with his commitment to self-expression and truth telling.

3. The concept of freedom is based in the idea of the North as a place where individualism is at least possible, though Wright will find out differently the further one reads in *Black Boy (American Hunger)*.

4. The role of literacy is to offer the black boy a sense of an alternative way of life defined first by an abstract American literary community (à la H. L. Mencken and Sinclair Lewis) and second by a leftist political community (the Communist Party in the North), both of which are seen as transcending racial divisions in the South, though in the end they do not nurture or sustain Wright, the alienated modernist artist.

I Know Why the Caged Bird Sings

1. Slavery is summed up in the sense of the ugly duckling mentality, unworthiness, youthful withdrawal and silence, and a paralyzing lack of self-esteem.

2. The identity ideal is the mother, Maya's literal mother, and motherhood, which Maya achieves at the end, as a way of proving her capability.

3. The concept of freedom is based in the idea of California as a place where she can become a new person, self-sufficient as she is after driving her father's runaway car, spending the month with the youths in the junkyard, and getting a job as the first black conductress on the San Francisco trolleys.

4. The role of literacy is not featured as prominently in this text, though clearly Maya Angelou, like Jacobs, has secrets to tell that allow the author liberation from past traumas.

SUGGESTED SECONDARY SOURCES

Andrews, William L., ed. *African American Autobiography: A Collection of Critical Essays*. Englewood Cliffs, N.J.: Prentice-Hall, 1993.

———. *To Tell a Free Story: The First Century of Afro-American Autobiography, 1760–1865*. Urbana: U of Illinois P, 1986.

Davis, Charles T. and Henry Louis Gates, Jr., eds. *The Slave's Narrative*. New York: Oxford U P, 1985.

Foster, Frances Smith. *Witnessing Slavery: The Development of Ante-bellum Slave Narratives*. 2nd ed. Madison: U of Wisconsin P, 1994.

Parker, Theodore. "The American Scholar." *The American Scholar*. Vol. 8 of *Centenary Edition of Theodore Parker's Writings*. Ed. George Willis Cooke (Boston: American Unitarian Association, 1907), 1–53.

Peabody, Ephraim. "Narratives of Fugitive Slaves," *Christian Examiner* 47 (July 1849), 61–93. Rpt. In Davis and Gates, ed., *The Slave's Narrative, 19–28*.

Rawick, George P. *The American Slave: A Composite Autobiography*. 19 vols. Westport, Conn.: Greenwood P, 1972.

Sekora, John and Darwin T. Turner, eds. *The Art of Slave Narrative*. Macomb, Illinois: Western Illinois U, 1982.

Starling, Marion Wilson. *The Slave Narrative: Its Place in American History*. Washington, D.C.: Howard U P, 1988.

Stone, Albert E. *The Return of Nat Turner: History, Literature, & Cultural Politics in Sixties America*. Athens: U of Georgia P, 1992.

"A RIP IN THE TENT"

Teaching (African) American Literature

Katharine Driscoll Coon
Noble and Greenough School
Dedham, Massachusetts

The interest in African-American events, studies, programs, history, literature, language, culture, is not peripheral. It has enormous weight. It's a catalyst for understanding many other disciplines and many genres. . . . What's interesting about Afro-American studies is that it's a rip in the tent, and you can get through it, not primarily to understand the experience or intellectual life of African-Americans, but to understand a number of things in the history, language, art and culture of this country. It's like an ignition, an engine that is turned on and distributes itself among virtually all of the disciplines in the humanities . . . and certainly most of the social sciences.

—TONI MORRISON,
"African-American Intellectual Life at Princeton:
A conversation"

I

The more I teach African American literature, the more I believe it must be taught. As soon as we think about studying the literature in the way that Morrison describes, as a rip in the tent, we can, I think, no longer see African American literature as marginal, as belonging to

31

a special interest group, as a literary ghetto. It belongs to all of us and, more importantly, it holds out a challenge to all of us.

One question that it asks of us is, "What does it mean to be an American?" As Albert Raboteau says in the same conversation, "In a sense, Afro-American studies speaks to a deeper meaning of the African-American presence in this nation. That presence has always been a test case of the nation's claims to freedom, democracy, equality, the inclusiveness of all."[1] When we teach, side by side, the Bill of Rights and sections of the Slave Codes, then we give students a powerful, if unsettling, lesson in what is meant by "liberty and justice for all." When they read the gripping, highly literate, account of Harriet Jacobs's *Incidents in the Life of a Slave Girl*, our students' views of nineteenth-century slavery are challenged and deepened. When they read contemporary texts such as Gloria Naylor's *Mama Day*, Charles Johnson's *Middle Passage*, and Toni Morrison's *Beloved* both as postmodernist literary achievements and as descendants of the nineteenth-century slave narratives and other vital forms of African and American cultural expression, they gain a rich sense of how "the clothesline of history"[2] stretches from the past to the present day. In teaching African American literature, we have extraordinary opportunities to teach the kind of critical thinking we know is so deeply important.

As a first step, we who are not African American must think about how we are to approach this subject with what I might call the right attitude or set of attitudes. Do we come, as James Baldwin said, "armed with spiritual traveler's checks,"[3] looking for some kind of fulfillment in the black experience? Are we coming to it simply as consumers? Are we voyeurs? Do our attitudes reinforce feelings of white superiority and black inferiority, or marginality and oppression, or do they reinforce feelings of dignity and honor and pride? Over the years I have come to think that the most important attitude I can bring to teaching African American literature is one of respectful attention. My African American students want to learn about their literary heritage from someone who has bothered to study it respectfully, and with the sustained attention that it deserves; they don't want to have to teach it to their teachers, nor should they be expected to, although too often that's what happens. We need to do our own homework and our own scholarship; we need to examine critically our own deeply embedded assumptions about race, American literature, and the true nature of diversity, in our classrooms and in our national life.

I'll be the first to admit that I write this from a perch of privilege. I teach in a selective independent school, stocked with bright, eager kids who are motivated to go on to college. Increasingly, it's a diverse student body, although nowhere near as diverse as those taught by my NEH Summer Institute colleagues at South Boston High, Snowden International School, and the John D. O'Bryant School in Boston, Massachusetts. I have an administration that encourages professional development and that supports teachers' initiatives. I am virtually free to design and teach the electives I want to teach, as long as they will "fly" in the demanding marketplace of student and parent expectations. If I want to team teach a course with my colleague in the history department, we can finesse our schedules to make it work. And we can even find an empty classroom to teach it in. As a mentor-teacher, I can suggest and model innovations in the "mainstream" (nonelective) curriculum. For example, we now teach *Beloved* right alongside *Hamlet* in the required English course that all juniors take, which is partially aimed at preparation for the English Literature Advanced Placement tests. If we need books, we have a budget big enough to order them. And the same is true for photocopying, a must when providing access to African American primary sources. I am not subject to the school board mandates and other political strictures that I know are constraints for most of my compatriots teaching in public schools.

But in the grand liberal tradition, I've always believed that with privilege comes responsibility. For me, that means that if I have the freedom to design and teach courses, they should be courses that provoke critical thinking and promote multicultural awareness. If the freedoms I enjoy could be seen not so much as luxuries but as necessities in the spirit of true educational reform, then the curricula that I am privileged to test-drive in my idyllic laboratory may help other teachers, in all kinds of settings, get ideas for theirs. And when more of us have access to such resources as the Internet and those I've described above, we just may be able to enlarge the conversation that enriches and empowers the many, not just the few.

In the meantime, there are potent intra-institutional benefits to offering African American literature at a school such as mine. In the six years that I've been formally teaching African American literature in "stand-alone" electives, many students have elected to continue their study of African American literature and history in a university setting. For students of color in an overwhelmingly white school such as mine, these courses offer some validation of their experiences and histories, and increase the likelihood of their voices' being heard freely and fully. And because many students of color do sign up for these electives, they often constitute a critical mass in the classroom, an otherwise rare experience in a school where they make up a small minority of the student body. They can and do exercise a diversity of voices and viewpoints and are no longer the only black student in the class— the one who serves as special consultant when it's time to read *The Color Purple* or to discuss the Dred Scott decision.

So not only are African American voices at the center of the classroom, for once they are also at the center of the curriculum. Indeed, they *are* the curriculum. Students encounter Richard Wright and Zora Neale Hurston, Charles W. Chesnutt and Francis E. W. Harper, John Hope Franklin and Lorene Cary not as adjuncts but as the main course. To have canonized African American literature, as it were, in the curriculum of a traditionally white college preparatory school is to say that it's important, that it carries academic weight, that it merits at least a full term's worth of sustained and scholarly attention—that respectful attention I spoke of earlier. It says that this is a body of books and important authors that we admire, that a great literary tradition is asking to be attended to.

Toni Morrison says of teaching African American studies,

> What interests me most in the work I do ... is the thirst among students and faculty, but especially among students—black students, white students—for a way to talk about these things, a vocabulary that allows them to talk about race in a manner that is not diminishing, demeaning, reductive or ad hominem. Race is a very difficult thing to talk about, because the conversation frequently ends up

being patronizing, guilt ridden, hostile or resentful. But for those interested in the study of literature and the writing of literature, it is something you have to confront and think about.[4]

I recognize that same thirst in our high school students, and many of the same difficulties. White students might find it particularly uncomfortable to confront notions of invisible white privilege and racial entitlement, but if they are willing (and I have found that, in most cases, they are), and enabled to do so they often find it a meaningful and liberating experience. In this regard, Peggy McIntosh's article "White Privilege: Unpacking the Invisible Knapsack"[5] and Alan Stoskopf's "Teaching about Racism in the Classroom: A Profile of Dr. Beverly Daniel Tatum's Research"[6] are valuable for stimulating discussion and self-examination of these issues. One (white) student wrote in her class journal, "This class brought about a different journey—one in which I was forced to evaluate my role in racism—by reading many books/articles I learned how well trained I was not to think about the issue." Said another, "I learned so much about myself as a person, and about my role in society as a white male. I got over a lot of prejudices which I hadn't noticed before, and I am much more sensitive now, or at least I hope. . . . This class should be required of everyone." These comments counter the idea that to examine internalized and systemic racism produces, or heightens, feelings of white guilt, or that there's a zero-sum game in which whites must sacrifice in order for people of color to advance. Both "races" stand to benefit from, and all of us need, a more balanced knowledge of our collective selves, our historical pasts.

Perhaps my favorite comment of all came last year from a student in a team-taught course called "African American Literature and History," who said, "What I've really learned from this course is that it's all a lot more complicated than I ever realized." That awareness suggests a first big step toward the critical thinking and intellectual curiosity that we hope to inspire in all of our students.

At Noble and Greenough, students may elect African American literature for one semester or two, in the fall of their junior and senior years, and elect African American literature and history, the interdisciplinary course offered each spring. We look at cultural, literary, and historical phenomena such as the oral tradition, the slave narrative, African survivals, creolization, sorrow songs, the great migration, and blues, jazz, and rap, to see how they have shaped a body of literature that is at once distinctly American, profoundly universal, and culturally specific. Discussion inevitably engages vital contemporary issues such as racism, class and gender privilege, violence, hatred, inequality, and political process. These discussions are part of the multicultural curriculum, emphasizing the importance of learning how better to "communicate across differences." Students keep journals, conduct and transcribe interviews and oral histories, write frequent papers that are both narrative and analytical, and present a final research project.

Syllabi change from year to year and from semester to semester. In African American literature and history, the team-taught course, we use a single history text as the chronological and conceptual framework for the semester. We have used Lerone Bennet Jr.'s *Before the Mayflower* in the past; this year we will use John Hope Franklin's *From Slavery to Freedom*. In addition to many short works found primarily in *Crossing the Danger Water*, we use texts such as Charles Johnson's *Middle Passage*, Anne Moody's *Coming of Age in Mississippi*, Alice Walker's *Meridian*, Cornel West's *Race Matters*, and Harriet Jacobs's *Incidents in the Life of a Slave Girl, Written by Herself*.

The fall semester has been shaped around the following statement by Dr. Bernard Bell, whose work appears elsewhere in this volume:

> [T]he tradition of the Afro-American novel is dominated by the struggle for freedom from all forms of oppression and by the personal odyssey to realize the full potential of one's complex bicultural identity as an Afro-American. . . . In short, *the Afro-American canonical story is the quest, frequently with apocalyptic overtones, for freedom, literacy and wholeness—personal and communal—grounded in social reality and ritualized in symbolic acts of African-American speech, music and religion.*[7]
> [Emphasis added]

Groupings of texts that I have found work well together under this aegis include:

- Maya Angelou's *All God's Children Got Traveling Shoes*; Gwendolyn Brooks's *Selected Poems*; Richard Wright's *Native Son*; Lorene Cary's *Black Ice*; James Baldwin's *The Fire Next Time*

- Ralph Ellison's *Invisible Man*; Toni Morrison's *Song of Solomon*; Harriet Jacobs's *Incidents in the Life of a Slave Girl, Written by Herself*

- Richard Wright's *Native Son*; Zora Neale Hurston's *Their Eyes Were Watching God*; Toni Morrison's *Sula*; James Baldwin's *The Fire Next Time*

One year I began the course with Richard Wright's short story "Bright and Morning Star" followed by the novel *Native Son*. Like the novel, "Bright and Morning Star" raises vexing questions about the possibilities of constructive as well as oppressive relationships across racial divides. It provides a powerful introduction to the issues that concern Wright in the novel—violence, resistance, speech, politics, racism, and redemption—but with some interesting differences. For one thing, it establishes a backdrop of the rural South as against the urban North, where Bigger is "born"; for another, it offers a sense of female agency missing from the novel. By reading it first, students were better able to see both some of the powerful absences in Bigger Thomas's story and some of the thematic material that drives the novel to its chilling conclusion.

Native Son, while deeply problematic, is an originary text that is as provocative today as it was in 1940, when it climbed rapidly to the top of the best-seller list, selling a quarter of a million copies as a Book-of-the-Month Club main selection and attracting lively critical attention. It was then, as it is now, a disturbing and electrifying read that achieved a major goal for Wright, "the exposure of the starkest realities of American life where race was concerned."[8] Those realities are still very much with us in the 1990s, as is Bigger Thomas. Contemporary black writers such as Brent Staples, Nathan MacColl, and Caryl Phillips often cite *Native Son* as the first book they read in which they encountered their own lives in the pages of a book. For these writers, and for some of the students in my class, this encounter was a conversion experience. One student wrote a twenty-three page memoir of his life in the projects; another wrote a ten-page essay called "The Bigger in Me" that explored his Indian family's experience with racial prejudice and his own bicultural identity. A female African American student wrote a paper that contrasted her own secure, middle-class upbringing with Bigger Thomas's while acknowledging similarities in encounters with white racism and feelings of powerlessness.

When a white student opened class the day after we read about Mary Dalton's death saying, "I think Bigger deserves to die," we came face to face with the white heat at the core of this book and stayed with this question through the weeks that followed. Bigger, of course, does die at the end of the novel, but understanding the moral, spiritual, and psychic journey that brought him there, and the political, social, and economic forces that make Bigger Thomas a "native son" is the challenge Wright extends to the reader. The novel is, as he promised, not "a book which even bankers' daughters could read and feel good about"; he hoped that "no one could weep over it; that it would be so hard and deep that they would have to face it without the consolation of tears."[9]

We followed *Native Son* with *Their Eyes Were Watching God*, by Wright's contemporary Zora Neale Hurston. Wright and Hurston's philosophical, political, and personal differences have been well documented (they each wrote hostile reviews of the other's work, for example), and their books provide a fascinating counterpoint to one another. As we set the texts side by side, we looked empirically at the differences between them, taking into account that they were written in the same time period. The students generated the following list:

- female vs. male protagonist
- rural South vs. urban North
- agrarian vs. industrial economy
- mules vs. cars, guns, movies
- social community vs. social isolation
- black self-governing community vs. white-controlled segregation
- economic self-determination vs. dead-end poverty

- protected early life vs. lack of protection

- romanticism vs. realism

- comedy vs. tragedy

- folklore vs. mass media

- voice vs. silence

- life vs. death (for the protagonist)

- color vs. somber tones

As one student said regarding the last point, "It's as though *Their Eyes Were Watching God* is in Technicolor and *Native Son* is in black and white." These differences inform our growing understanding of the Afro-American canonical story as described by Bernard Bell: as a "quest . . . for freedom, literacy, and wholeness—personal and communal—grounded in social reality and ritualized in symbolic acts of African-American speech, music, and religion."[10] Janie Crawford's quest ends, significantly, with a homecoming and with the telling of story. "'Lawd!' Phoeby breathed out heavily, 'Ah done growed ten feet higher from jus' listenin' tuh you, Janie.'"

Next came Toni Morrison's *Sula*, providing a bridge from the first two books into a more recent literary past. Sula is interesting in the tradition of, as Sterling Brown puts it, "the best foot forward." She is a woman allowed to be *bad*. Sula does mean things: she steals her best friend's husband; she turns her grandmother out of her house and puts her into a substandard nursing home; she watches her own mother burn; and she lets a little boy drown and doesn't tell. In this way, she's like Bigger Thomas, whose amoral actions (e.g., what he does to Bessie) upset us; he, too, is "bad." But Sula is, unlike Bigger, a "bad" *woman*. She is not chaste, as a "good" woman would be (neither is Janie); she stands up to authority in a way a "good" woman would not. She helps herself to whomever and whatever she wants, including her best friend's husband, disrupting the conventions of best friendship and marital fidelity. She leaves (as Janie Crawford did and Bigger tried to) to seek her personal freedom.

As a female, Sula Peace is no victim, no creature of muted, powerless

39

suffering. Think of how different she is from Bigger's mother and sister, from Bessie, despite similarities in their situations: poverty, racial discrimination, male abandonment and betrayal (Boy-Boy) or ineffectuality (Plum, Tar Baby), severe trauma, and death. Or from the women in James Baldwin's novels who are suffused with mother love, fear, submissiveness, and religous piety, a claustrophobic kind of hopelessness and infinite capacity for suffering.

By contrast, Sula shows us early on, when she slices off the tip of her finger in front of the Irish boys, that she certainly can endure suffering as her virtuous literary foremothers did, but she won't be a victim. She'll inflict her own suffering rather than have the Irish boys or anybody else do it for her. She will be an agent of her own fate, the protagonist of her own story.

Both Sula and Janie defy yet another convention of the "good" woman, the convention of the good mother. This is a tender issue in the African American tradition, for one of the searing tragedies of slavery was the agonizing separation of mothers from their children, a subject that is at the heart of many African American writings of the nineteenth and twentieth centuries. That the mother-child bond, arguably the most primal and elemental of human bonds, took on almost sacred proportions is not hard to understand in light of the repeated cruel and deliberate ruptures of that bond throughout generation after generation of slavery. It takes nothing away from the heroism of those mothers both real and fictional who fought with their lives to hold on to their babies, to hold on to their children and families, to say that some women would reject the role or would at least complicate it, as Sethe does in *Beloved*. We don't know why Janie and Sula do not have children, they just don't.

Fully female, exuberantly heterosexual, and decidedly childless, Janie and Sula seem never to hear their biological clocks ticking away or to express regret. There is no mention of "lost" babies or of maternal feelings; the subject never surfaces. In becoming something other than the socially sanctioned "good" woman, or "good" black woman, they command an expanded range of human possibilities. They refuse to be constrained by a narrow definition of race, gender, or personhood and instead claim the right to be free and triumphant. With Janie's story, *Sula* deservedly joins the ranks of the canonical Afro-American story.

Finally, we ended the course with James Baldwin's incandescent, brilliant, timeless, and timely essay "The Fire Next Time." Perhaps it's obvious that putting this work at the end provides an almost perfect frame to beginning with *Native Son*, but I'll say it anyway. Baldwin's voice is prophetic and uncompromising and, like Wright's, radical in its reach and resonant even today. Here are the "apocalyptic overtones" Bell speaks of, writ large. Here is a challenge to all of us, the "test case of the nation's claims to freedom, democracy, equality" that Raboteau described:

> And I repeat: The price of the liberation of the white people is the liberation of the blacks—the total liberation, in the cities, in the towns, before the law, and in the mind. . . . In short, we, the black and the white, deeply need each other here if we are really to become a nation—if we are really, that is, to achieve our identity, our maturity, as men and women.[11] . . . If we—and now I mean the relatively conscious whites and the relatively conscious blacks, who must, like lovers, insist on, or create, the consciousness of the others—do not falter in our duty now, we may be able, handful that we are, to end the racial nightmare, and achieve our country, and change the history of the world. If we do not now dare everything, the fulfillment of that prophecy, recreated from the Bible in song by a slave, is upon us: *God gave Noah the rainbow sign, No more water, the fire next time!* [12]

Clearly we have not yet "ended the racial nightmare," nor managed fully to "achieve our country." Nor may it ever be within our reach to "change the history of the world." But asking students to encounter the moral and intellectual challenge of Baldwin's bold, sometimes difficult ideas can change their worlds, and that's not a trivial consequence. Once again, through Baldwin we provide a forum for sophisticated, critical thinking, for enlarging students' sense of historical context and complexity, and for experiencing directly the power of language.

II.

Another crucial forum for this kind of critical thinking and exploration is available to those working within what is commonly considered the mainstream or traditional curriculum of the American high school. Unfortunately, not every high school will offer the kind of electives I've been describing. But what high school in this country doesn't teach American literature, usually with our river-rafting young friend Huck Finn smack in the middle of that mainstream? What opportunities does his presence in the canon provide for new approaches, informed by readily available scholarship in African American studies? Here is a "rip in the tent" of significant proportion. As Shelley Fisher Fishkin says, "A shift in paradigm is in order. Understanding African-American traditions is essential if one wants to understand mainstream American literary history."[13]

Few books have a more contentious history than *Adventures of Huckleberry Finn,* and few novels enjoy more pride of place in our high school English curricula. The latest round in "the culture wars" surrounding Mark Twain's famous story was an exchange of essays between author Jane Smiley ("Say It Ain't So, Huck: Second Thoughts on Mark Twain's 'Masterpiece'" in *Harper's Magazine,* January 1996) and critic Justin Kaplan ("Selling 'Huck Finn' Down the River" in *The New York Times Book Review,* March 1996). To summarize their complex lines of argument is to trivialize them, but it's worth noting that the battle lines in these essays, as in others of recent vintage, continue to be drawn largely around defending or denouncing the novel's place in the American literary canon. Jerry W. Ward, Jr. of Tougaloo College, who moderated a panel at the 1996 conference of the College Language Association at which a version of this paper was presented, suggested that what we ought to be looking at is "how we are behaving historically, what interventions we are making now," as we consider these contested texts and related issues.

Ever since William L. Andrews spoke at our NEH Summer Institute in African American Literature in 1993, I've been intrigued by the connections he pointed out between slave narratives (which Toni Cade Bambara says should more properly be called "freedom narratives") and some of the most popular and revered works in the American literary canon. Two works in particular, *Uncle Tom's Cabin* and *Adventures of Huckleberry Finn*, owe the deepest of debts to the African American literary tradition in general and to "freedom narratives" in particular. Yet many high school English and history teachers are not familiar with the slave narrative, with its literary conventions or with its place in history. In the interest of time and space, I'll focus here on *Adventures of Huckleberry Finn*, mentioning the research presented by Andrews along with the groundbreaking work of Shelley Fisher Fishkin in *Was Huck Black? Mark Twain and African-American Voices*.

Too often the African American literary tradition is viewed as marginal to, alongside of, separate from, and secondary to the real American literary tradition (Faulkner, Hemingway, Twain, Hawthorne, Melville, et al.) and not at the center, not woven so deeply into the fabric of American letters as to be integral, inseparable, indispensable. Yet as Ralph Waldo Ellison says in his 1970 essay, "What America Would Be Like Without Blacks"

> [T]he melting pot did indeed melt, creating such deceptive metamorphoses and blending of identities, values and life-styles that most American whites are culturally part Negro American without even realizing it. . . . [I]njustices have failed to keep Negroes clear of the cultural mainstream; Negro Americans are in fact one of its major tributaries.[14]

Theodore Parker, the celebrated Unitarian minister from Boston, claimed that the slave narrative is, in fact, our most original indigenous American literary form. This claim is echoed by Ralph Waldo Emerson, that quintessential American man of letters who deemed this "discourse of the living" of vital interest and importance to the writing and thinking of the day.[15] As Andrews and others document, this immensely popular genre spawned a whole side industry of fictionalized accounts, sentimental novels (many by white authors, abolitionists, and others), lecture tours, newspaper editorials, and spirited contemporary commentary. The Reverend Ephraim Peabody compared the narratives of the fugitive slaves to Homeric epics, saying, "[The fugitive slaves] encounter a whole *Iliad* of woes . . . or if the *Iliad* should be thought not to present a parallel case, we know not where one who wished to write a modern *Odyssey* could find a better subject than in the adventures of a fugitive slave."[16] Mark Twain would, perhaps, agree.

Not everybody was pleased by this wildfire popularity. Wrote one disgruntled correspondent, "It's all very well for the South to talk of Negro excitements, and to take things to heart. If they had to read all those Negro books that overflow us, north of Mason and Dixon's line, then, indeed, we should despair of them. We don't want, therefore, to hear any more complaints from Georgia or Carolina."[17]

So, slave narratives, or freedom narratives, were all the rage in Twain's time, and very much at the center of public discourse. In the late 1860s and 1870s, Twain was impressed by the narrative skills of black speakers such as Frederick Douglass, as he wrote in a letter to his future wife: "Had a talk with Fred Douglas (sic), to-day, who seemed exceedingly glad to see me—& I certainly was glad to see him, for I do so admire his 'spunk.'" Andrews argues convincingly that Twain would also have come across the Reverend James W. C. Pennington and his narrative, published in 1850, *The Fugitive Blacksmith*. As Andrews says,

> Mark Twain knew about the fugitive slave narrative genre and owned a copy of Charles Ball's *Slavery in the United States: A Narrative of the Life and Adventures of Charles Ball, A Black Man*, which he used as a source for *A Connecticut Yankee in King Arthur's Court*. Fugitive slave narratives were the sort of book Mark Twain liked to read combining, as they do, the staples of his literary diet: 'History, biography, travels, curious facts and strange happenings.' These literary preferences, his life-long interest in Afro-Americans, and the evidence of his knowledge and use of one slave narrative all suggest that, given the opportunity to read a short and exciting account like Pennington's, Mark Twain may well have done so.[18]

A much fuller discussion of this matter of direct literary influence and probable appropriation can be found in Andrews's chapter of this book.

Prefiguring the arguments of Toni Morrison in *Playing in the Dark* and of Shelley Fishkin in *Was Huck Black?*, Ellison also told us in 1970:

For one thing, the American nation is in a sense the product of the American language, a colloquial speech that began emerging long before the British colonials and Africans were transformed into Americans. . . . It is a language that began by merging the sounds of many tongues. . . . And whether it is admitted or not, much of the sound of that language is derived from the timbre of the African voice and the listening habits of the African ear. So there is a de'z and do'z of slave speech sounding beneath our most polished Harvard accents, and if there is such a thing as a Yale accent, there is a Negro wail in it—doubtless introduced there by Old Yalie John C. Calhoun, who probably got it from his mammy.

Whitman viewed the spoken idiom of Negro Americans as a source for a native grand opera. Its flexibility, its musicality, its rhythms, free-wheeling diction, and metaphors, as projected in Negro American folklore, were absorbed by the creators of our great nineteenth-century literature even when the majority of blacks were still enslaved. Mark Twain celebrated it in the prose of *Huckleberry Finn; without the presence of blacks, the book could not have been written. No Huck and Jim, no American novel as we know it.*[19] [Emphasis added]

Fishkin's book examines in meticulous detail just how, exactly, "the black man is co-creator of the language [of] Mark Twain." Without, quite specifically, "Sociable Jimmy" and a young slave named Jerry, without Mary Ann Cord and George Griffin, real-life African Americans Twain knew and admired and whose stories he recorded and told, the book would not exist.

"Sociable Jimmy" was Twain's first published work in which the voice of a child took center stage, a fact that, Fishkin points out, should have attracted scholarly interest but has, instead, been almost totally ignored.[20] When he met "Sociable Jimmy," Twain was so captivated by the youngster's speech that he wrote down what the child said and sent it home because he "wished to preserve the memory of the most artless, sociable and exhaustless talker I ever came across. . . . [H]is talk got the upper hand of my interest, too, and I listened as one who receives a revelation. I took down what he had to say, just as he said it—without altering a word or adding one." Shortly thereafter, he wrote to Livy, "I think I could swing my legs over the arms of a chair &

that boy's spirit would descend upon me & enter into me." It was, says Fishkin, "a crucial step on the road to creating Huck."[21]

Fishkin writes that in the same month (November 1874) the *New York Times* published "Sociable Jimmy," Twain's "A True Story" appeared in *Atlantic Monthly*. Called "Aunt Rachel" in the article, Mary Ann Cord was an ex-slave who worked as a servant at the Twains's summer home in Elmira, New York. The author was captivated by her story and took great pride in setting it down for *Atlantic Monthly*'s readers exactly as he had heard it. "She told me a striking tale out of her personal experience, once, & I will copy it here—& not in my words but her own. I wrote them down before they were cold."[22] Fishkin argues that

> That evening in 1874 when Mary Ann Cord captivated Twain and Livy on the porch of Quarry Farm may have been almost as important a step on the road to *Huckleberry Finn* as Twain's encounter with Jimmy two years earlier. For, while Jimmy's vernacular speech intrigued Twain, Mary Ann Cord showed Twain the possibilities of combining vernacular speech with accomplished narrative skill. . . . Her story impressed Twain as a "curiously strong piece of literary work to come unpremeditated from lips untrained in literary art."[23]

Another telling influence on Twain was Jerry, whom Twain once described as "the greatest man in the United States, though in the version printed posthumously he was just the greatest orator." Fishkin says, "One can imagine Twain having listened to Jerry much as he had listened to Jimmy: 'as one who receives a revelation.' The revelation in this case was of the power of satire—satire in an African-American vein, the indirect, double-voiced variety of satire known as 'signifying.'"[24] Twain writes,

> Fifty years ago, when I was a boy of fifteen and helping to inhabit a Missourian village on the banks of the Mississippi, I had a friend whose society was very dear to me because I was forbidden by my mother to partake of it. He was a gay and impudent and satirical and delightful young black man—a slave—who daily preached sermons from the top of his master's woodpile, with me for the sole audience. He imitated the pulpit style of the several clergymen of the village, and did it well, and with fine passion and energy. To me he was a wonder. I believed he was the greatest orator in the United States.[25]

The kind of "signifying" speech that so fascinated Mark Twain in Jerry's sermons is absolutely central to the language and the satire in *Huck Finn*. Fishkin gives a plethora of examples, including Pap's speech railing against the "guv'ment" and the scene where George leads Huck to Jim with a fable about water moccasins. Fishkin proposes that Jerry's great appeal for Twain was his "ability to harness the power of satire to his own ends, an ability Twain himself would hone throughout his long career."[26] She poses the question whether Huck, like Jerry, is a classic "trickster" figure, "a master of 'signifying' who rhetorically outwits his stronger, more powerful adversaries." [27]

The case of Jim's voice is a complicated matter and is taken up at length in Fishkin's book. She writes:

> [R]eading *Huckleberry Finn* in an American secondary-school class-room can be an enormously painful experience for a black student. Twain's sympathy for Jim may have been genuine, but Jim's voice retains enough of minstrelsy in it to be demeaning and depressing. Black students reading the book may well identify—as Ralph Ellison and his brother did—with Huck, instead of Jim. Given our awareness now of the extent to which Huck's voice was black, black students who find themselves identifying with Huck may feel somewhat less ambivalence. After all, they are not identifying "against" their race: rather they are choosing which of two black voices in the book they find more appealing. Nonetheless, Jim, the major figure in the book who sounds black, looks black, and is black, is still there, and must be dealt with.
>
> One cannot get around the fact that Jim's voice is, ultimately, a diminished voice, a voice cramped within boundaries as confining as his prison-shack on the Phelps Plantation. It is not a voice with which any student, black or white, whose self-esteem is intact would choose to identify for very long. Yet it is often the only black voice on the syllabus.[28]

As Ward points out, the novel presents us with a problem of subject position, with the issue of who *staged* the voices that we hear in the story.[29] There are indeed black voices throughout *Huck Finn*, but Twain is always there, too, of course, pulling the authorial strings of plot, character, and voice; splitting, in a sense, the black vernacular and drive toward freedom that are so central to the African American

idiom, into two characters, one white and one black, in ways that ultimately diminish and distort the obviously black-voiced character of
Jim.

I asked tenth-grade students who had read both *The Narrative of
the Life of Frederick Douglass* and *Adventures of Huckleberry Finn* to tell
me what they saw as important similarities between the two texts.
Interestingly, most students more readily volunteered differences. "It's
hard for me to think about the similarities between *The Narrative of
the Life of Frederick Douglass, Written by Himself* and *Huck Finn*. I could
mention the burning desires of Jim and Frederick while they are both
slaves. That's similar. I can also mention the importance of travel in
both books. They seem to have more differences to me than anything
else" (Sydonya Barker). Another: "Frederick Douglass is portrayed as an
African-American of high importance. He was a very determined man,
who strongly believed in his rights as a human being. *Huck Finn's*
African-American figure is Jim, who is not as educated and determined
for his rights as Douglass" (no name). And, "In *The Narrative of the Life
of Frederick Douglass,* he [Douglass] is portrayed as a pious and well-
educated man who had fought for his freedom, while Jim in *Huck Finn*
is shown in such a way that demeaned him as a person" (Michael
Birmingham). Douglass and Twain were not only contemporaries, but
knew each other. Both wrote books that "capture the reality of slavery
in the south," but "the narrative just shows the treatment of black
slaves more thoroughly and with more detail" (Latoya Linton).

Students, at least at this age, perceive in *The Narrative of the Life of
Frederick Douglass, Written by Himself* a portrayal "from a black perspective, [as having] less stereotypes . . . [in] a more dignified fashion about
blacks."[30] The undignified portrayal of Jim is but one of the problematic aspects of how Twain has "staged" the voices in the novel. The
whole question of what happens to Jim at the end of the novel is also
troubling. Fishkin takes up the question in her book, in a provocative
analysis of Twain's thinking on Reconstruction and race. (See especially
Part Four: "Break Dancing in the Drawing Room.") For further discussion, the essays in *Satire or Evasion? Black Perspectives on Huckleberry
Finn*[31] are invaluable.

As we teach *Huck Finn*, it may be interesting to think of the novel as a thwarted slave narrative. At a crucial point, the raft conveying Jim toward freedom veers deeper south. Not only that, Tom shows up and stages an elaborate "escape" plan that serves to shackle Jim all over again, psychologically as well as physically. This is a startling reversal of the classic slave narrative pattern Andrews describes, one in which the journey is from the South to the North, from bondage to freedom. Indeed, at the end of the novel Jim virtually disappears; we don't really know what becomes of him.

What's to be done, then? Toss the revered text out of the curriculum? Continue to enshrine it as the book from which all American literature derives, like tributaries from the mighty Mississippi? Should *Huck Finn* be the "race novel," the vehicle through which teachers and students attempt to struggle with some of the thornier issues of our time? Clearly not. Fishkin states,

> Jim must not be the only African-American voice from the nineteenth century that is heard in the classroom. Twain's novel must not be the only book that raises issues of American race relations. The only way to counter the demeaning experience of encountering Jim's voice is by adding others, by exposing students to the eloquence of Frederick Douglass and W.E.B. Du Bois, to the "signifying" wit of Charles W. Chesnutt and Paul Laurence Dunbar, to folk tales and folk sermons, to the rhetorical power of Sojourner Truth, to the lucid anger of Ida B. Wells. . . . Mark Twain's use of black voices in *Huckleberry Finn* may have been an act of appreciation, rather than appropriation. . . . Our classrooms must be as open to and appreciative of African-American voices as was Mark Twain's imagination.[32]

As my NEH colleague Marcelline Rogers says, "Mark Twain's Jim needs to meet Charles Chesnutt's Uncle Julius." Knowing that Mark Twain knew Charles Chesnutt and, on at least one photographed occasion, had him over for dinner, merely strengthens the argument of historical and literary propinquity.

We must reclaim the history that nourished this rich and complicated novel, as Fishkin and Andrews and Ellison and other scholars have done. We must teach it to our students. When Hemingway said,

"All modern literature comes from one book by Mark Twain called *Huckleberry Finn*. . . . There was nothing before. There has been nothing as good since," we may allow for the hyperbole, but we shouldn't fall for the idea.[33] There was a great deal before, and it needs its place not at the margins, but at the center of our appreciation and our discourse.

Notes

1. Toni Morrison, "African American Intellectual Life at Princeton: *A Conversation*," (Princeton University Office of Communications and Publications: Stanhope Hall, Princeton, NJ) p. 5.

2. Inez Dover, participant, NEH Summer Institute in African-American Literature, 1993–1994.

3. James Baldwin, *The Fire Next Time* (New York: Vintage International, 1993), p. 96.

4. Morrison, op. cit.

5. Working paper 189, "White Privilege and Male Privilege: A Personal Account of Coming to See Correspondences through Work in Women's Studies" (1988); available for $4 from the Wellesley College Center for Research on Women, Wellesley, MA 02181.

6. Alan Stoskopf in "Facing History and Ourselves Newsletter," Winter 1990–1991. Facing History, 16 Harvard Road, Brookline, MA.

8. Bernard Bell, *The Afro-American Novel and Its Tradition* (Amherst: University of Mass Press), pp. 142–43.

9. Arnold Rampersad, quoting Richard Wright in Introduction to *Native Son* (HarperPerennial, 1993), p. xviii.

10. Ibid.

11. Bell, *The African American Literary Tradition*, pp. 142–43.

12. Baldwin, *The Fire Next Time*, p. 97.

13. Ibid., pp. 5–106.

14. Shelley Fisher Fishkin. *Was Huck Black? Mark Twain and African-American Voices* (New York and Oxford: Oxford University Press, 1993). p. 143.

15. Ralph W. Ellison, *Going to the Territory* (New York: Random House, 1986), p. 108.

16. From lecture notes, William Andrews, NEH Summer Institute in African-American Literature, 1993.

17. Marion Wilson Starling *The Slave Narrative: Its Place in American History* (Washington, DC: Howard University Press, 1988), p. 97.

18. Ibid., p. 37.

19. William L. Andrews, "Mark Twain and James Pennington: Huckleberry Finn's Smallpox Lie." *Studies in American Fiction 9* (Spring 1981): pp. 107–108.

20. Ellison, *Going to the Territory*, pp 108-109.

21. Fishkin, Was Huck Black? p. 14.

22. Ibid., pp. 14–15.

23. Ibid., p. 31.

24. Ibid., pp. 36–37.

25. Ibid., p. 55.

26. Ibid., p. 54.

27. Ibid., p. 65.

28. Ibid.

29. Ibid., p. 107.

30. College Language Association, April 1996, oral remarks.

31. Students in the class of 1998 at Noble and Greenough School, Dedham, MA.

32. James S. Leonard, Thomas A. Tenney, and Thadious M. Davis, *Satire or Evasion? Black Perspectives on Huckleberry Finn* (Durham, NC: Duke University Press, 1991).

33. Ibid., p. 108.

34. Ernest Hemingway, *Green Hills of Africa* (New York: Macmillan, 1963, rpt. 1987), p. 22.

❊ 3 ❊

MULTIPLE VOICES,
MULTIPLE IDENTITIES
Teaching African American Literature

Jane Skelton
*Muriel C. Snowden International High School
Boston, Massachusetts*

> *I envy neither the heart nor the head of any legislator who has been born to an inheritance of privileges, who has behind him ages of education, dominion, civilization, and Christianity, if he stands opposed to the passage of a national education bill, whose purpose is to secure education to the children of those who were born under the shadow of institutions which made it a crime to read.*
>
> —FRANCES E. W. HARPER,
> "Women's Political Future"

I

As a teacher of English and theater in the Boston Public Schools for almost nineteen years, I am more than aware of the significance the learning environment can have on identity issues. This is especially true at Snowden International High School, where we emphasize world cultures and languages and where the students come from all over the city of Boston and represent the increasing diversity of the city. The students at Snowden are predominantly African American and Latino/a, but also Caribbean, white European, and Asian. There is a constant need to engage in dialogue about the cultural beliefs that form our conceptions of identity in terms students will recognize and understand. For these students, multiculturalism often becomes the umbrella for understanding and balancing the images, identities, and experiences in the material presented for study with the diversity of the classroom.

In creating a positive and engaging learning environment in schools with diverse cultural and ethnic populations, then, we need to consider the dynamics of identity development as a variable of instruction. Beverly-Daniel Tatum, who has done extensive research on racial identity and assimilation issues for African American students, concludes that students' expectations for the future are strongly affected by the role models they encounter in their home and school communities.[1] If school curriculum presents a limited and marginalized representation of the past, the ultimate impact for the African American student may be a reinforced sense of powerlessness and marginal involvement in the present and future.

Like all teachers, I bring my own experiences into the classroom. Growing up in the South, I can recall all kinds of people who looked like me, from domestics to college librarians and from factory workers to military officers; yet I also remember that no similar images appeared in the history or literature I was required to read as a student. The curriculum I encountered simply wasn't open for direct ownership, and that extended to extracurricular activities as well. Because of color casting, for example, I and other black students could be part of the drama club in high school only as stage hands or box office help. It wasn't until I was in college that I discovered the full extent to which African Americans had participated in and influenced American society and culture. Even in college, however, this information was hard to come by. It was mostly through discussions with black faculty or artists working in the community that I knew what to look for and where to find it, not through any formal course work as a teacher in training—just as, I would argue, the case is for many of my students today.

My interest in African American literature, nevertheless, has had a tremendous impact on how I view the power of language and literacy and the influence that it can have on self-identity.

Whenever I incorporate information about African Americans in

53

my classroom instruction, I am met with awe from students confronting for the first time the diversity of social, political, and economic statuses held by African Americans throughout our history here, from the enslaved to the free-born, to illiterate sharecroppers, educated scholars, and artists—and everything in between. Perhaps their confusion stems from the fact that the schema they use to access and organize information is undergirded by stereotypes. I remember showing a documentary film on the life and work of Langston Hughes. The film depicts well-educated, middle-class Harlem blacks (somewhere in American history between slavery and civil rights), well-dressed, well-traveled, holding literary soirees and sailing off to Europe and to Africa, reflecting, in other words, a black experience far from that of the slave or the disenfranchised. After watching the film, one of the seniors blurted out, "I didn't know black people lived that way back then."

While innocent, my student's disclosure reflects a perception shared by most students and, indeed, most of their teachers. That is to say that although Hughes and other African American writers are anthologized at varying levels in today's curriculum, they are seldom presented *in context*; and rarely is individual meaning attributed to the work or the author. The assumption is that all black authors write about slavery and oppression; that we have all lived the same life. This view also makes it easy to assume that reading one piece of literature by a black American is like reading any other. Even the writers of the Harlem Renaissance, a literary movement with profound implications regarding how and for whom African American writers created art, are seldom presented in texts for teachers as being part of an historical continuum of American letters. Rather they are construed as an elite (and aberrational) group of black, predominantly male writers who were fortunate enough to enjoy white patronage and permission. Thus, a rich array of poets, novelists, essayists, and visual artists—multiple voices and multiple identities that our students might access—barely make it into school curriculum and, if they do, go uninterpreted in the wider domain of cultural production.

When students ask me, "Why read?" I tell them that they'd better, because what they see on television has already been censored and approved for public consumption. After all, next to school, and in some cases more so, television is their main source of cultural knowledge. But the media are guided by consumer principles of supply and demand, and its images of black people are gleaned from popular opinion and codes of acceptability organized along the least common denominator.

In fact, most of the black people our students see and hear about through the mainstream media are the subjects of insidious "real-life" crime shows, the products of "broken" homes or single-parent families. As a result, our students develop a sense of identity in a society highly mediated by stereotypes of black people: the athlete, the rapper, the welfare mother, the gang-banger. Even the more benign situation comedies place amiable black people in totally deracialized, middle-class environments where lightness reigns and problems are solved within one or maybe two story lines. I'm not interested in media bashing, nor do I think the responsibility for educating kids should be left up to an industry whose overall objective is ultimately to entertain and to sell advertising. Rather I am convinced that as educators we need to balance these images so that students have access to a range of role models with which they might identify. I teach African American literature because it offers rich opportunities to help me achieve this balance and because I could not conceive of teaching English in any way without it.

II

If our students' perspectives on black people in the present are bleak, their ideas about the past are even worse. A focus on African American literature from the nineteenth century not only deconstructs the myth that African American identity can be construed solely in terms of oppression and disenfranchisement, but also reveals other possibilities of human existence under such circumstances. For thinking about identity issues, the nineteenth century provides an especially apt historical context, as it highlights a time when both America and Afro-America were undergoing simultaneous identity transformations. America was a nation in flux, pulling further and further away from its

European roots and moving rapidly toward industrialization and urbanization. Afro-America, on the other hand, was responding to new freedoms, migrating north, from field to factory, and finally gaining political representation. In this context, we find black women at the forefront of political leadership and social change.

My emphasis on the nineteenth century comes as a result of an informal survey I conducted with about sixty of my students some five years ago. I wanted to test what my students knew (or thought they knew) about the history of black women in this country. Their responses reinforced what I'd already suspected: slaves and victims. True, some of the students had a passing familiarity with Phillis Wheatley, Harriet Tubman, and Sojourner Truth, but most of them had no real sense of who these women were and what they represented, nor could they name others, such as poet, novelist, essayist, and activist Frances Ellen Watkins Harper, a popular and prolific writer and one of the most respected leaders in the abolitionist movement; or Anna Julia Cooper, who, though born a slave, went on to teach mathematics and earn a Ph.D. in French at the University of Paris; or Pauline E. Hopkins, a Bostonian who at the turn of the century wrote for *Colored American Magazine*, one of the most important black periodicals of its time. This list of heroic black voices could continue into the 1920s, 30s, and forward, although I hope I've made my point. I don't mean to imply that a list of heroic black voices would be exclusively female; however, access to these writers is especially significant as our children continue to receive mixed messages about black women's sexuality, social status, and intellectual ability. What might they make about the fact that a black woman, Maria W. Stewart, was the first woman ever—of any color—to address publicly a mixed group, men and women together, that is, and that a black woman challenged the Christian authority of the patriarchy long before the women's movement of the 1970s? Far more than mere symbols of oppression, these women went well beyond what was expected of them, and that is precisely what I want for *all* of my students: for them to exceed the limitations of a race-conscious society. And I want them to know that they come by it honestly.

Let me try to illustrate how I help students respond to literature personally and contextually. About three years ago, I put together a packet on African American poetry for a tenth-grade English class that included works by Frances E. W. Harper, Jupiter Hammon, George Moses Horton, and Sterling Brown, among others. My selections were designed to fill in some of the gaps in their knowledge and also to discuss the ideas of accommodation and protest in African American poetry. In this class, the students were assigned approximately ten poems per week to which they were to respond in their journals, focusing especially on theme and topic and identifying literary structures and conventions in the poem. In class, they would be asked to read aloud a poem of their choosing and to discuss their personal connection to it.

One of Harper's poems, "A Double Standard," about a woman who can't escape the stigma of an affair, even though her male lover, "gay and proud/Still bears an honest name," emerged as a clear favorite, especially among the girls (nearly all of them had selected it as the one they would read in class).[2] Though my students were surprised that they could interpret and would actually like nineteenth-century poetry, I wasn't. The poem's ballad structure is a familiar one, and its rhythm and rhyme makes it inviting to students at various reading levels. And, after all, "Double Standard" is about thwarted love, and to what teenager does that not appeal?

As we usually do, we talked about the nature of poetry and identified specific formal elements such as metaphor, simile, and other forms of figurative language that poets use to create imagery and convey meaning. We asked of the poem the usual questions about form: what kind of metaphors does it contain? What is the mood or tone of the poem? Does it use repetition?

To give context to our interpretations, on the other hand, we talked about the cult of true womanhood, piety, and domesticity. I recommend to teachers wanting to have this same discussion Hazel Carby's *Reconstructing Womanhood* for its thorough understanding of the sexual ideologies that black women sought to reinterpret in their writing during the nineteenth century.

Our discussion continued as we looked at Harper as a protest writer.

57

We talked about the significance of Harper as an African American woman publicly challenging the status quo. The students, especially the girls, were mindful of the fact that in the 1850s, women struggled with some of the very same problems they struggle with in the 1990s. Asked how the poem relates to what they know today about the status of women, they pointed out that girls always have "to know better" and "it's always up to the girl not to get pregnant." The "double standard," they charged, is about "how girls always get blamed for everything!"

The boys in the class, interestingly enough, although they were invited to comment on the accuracy of the girls' perceptions, were mostly observers during this process. Thinking back on the dynamics of this particular moment of this particular class, I can only speculate as to whether their silence signaled agreement or disagreement, or whether they were simply listening to what the girls had to say. I will say that I recall a respectful silence, and also that I never worry about "neglecting" the boys when I'm teaching women writers. I settled that decision long ago. In fact, I think boys are very interested in the female perspectives, just as I think students who aren't African American are interested in black perspectives.

As a teacher, I believe that in the development of life-long learners it is crucial for students to have a "true" awareness of not only what is common to, but what is contradictory to, their beliefs. To bestow authority of the human experience or identity to one particular gender, race, or culture substantially limits the potential for critical discussion and the dynamics of personal discovery in a classroom setting.

III

Because I love exploring the possibilities of language and its dynamics within social and cultural constructs, I often use drama as an interactive pedagogy to promote language development. Last year I taught Alice Childress's *Trouble in Mind* in a developmental reading class of eleventh- and twelfth-graders who have been identified as having substantial difficulties with reading and writing.[3] Drama is especially suitable for developmental classes because it requires a high level of student engagement with linguistic issues and yet allows them to explore these issues "in character."

You can imagine that by the time these kids find themselves in a developmental class, they have limited expectations about the approval they are likely to receive as to their own use of language and the achievement they are likely to attain. So the play gave us a chance to talk about some of the linguistic issues that tend to frustrate developmental readers and writers, especially the differences between written and spoken texts, while taking on the personae of someone else. Speech patterns in *Trouble in Mind,* for example, range from standard English to regional and cultural dialects. This means these students, some of whom speak English as a second language, had to ask (and answer) some pretty sophisticated questions about the nature of orality. Which characters in the play speak in dialect, and which use standard English? How can we tell? Does situational context make any difference? Which characters code shift and when do they and why? How does the ability or inability to shift codes suggest relationships between characters? Though I'm not willing to take on the Ebonics debate currently raging, I will say that my emphasis on linguistic contexts is meant to move students toward further literacy in standard English while tapping what they already know about how language is used and to what ends.

I also like to teach plays because, more than any other literary form, they invite students to participate. For students to get into character, however, contextual knowledge is critical. *Trouble in Mind* is about a group of actors who are rehearsing a play called *Chaos in Belleville,* a lynching melodrama written and directed by whites. One character, Wiletta, an actress who is well acquainted with many such productions, refuses to work in protest of the offensive stereotyping of the play's black characters.

Before we begin reading, I tell the students a little bit about Childress herself. And because I want to highlight Childress's example of resistance as it will appear in *Trouble in Mind,* I ask them to respond in their journals to a philosophical statement by Childress:

A part of Black Liberation struggle is to constantly evaluate or to
reevaluate ground we have covered, making sure that we are not judg-
ing our struggle by appearances; substituting appearances for struggle
. . . dashiki, jewelry, language, stance, attitudes, music preference,
soul food . . . used in place of concrete action, or used as delaying
action because we may not know exactly what to do at the moment.
Knowing we are in trouble and knowing we do not exactly know
what to do . . . is true knowledge and gives us a clean slate to start
with. We are varied people and our ideas are bound to clash . . . but I
remind myself frequently that symbols may trick us.[4]

I like this statement not only for the historical and sociopolitical contexts it provides, but because it problematizes those symbols that pass
for markers of cultural and ideological identification and affiliation.
During the height of black liberation, "dashikis" and "soul food," as
Childress points out, sometimes became signifiers that took the place
of "concrete action." More recently, I reminded my students, those
ubiquitous "X's" gracing any manner of adornment purchased by
black youth took on a similar (a)political function.

My students' interpretations of Childress's statement didn't go very
deep at first; their interpretations ranged from "You can't be satisfied
with things" and "You have to speak up" to "Just because you wear the
right hair or say the right thing doesn't mean you're smarter or better
than someone else." But since this was a prereading discussion, I was
willing to wait for a less superficial response. I knew we were on to
something, however, when postreading discussions took up a slightly
different line of discourse. One of my students who comes from a
country in the Caribbean wrote, for example, "People lump us all
together as black. They think that because you look black, you are all
the same but African-Americans don't necessarily see us the same . . .
we don't know the same history." Another student pointed out that "if
you're Black, you're supposed to like rap and to dress hip hop." In
doing so, they were registering important protests of their own: that
they are expected to accommodate a variety of perceptions about what
it means to be black, perceptions that are at times simply inaccurate
and at other times no more than stereotypes.

Although my goal was not to produce a staged performance of the play, I wanted to emphasize the kind of knowledge necessary for directors to convey subtext and to achieve context. To help them realize that understanding that "setting" means much more than mere dates and locality when interpreting drama, then, the students were instructed to bring to class information on events happening in 1955, the year the play was written. We discovered that 1955 was the year Rosa Parks refused to give up her seat on a Montgomery, Alabama, bus; that fourteen-year old Emmet Till was murdered that year; that the Supreme Court outlawed segregation in public facilities in 1955; and that even though black people and white people were dancing to Chuck Berry's hit single "Maybelline," the burgeoning civil rights movement was fueling increased racial tensions all over America, and especially in the South. To facilitate a contextual reading of the play, I also suggested they take notes as they read in order to locate where the play makes references to lynching [which of course necessitated an explanation of the term and the widespread practice of lynching in the South], segregation, social status, the civil rights movement, and access to employment and education. These notes would become the focus of pre- and postreading discussions. Against this background, *Trouble in Mind* became interpretable and Wiletta's objection to her role in *Chaos in Belleville*—for example, that Manners expects her to portray a woman who would actually try to convince her son that he must face his lynch mob with dignity, took on its full import.

On the surface, *Trouble in Mind* isn't particularly "in your face." Often it makes its point gently, and not without laughter. Much of the confrontation with white racism is explicated through dialogue between the black actors who must justify why they stay in the business. In this early scene, Wiletta and Millie, who are veterans of more than one *Chaos*, point out to the younger, disbelieving John the absurdity as well as the banality of life as a black actor in 1955.

> MILLIE: Last show I was in, I wouldn't even tell my relatives. All I did was shout "Lord, have mercy!" for almost two hours every night.
> WILETTA: Yes, but you did it, so hush! She's played every flower in the garden. Let's see, what was your name in that TV mess?

61

MILLIE: Never mind.

WILETTA: Gardenia! She was Gardenia! 'Nother thing she was Magnolia, Chrysanthemum was another. . . .

MILLIE: And you've done the jewels . . . Crystal, Pearl, Opal! (Millie laughs)

JOHN: (Weak, self-conscious laughter) Oh, now . . .[5]

Nevertheless, this is grim business, and the double-bind, as the students were quick to point out, was that were it not for those stereotypes, the actors would have no place on the stage. Class discussion suggested that students were thinking hard about what we are willing to do to be accepted. Some students felt that Wiletta also jeopardizes her fellow actors' jobs when she quits the play. For textual "proof," they cited how Sheldon says to Millie, "You holler when there's no work, when the man give you some, you holler just as loud. Ain't no pleasin' you!" (216)[6] Others thought that she did the only thing she could do and that although Wiletta's protest came with a price, it had also prompted some of the other characters to consider their own collusion in the dehumanization of African Americans.

Although the characters can at times laugh at their situation, the gravity of Wiletta's protest is always present. Upon reflection, this would have been a great moment to bring in the concept of masking ("We wear the mask that grins and lies, / It hides our cheeks and shades our eyes—") as expressed by nineteenth-century poet Paul Laurence Dunbar, who, ironically, was himself criticized for perpetuating stereotypes in some poems he wrote in plantation dialect. *Trouble in Mind* is, after all, about wearing the masks of oppression—and choosing to take them off.

We also talked about how although the play predates Lorraine Hansberry's 1959 *Raisin in the Sun, Trouble in Mind* never made it to Broadway because Childress refused to change the ending of the play to make it more palatable to white audiences. In the version the students read, the play ends with Wiletta refusing to play her role as scripted and with the players not knowing what will come next. I asked them to think about the revisions Childress might have been asked to make given what they now know was going on in 1955. In doing so, I was not much interested in coming to a definitive conclusion as I was in getting the students to speculate about the author's decision based on what they knew of the play's historical context. The level of student comprehension and engagement is reflected in the following response by one twelfth-grader:

> She [Wiletta] didn't want her son to be killed and probably the producers said to make the play say the boy had to be sent out [to a lynch mob]. That's the way it had to be. Maybe it was also because Wiletta stuck up for herself against a white man by saying she refused to do the play. . . . Maybe it was because she felt that no one in their *right mind* would send their son out to be murdered [emphasis added].

Maybe, indeed.

IV

That children hardly read anymore is no secret, and indeed, many of our students are barely literate. And yet we continue to draw battle lines around what we might teach, as my colleague Kate Coon reminds us elsewhere in this volume, instead of thinking wisely about what might compel kids to read more—what might inspire them to full literacy. And so I want to conclude by saying that teaching African American literature is not about making political concessions to black students. Rather it is about offering *all* of our children a range of possible identities so that they might recognize many different voices and claim new identities for themselves. Teaching African American literature is about putting children in touch with those who have triumphed under the direst of circumstances so that they might understand how indestructible the human spirit is: even though it was a crime for George Moses Horton to read, he still wrote Romantic poetry. It's about reminding them that our physical environment doesn't necessarily limit what we might become: Francis E. W. Harper earned her living as a domestic before becoming one of the most well-respected public figures of her day. It is about persuading students to think about their education as a process and not just some means to an end, especially when the rewards for getting a high school diploma simply aren't there anymore.

When we talk about exploring identities we're really talking about life options. The kids that come back and see us during alumni week at Snowden come back because some emotional support was provided for them, or because they found out something about themselves while they were there. It is my hope for them that even if they haven't figured out that one thing they think they're going to be when they grow up, the journey through school will have had its great moments.

Notes

1. Beverly-Daniel Tatum, "African-American Identity Development, Academic Achievement, and Missing History," *Social Education:* 56 (1992): 331–34.

2. Frances, E. W. Harper, "A Double Standard," in *African American Poetry of the Nineteenth Century: An Anthology*, ed. Joan R. Sherman (Urbana: University of IL Press, 1992).

3. Alice Childress, *Trouble in Mind*, in *Black Theatre*, ed. Lindsay Patterson (New York: Plume, 1971).

4. Elizabeth Brown-Guillory, *Their Place on the Stage: Black Women Playwrights in America* (New York: Greenwood Press, 1988).

5. Childress, *Trouble in Mind*, p. 216.

6. Ibid.

LITTLE HAM'S SELF-INVENTION
Teaching Langston Hughes

Leslie Catherine Sanders
York University

> *Performance . . . records the way in which black people, through a*
> *communicative action, engender themselves within the American*
> *experience. . . . [P]erformance presumes an existing tradition and*
> *an individual or group of people who interpret that tradition in*
> *front of an audience in such a way that the individual or group of*
> *people invent themselves for that audience.*
> —MANTHIA DIAWARA,
> "Cultural Studies, Black Studies"

In the summer of 1994, I was invited to participate in an NEH Summer Institute on African American Poetry and Drama for high school teachers. My week of lectures took up the history of African American theater; I had assigned about fifteen plays for reading, and the students were required, over the course of the week, to organize themselves into three groups and prepare a scene from any of the plays. I made no suggestions, so I was surprised and delighted to see that a large group had gravitated toward Langston Hughes. The biggest hit was two scenes from his 1936 comedy *Little Ham*: blind casted and using the flimsiest of props, it brought down the house. Particularly surprising was how little his comedy has aged. This play, which even in its own time was regarded by some as pandering to degrading comic stereotypes, endured, one might even say triumphed, in a racially mixed group, whose members were not entirely comfortable with one another—which is to say, a group in which one would not expect the comedy of type to play well.

On one level, the teachers' attraction to Hughes's comedy is easy to understand. Hughes is very funny. The action in *Little Ham* is playful, and the character of type is a familiar and engaging comic mode. The teachers chose scenes containing many characters, so groups could work collectively. Also, not only is Hughes funny, performing him is fun. Besides, Hughes is *always* popular, beloved. He has engaged readers since the beginning of his career with his apparent simplicity; his wit and indirection, his irony and poignancy; his ability to capture, depict, and represent the tone, angle of vision, and point of view of ordinary African Americans, particularly the urban working class. He is best known, of course, for his poetry and prose, particularly his great comic creation Jesse B. Simple, whose wit and wisdom first engaged readers of the Chicago *Defender* in 1943. Later, the columns were republished in five collections and reached a wider public. His work on stage is less well known, and its success was uneven. Yet particularly between the mid-1930s and the early 1940s, and then again in the 1960s, with his gospel plays, Hughes did achieve a measure of theatrical success.

In the history of African American theater, *Little Ham*, Hughes's first comedy and second play to be produced, is important for a number of reasons, and its achievement still has contemporary significance. As a response to the long and complex tradition of black humor—and the black as comic figure within a dominant culture—*Little Ham* comprises a thoughtful revision of black comic stage traditions. In fact, it sought to revolutionize the genre. Its approach, both as a racial and theatrical statement, relies on what only recently has become a site of theoretical exploration, an understanding of racial identity as performance. In its display of black style and styles, *Little Ham* asserts and celebrates a principal cultural mode of communication and self-definition. Thus it alters the terms of black comic performance by producing it within its own space. Moreover, though the script, which depicts the 1920s and was written in the 1930s, is clearly dated in many respects, its mode of self-definition leaves it open to revision in a variety of ways; it begs to be updated, redone in contemporary styles, and so, I will suggest, is a teacher's delight.

The plot of *Little Ham* is quite simple. Little Ham breaks with one woman to take up with another, who also discards a lover to be with him; his number hits, he gets hired as a runner by the white mobsters who take over the game halfway through the play; he is arrested and released, and he and his new love win a Charleston contest in the comic finale. But essentially the plot is simply an excuse to situate the wit of the black comic within the "play of history, culture, and power" that has produced it.[1] Social critique is muted but implicit in *Little Ham*. It emerges in the centrality of the numbers game to the hopes and aspirations of all the characters, in the takeover of the game by white gangsters halfway through the play, in the Shabby Man who announces that his good luck is not at the numbers, as everyone assumes, but that he may have a job. Virtually all of the characters are preoccupied by how best to choose a number to play, and how to get the money to play it. The romantic plot, however, finally dictates the action. Ham succeeds at love, and even hits with the number he saw reflected in his loved one's shoe.

Little Ham himself, or Hamlet Hitchcock Jones, represents an amalgam of comic types, and his repartee is reminiscent of the routines that were the bread and butter of any number of black comics.[2] A womanizer and something of a hustler, Little Ham is always on the edge of trouble, but "me and weapons don't mix," he tells a former lover and his current employer, Madame Lucille Bell, who worries his philandering will end tragically. Ham is sweet as well as a sweet talker, genial, and even kind—he gives Shabby Man a free shoeshine for his first day at work—and in the trickster tradition, he extracts himself from situations by his wits. Ham is inclined to retreat from confrontation; his grandiose name and diminutive stature suggest the comic pretension of the dandy, but there is nothing pompous about him.

In *Little Ham*, all the characters speak black argot; however, their grammatical and linguistic turns are not in themselves a subject for humor, as they were in black musical comedy and vaudeville or burlesque routines, or in the radio show that was virtually transfixing the country, *The Amos 'n' Andy Show.*[3] In fact, *Little Ham* sets out to recuperate comic black speech by setting it in context: most of the play takes place in either a Harlem shine shop or a beauty parlor. In these settings, black comic speech, black comedy, is naturalized and reclaimed. The diversity of characters who wander through these settings will be meaningful only to a black audience; the jokes in *Little Ham* are "in-jokes," private rather than public humor—intragroup signifying, as it were. For example:

> (Enter an EFFEMINATE YOUTH)
> YOUTH: Can I get a polish?
> HAM: You mean your nails?
> YOUTH: I mean my slippers. (*Mounting the stand*)
> HAM: Well, . . . er, are you . . . er, what nationality?
> YOUTH: Creole by birth, but I never draw the color line.
> HAM: I know you don't. Is you married?
> YOUTH: Oh no, I'm in vaudeville.
> HAM: I knowed you was in something. What do you do?
> YOUTH: I began in a horse-act, a comic horse-act.
> HAM: A who?
> YOUTH: A horse-act. I played the hind legs. But I got out of that. I've advanced.
> HAM: To what?
> YOUTH: I give impersonations.
> HAM: Is that what they call that now?
> YOUTH: I impersonate Mae West.
> HAM: Lemme see.
> YOUTH: Of course. (*Begins to walk like Mae West, giving an amusing impersonation of that famous screen star*)
> HAM: You a regular moving picture!
> YOUTH: Indeed I am. (p. 63)

Or,

> (Enter a WEST INDIAN)
> WEST INDIAN: I wahnt a parfick shine!
> JASPER: You got perfect shoes? . . .
> WEST INDIAN: I'm a Church of the Englander, lady. Firm and true.
> DEACONESS: Well, I'm a Wash Foot Baptist. Touch my foot and you'll find it clean. My soul's the same way! How about you, son?

YOUTH: Oh, you're speaking to me? I'm New Thought—and we don't bother with such common things as washing feet.
DEACONESS: Well, you better, 'cause God ain't gonna let nobody in heaven 'thout their feet is clean. How about you, son?
HAM: I was baptized and everted when I were 10 years old, and I ain't had a dirty foot since. Amen!
JASPER: Amen, hell! (pp. 64–65)

The satire in *Little Ham* is always gentle; the point of the comedy is a celebration of the community's diversity and inclusiveness.

In choosing to restore black comic practices to their context—at least as representation—Hughes displays the effects of his earlier associations with Zora Neale Hurston and their abortive collaboration on *Mule Bone*. Both in that play and in her 1935 folklore collection *Mules and Men* (which includes material collected on trips on which Hughes accompanied her), Hurston dramatizes not only the tale but the verbal play surrounding it. In *Mule Bone*, she situates that verbal play on the front porch of the store in Eatonville; in *Mules and Men*, in a variety of locales. "Ethnography operates on the cusp of text and performance; indeed, 'writing culture' might be thought of as a process of turning performances into texts," writes Joseph Roach in "Bodies of Doctrine." Conversely, he continues, "Like texts, bodies carry messages, posted in the historical past, but continuously arriving in the present, delivered by the performers themselves."[4] Performance of the text creates what he calls "'genealogies of performance,' the historical transmission and dissemination of cultural practices through collective representations."[5] The setting for the love plot in *Mule Bone*, then, is the same storefront now well known through *Their Eyes Were Watching God*.

In *Little Ham*, Hughes attempts an urban context for what he and Hurston had long discussed and had undertaken in their collaboration: a "real" Negro folk play. No anthropologist, Hughes rather depends on his skill at reproducing and representing urban folk as he sees, understands, and celebrates them. Parading through both shoeshine shop and beauty parlor is an array of Harlem types: showgirl, Shabby Man, West Indian, janitor, follower of Father Divine, Hot Stuff Man, and so on. None is introduced simply as the butt of humor, for although some are satirized, all make up the fabric of the community. In her discussion

69

of Hurston's play *Color Struck,* Sandra Richards argues that cultural literacy is critical to an understanding of how the play works.[6] The same is true for *Little Ham,* for the social rituals of the shine shop and beauty parlor are not incidental to the play's "in-group" atmosphere. The play was written for the black Karamu Theatre in Cleveland; white spectators are welcome to look in, but the play is not for their benefit.

Although *Little Ham* insists on itself as comedy, its world is portrayed as being under threat of takeover, as when white mobsters take over the numbers racket. This aspect of the plot is topical as well as symbolic. White mobsters had won the battle for turf in Harlem. When his new love, Tiny, says, "I thought [the shop] belonged to colored folks," Little Ham explains, "It do, but whites run it."[7] Moreover, both literally and symbolically, the numbers provide the only material and substantial hope for the residents of this community, and whether or not the winning numbers are honored is by the end of the play in the hands of whites. Yet the play remains resolutely benign. Guns are fired—by an unruly customer, and by the errant husband of Ham's discarded girlfriend—but no one is hurt. Not only do Ham and Tiny win the Charleston contest, which is how the play closes, but all the play's couples are reconciled.

Hughes's representation of both men and women in *Little Ham* is also noteworthy. "[T]raditionally there has been an uneasy accommodation to women in comedy," writes Mel Watkins. Even those women who did breach the gender line in mainstream stage comedy often had to endure public opprobrium; they were regularly shunted into stereotypical roles as mannish or dumb, or as virtual harlots."[8] Minstrelsy typically relied on female impersonation for male-female encounter, and thus rendered complex and unstable all gender representation within that comic tradition. As Eric Lott so ably demonstrates in *Love and Theft: Blackface Minstrelsy and the American Working Class,* representations of black masculinity, whether by whites in blackface or "blackened" blacks, fetishized the black phallus as a site of threat and danger. Accordingly, female impersonation within the minstrel tradition gestured to the feminized male slave stereotype, or the Uncle Tom of Stowe's novel and countless stage and film retellings. Gender as performance is, of course, literalized in this scenario; its contours are grotesque and misogynist. Until well into the twentieth century, a taboo existed on the American stage against any portrayal of love between a black man and a black woman, and so what mention could be made of sexual desire, especially within the comic mode, of necessity cast the male character as predator, or at least preoccupied with somewhat grotesque objects of desire, which, of course, also commented on his own sexuality.[9]

Little Ham presents a genial challenge to the troubled comic representation of black sexuality in several ways. Particularly in Tiny's Beauty Shop, but also in Paradise Shining Parlors, a variety of female characters play out their comic type: Staid Lady, Deaconess, Pretty Woman, Masculine Lady, Lodge Lady, Sugar Lou Bird (a Harlem chorus girl), and others. There is nothing nasty in these portraits, nor is femininity itself the object of humor. The more delineated female characters—Madame Lucille Bell, proprietress of the Paradise Shining Parlors, Mattie Bea, Ham's discarded lover, and Tiny—convey a more complex statement about black women and gender relations as a subject of comedy. All three women pursue an active sexual life: Ham and Madame Lucille recollect their earlier liaison fondly, its afterglow having become maternal, a turn that Ham much appreciates for it allows him to take great liberties on the job. Madame Lucille is paired with the deposed Boss LeRoy, his name and deposition itself a comment on his gender role. Mattie Bea is quite unceremoniously dumped by Ham, and she responds stereotypically, by becoming a suspicious shrew. Ham's callousness is softened in the (a)morality of the play's world because she is married—and is reunited with her philandering husband, Gilbert, whom Tiny discards for Ham. In Tiny, however, Hughes addresses a variety of comic stereotypes head on—while also employing them.

In their first encounter, the boxer Joe Louis is said to be passing by. Everyone rushes outside, leaving Ham and Tiny alone:

> TINY: I done seen Joe Louis. I was at his last fight.
> HAM: You was? Who took you, high as them seats were?
> TINY: I took myself. I make money.
> HAM: Don't you need somebody to escort you places?
> TINY: Where'd you get that idea?

HAM: A sweet little woman like you's got no business at a fight all alone by her little she-self.

TINY: Now you know I ain't little. (*Coyly*) Don't nobody like me 'cause I'm fat.

HAM: Well, don't nobody like me 'cause I'm so young and small.

TINY: You a cute little man. You mean don't *nobody* like you?

HAM: (*Woefully*) Nobody that amounts to nothin'.

TINY: (*Impulsively*) Well, from now on Tiny likes you.

HAM: (*Holding his shine rag*) You really gonna like me, baby?

TINY: Sure I'm gonna like you, and they better not nobody else dare look at you neither.

HAM: Who would want to look at me? I know I won't look at nobody myself. But, I'm gonna be the boss, ain't I, Tiny?

TINY: Certainly—long as I boss you! (p. 57)

Tiny's most salient feature is her size; as bodies, Ham and Tiny comprise a running sight gag and subvert conventional ideas of sexuality, less because she is big than because he is small and yet not overwhelmed by her in any way. Moreover, again as body, Tiny promises to be a Sapphire, a domineering scold. Yet she is neither; she is sweetness itself with Little Ham, as well as a shrewd businesswoman who handles her workplace with authority and traps her blustering and armed ex-lover Gilbert with aplomb. The performances of (hetero)sexuality thus implied in *Little Ham* are utterly conventional, although they avoid stereotypical extremes of machismo and either domination or dependency.

As stage comedy, *Little Ham* certainly broke new ground in providing comic female roles that extended beyond the ingenue or tart of black musical comedy. Working women abound in this play (the two proprietors are women). In fact, on the whole, women have more dignity than men in *Little Ham*, despite a pretty intense verbal exchange between Tiny and Mattie Bea that ends in physical battle. Yet the presence of a female impersonator as one of the characters that floats through the Paradise Shining Parlors (there is also a Masculine Lady) gestures to a deeper sense of the performance of gender and its instability.

In its revision of the "performance of race" that marked the black comic tradition, *Little Ham* sets out to authenticate, to counteract its endemic self-parodying style. Yet, its comic display is also about the performance of style, about "'rappin' and stylin' out" within the community—or in contemporary terms, the 'hood.[10] In terms of the performance of gender, this groundbreaking work insists on a full range of sexual expression in its normalized inclusion of both the Effeminate Youth and the Masculine Lady. The diversity of the community is also clearly sexual.[11] In its recuperation of the humanity of the black comic figure, male and female, *Little Ham* enacts gender in ribald but ultimately conventional ways. Yet it also subverts conventional representations of heterosexual gender relations with powerful women who are also submissive, the sexual diversity of its characters, and the antics of a hero, Little Ham, whose performance or masculinity is, at root, gentle and sweet.

Most critics have regarded *Little Ham* as lightweight in the extreme. Arnold Rampersad's comment is relatively balanced:

> Always, Langston has found black laughter, like the blues, which often evoked laughter, a deeply serious matter; both were essential to the endurance of the race and its will to prevail. He affirmed the existence of a blues-sanctioned ambivalence between tears and laughter in his work; whether many of those who laughed also sensed the sorrow is, however, debatable.[12]

As Rampersad acknowledges here, *Little Ham* has a serious undercurrent, which Hughes himself insisted was present in all his plays.[13] The complexity of that undercurrent has never been fully explored, and the discussion here is intended to inspire further exploration.

In the classroom, then, *Little Ham* provides the opportunity to raise a variety of questions. The social history of the Harlem of the period is everywhere in the text. Hughes himself did research on the numbers game while writing it; the history of mob control in Harlem is also relevant. If a reading of the play as recuperating the tradition of black comedy is to be meaningful, that history is also of relevance. As well, the play can provide the occasion for a study of contemporary African American comedy, particularly on television, which is probably closer in type to *Little Ham* than, for example, George Wolfe's *The Colored Museum*—although evolution of the African American comic stage also, of course, flows from Hughes's theatrical work in the 1930s. Finally, *Little Ham* lends itself to study, performance, and updating. It is a comic play of the 'hood, and invites both interpretation and reinvention.

Notes

1. Stuart Hall, "Cultural Identity and Cinematic Representation," in *Black British Cultural Studies: A Reader,* eds. Houston Baker Jr., Manthia Diawara, and Ruth Lindeborg (Chicago: University of Chicago Press, 1996), p. 210–22.

2. Mel Watkins, *On the Real Side: Laughing, Lying, and Signifying—The Underground Tradition of African American Humor that Transformed American Culture from Slavery to Richard Pryor* (New York: Simon and Schuster, 1994).

3. *The Amos 'n' Andy Show,* which until the late 1930s used only white performers, was immensely popular with black as well as white audiences, although some black groups objected strenuously to it. See Melvin Patrick Ely, *The Adventures of Amos 'n' Andy: A Social History of American Phenomenon* (New York: Free Press, 1991).

4. Joseph Roach, "Bodies of Doctrine: Headshots, Jane Austen, and the Black Indians of Mardi Gras," in *Choreographing History,* ed. Susan Leigh Foster (Bloomington: Indiana University Press, 1995), p. 158.

5. Ibid., p. 156.

6. Sandra L. Richards, "Writing the Absent Potential: Drama, Performance, and the Canon of African-American Literature," in *Performativity and Performance,* eds. Andrew Parker and Eve Kosofsky Sedgwick (New York: Routledge, 1995), pp. 64–88.

7. Langston Hughes, *Five Plays by Langston Hughes,* ed. Webster Smalley (Bloomington: Indiana University Press, 1968), p. 77.

8. Mel Watkins, *On the Real Side,* p. 390.

9. Eric Lott, *Love and Theft: Black Face Minstrelsy and the American Working class* (New York: Oxford University Press, 1993).

10. The phrase is taken from a text that provides much useful background for the analysis of linguistic behavior, *Little Ham, Rappin' and Stylin' Out: Communication in Urban Black America,* ed. Thomas Kochman (Urbana, IL: University of Illinois Press, 1972). See also, Geneva Smitherman, *Black Talk: Words and Phrases from the Hood to the Amen Corner* (Boston: Houghton Mifflin, 1994), and Geneva Smitherman, *Talkin and Testifyin: The Language of Black America* (Detroit: Wayne State University Press, 1986).

11. This sympathy is also present in his poetry; see Anne Borden, 'Heroic "Hussies" and "Brilliant Queers" Genderacial Resistance in the Works of Langston Hughes,' *African American Review.* 28.3 (Fall 1994): 333–45.

12. Arnold Rampersad, *The Life of Langston Hughes: Volume I: 1902–1941: I, Too, Sing America* (New York: Oxford University Press, 1986), p. 326.

13. Ibid.

◻ 5 ◻

FREEING THE FEMALE VOICE
New Models and Materials for Teaching

Constance Borab

*I am myself—a Black woman warrior poet doing my work—come
to ask you are you doing yours?*
　　　　　　　　　　　　　　—AUDRE LORDE,
　　"The Transformation of Silence into Language and Action"

Having taught literature, theater arts, and film criticism for twenty-three years in what is now an inner-city, culturally mixed, predominantly African American all-girls school, I find myself thinking about Lorde's question as I go about the business of transforming the silence of adolescent girls into language and action. I have spent more than two decades listening to and trying to understand the female voices that I hear, my own included.

When I began teaching in 1974, I did so as a rebel—at least I thought I did—rejecting the model of the teacher as imparter of knowledge. Instead, I would engage my students in a version of Socratic dialogue that I thought, naively as it turns out, would call them to higher learning and would develop their ability to think critically and express themselves clearly. Through discussion of literature and subsequent critical inquiry, I envisioned that each of my students would recognize her life, dreams, and story.

75

Yet despite my intention to have them tell their own stories as they explored the stories of others, my students' voices were too often disconnected from the literature they were studying. Fortunately for me, they did not remain so when I asked for feedback about the lack of interest that marked our discussions in class. "Ms. Borab, you don't let us say what we think," I remember Donna saying to me. "You keep saying that you don't want to teach us *what* to think, but *how* to think. Yet sometimes when we start to tell you what we feel, you cut us off."[1] Other students agreed and cited plenty of examples, but it was what Donna said next that really made me hear what they were saying. "Yesterday when we talked about the Emily Dickinson poem about death ("Because I could not stop for death"), I started to tell you about how I see death. But you said, 'Let's first focus on how the author sees it and the images she creates.'" Donna's comment helped me realize that my insistence on beginning with what I saw as an objective analysis of literature—using an exclusively Anglo canon, no less—was impeding rather than facilitating the freeing of their voices and their proclaiming of knowledge. And so, for me, a paradigm shift in teaching began.

This shift had two major phases. The first concerned pedagogical changes; the second (and the more fun) was the realization of these changes through the curriculum. To make these changes, I had to understand my own conceptual framework about the role of the student as well as the role of the teacher and how it colored both my interpretations of the literature I was teaching and the interpretations I elicited in class. It was in those early years of teaching that I learned to trust my students' feedback, whether it manifested itself in direct comment on my methodology or in more subtle forms of silence, frustration, or apathy. I learned to ask about and to listen to the messages and motivations of my students.

Carol Gilligan's book *In a Different Voice*, which I read in 1982, my eighth year of teaching, was enormously instrumental in the naming and reshaping of my pedagogy.[2] Though familiarity with the book and its critique of the gender biases that challenge the universal application of Kohlberg's theories of moral development is considered requisite by many today, it has not lost any of its impact on my work. At the risk of stating the obvious about this landmark work, I will try to summarize her points here only insofar as they provide insight into my experiences in the classroom and lay the groundwork for new models of teaching. Especially relevant here is her conclusion that boys' identities are formed by separation from their parents, especially their mothers, but girls continue to identify with their mothers as they develop their identities, all along being taught that connection is important and that cooperation and maintenance relationships are key to their (good) natures. Gilligan also points out that Kohlberg's hierarchical model of moral development, based on an "objective" understanding of justice, is male-biased because separating from one's own self-interest or group interest in order to stand up for a "universal" sense of justice favors those who are taught that separation is key to identity and personhood. In having done so, Gilligan helps us hear the female voice in a new way and measure it against a different scale of moral development. For example, in the attempt to resolve Heinz's dilemma, (i.e., Should Heinz, whose wife is dying, steal the unaffordable life-saving drug?), one of the boys in the study suggested, among other things, that, life being more important than property, Heinz should steal the drug. Though the full answer he gave was not totally logical, because he brought in objective principles of justice, for example, life versus property, he was rated higher on Kohlberg's scale than was a girl who thought out loud in what appeared to be a halting manner about ways to preserve relationships (including that with the druggist who owned the medicine). Because she seemed to bring in issues not mentioned in the original problem, her reasoning was deemed muddled and confused. Gilligan goes on to state that for girls, the most just and salient decision is one that maintains care and relationships.

Gilligan's critique of these conclusions helped me listen to the different voices of my students. At times, I had been dismissing as invalid, irrelevant, and even confused my female students' attempts to name and discover meaning in the literature we read when they didn't follow my prescribed agenda for understanding literature.

Gilligan's work brought me right up against the walls of my own conceptual framework, a framework Karen Warren in her article "Feminism and Critical Thinking" would say is patriarchal.[3] Warren states that a patriarchical conceptual framework, which is marked by value-hierarchical thinking, value dualisms, and logic of domination, is not the only point of view.[4] Further, Warren argues that "objectivity" is not neutral: "Critical thinking does not occur in a vacuum; it *always* occurs in some conceptual framework. . . . The so-called ideal of a 'neutral observer,' i.e., one who has no point of view is, at best, an ideal, and at worst, an 'ideological prejudice.'"[5] Her work echoes not only Gilligan's thesis but, more important to me, my students' complaints that I hadn't been listening. By insisting that my students analyze objectively—separately, in other words, from their emotional, spiritual, and psychological experiences—I was requiring that their voices "go underground," a common misstep that Gilligan explores in her later works. Certainly my own training at Boston College in the 1970s had exalted a patriarchal conceptual framework by insisting that value dualisms, objectivity, and logic were the only truly valid forms of knowing. By asking my students to stay within value-hierarchical thinking and the limits of logic, however, I was cutting off their access to the literature and subsequently stifling their voices.

Some have questioned the applicability of Gilligan's findings to African American girls. Articles in the 1986 winter edition of *Sign* point out that Gilligan's subject pool did not contain a significant number of African American females. Questions were raised about differences in the formation of African American adolescent girls' voices because of cultural and, particularly, racial influences. I turned to other sources to understand these differences and how they might be integrated with Gilligan's theories rather than supplant them. I found a collection of essays called *Women, Girls and Psychotherapy: Reframing Resistance*, which attempts to "reframe the clinical understanding of resistance to include the notion of resistance as a healthy sustaining process."[6] In "'A Belief in Self Far Greater than Anyone's Disbelief': Cultivating Resistance Among African American Female Adolescents," for example, Tracy Robinson and Janie Victoria Ward point out that within many African American communities, a great value is placed on developing a "resistance of liberation," and a strong voice that speaks out against oppression, particularly racism. In forming her identity as an African American, often an adolescent girl develops a voice resistant to racism; but she is empowered to do so because of her connections with a culture and community that reinforces this resistant voice.[7] Thus, resistance and identity become positively linked to community rather than at odds with it.

It was in my classroom that I first heard this willingness to give voice to racial and cultural identity. Robinson and Ward only confirmed for me what I had already discovered: when an African American girl speaks of resistance to racism and social oppression, her voice is strong, her message confidently and definitively delivered. Asked what the number one threat to her life and happiness was, Kenji wrote in her journal, "We are all racist, confused and narrow minded, we're in hell and as Tupac quoted—'a nation under stress.'"[8]

Yet, what happens when my students' resistance is not, in their own understanding, clearly connected to fighting group oppression against their community? Alaycia's voice, which is ever vigilant about naming racism and ways to overcome it, loses its clarity and dynamism when she writes of a personal dilemma: "I wish to be found, I wish someone could understand my needs and my wants." Daphnay had also spoken in class about difficulties between her and her mother, and comments in her journal capture a conflict that many of her classmates have raised as well:

> If you saw my mother, you would see by her looks, the way she dresses and speaks that she is a strong and beautiful woman. There is so much pressure to be the perfect proud Black woman that my mother is and wants me to be. . . . It does no good to tell her what I want, what I feel, she doesn't listen. . . . So I take care of my little brother, even if it means I will miss school and other things I want to do. What am I supposed to do, leave him alone? I love him, but I want to love my own life.

As Daphnay's journal entry suggests, when the "resistance of liberation" moves from a communal and cultural context to an individual one, the girls' voices often weaken. Faced with a situation in which her own desires are at odds with those of others, she submerges her voice and identity for the sake of relationships, and her choice reflects the choices of many of her classmates.

Audre Lorde's words, "And where the words of women are crying to be heard, we must each recognize our responsibility to seek those words out, to read them and share them and examine them in their pertinence to our lives," define the essential focus of the next stage in the evolution of my teaching: to include more women writers, especially African American women.[9]

Recently a group of seniors and I completed a unit on Zora Neale Hurston's *Their Eyes Were Watching God*, a novel, in part, about "the words of women . . . crying to be heard."[10] This unit reflects many of the pedagogical and methodological changes I have made in the classroom. We still identify and analyze literary devices, the author's style, the relevant historical, philosophical, biographical, and cultural influences, and the place in the canon of American literature that *Their Eyes Were Watching God* has come to assume, but we also explore the work in terms of its pertinence to our own lives, identifying and using our own conceptual frameworks. Our discussions focus on connecting the voice of Hurston and her characters to our inner voices.

This is not to say that the students simply talk about their lives and that the literature is just a footnote. Of course they are accountable for knowledge beyond their own lives and will continue to be as they prepare for and attend college. To me, however, it's a "constructed knowledge,"[11] a dialogue between what they know and what others know, whether we are talking about scholarly sources, historical context, biographical information about the author, or experiences shared in class discussion.

Teachers may recognize the beginnings of my constructivist approach to learning—the resolution to "Start with what they know." This has become for me an important directive for getting students to name their own knowledge while making connections to that of others. For our unit on *Their Eyes Were Watching God*, the students used daily freewriting in journals as a starting point. When we began this unit, the seniors had been freewriting in journals for more than a year, in part to help them overcome the sometimes paralyzing phobia that they "can't write" or that they "don't have anything to say." Their entries also provided the first draft of many pieces that they would develop into finished writing. For the Hurston unit, we used a quote from the novel as a prompt to begin an entry. These journal entries became their first points of analysis and understanding of the novel, and every so often they were asked to read an entry of their own choosing to the class.

One student, Marie, when freewriting an entry prompted by Hurston's line "Common danger made common friends,"[12] wrote:

> These were the words that were silently uttered within her soul. These powerful syllable words can only be expressed within her heart because she had only experiences but can't define them in words. It will be like trying to get hold of water with her bare hands. Yes, she had friends who went through similar agony, pain, loneliness that she beared for the last few years. But her pain was more unbearable. She can only visualize these moments, and cherish the scar that is left hidden inside and will never be revealed to a single soul. Her mouth is sealed forever not allowing a single word to penetrate. But only allowing her eyes to seek as far as her sight can prolong and her lonely heart can bear.

Marie's words reflect a young woman's voice yearning to break its silence. When I met her last year in Junior English, Marie, who is often an absorbing silence in class, was much more confident of received knowledge than of her intuitive and experiential knowledge. Yet as evidenced in this passage from her journal, in the third person, she is willing to name what she knows about "agony, pain, loneliness." Because of the atmosphere of openness, respect, affirmation, and trust that we have built as a class, Marie has moved from hesitancy to eagerness to share her work.

During class discussion, Marie's entry served as a bridge between personal experience and the text. Students responding identified phrases from the novel that spoke to their own experiences and to those Hurston's Janie undergoes. Melissa, for example, pointed out that "Her mouth sealed forever" echoed Janie's feelings of entrapment and loss of voice during her marriage to Jody. Another student reminded us that Marie's words "cherish the scar that is left hidden inside and will never be revealed to a single soul" reminded her of Janie's hidden scars and her soul's journey to inner peace.

In another entry that started with the Hurston quote "Two things everybody's got tuh do fuh theyselves. They got tuh go tuh God, and they got tuh find out about livin' fuh theyselves,"[13] Jeany wrote:

> This is a true statement for me because sometimes I feel trapped and it feels as though some people are living my life for me. They decide where I'm going, who I'm going with, what I am to eat, what I'm to wear and not to wear, what my goals in life are and who I'm to go to and not to go to for help. One may see this as a carefree life, but it isn't. Trust me, this isn't a life because you're not living it. You don't develop your own voice and make others acknowledge your presence. I also believe that in order to live for yourself, you must allow God to give you strength to discover life for yourself. Because sometimes it only takes one personal experience with God for one to learn who they really are and what they are capable of.

To Jeany, the most sacred knowledge is that of the self, a God-given self, and one that is too often surrendered to the will of others. After Jeany read her entry to the class and they responded, I asked them, "Could Janie have written this?" I wanted to suggest some connections between issues Jeany had raised and things that happen to Janie early in the book. Students noticed, for example, that Jeany's "people are living my life for me" reflects a similar tension between Janie and her grandmother, and they made much of the fact that Nanny wants to control the course of Janie's life when she arranges her marriage to Logan. Like Jeany's very traditional parents, Nanny could impose her will on her granddaughter. But the students also brought up the fact that very real dangers shaped their elders' points of view. The students respected Nanny's view much as they did their own family members' views, but like Janie, many of them felt suffocated. As Jeany put it, you have a right to "live for yourself."

The empathetic connections that begin in journal writing help the subjective knower move to cognitive insights and to procedural and constructed knowing.[14] Delores Gallo, who makes a strong case for the role of empathy in effective critical thinking, states in her article "Education for Empathy, Reason, and Imagination" that, "In the field of social psychology, one can find the term empathy used in at least two ways: to mean a predominantly cognitive response, understanding how another feels, or to mean an affective communion with others."[15] The journal writings and follow-up discussions help develop the affective and the cognitive as well as interpersonal and intrapersonal intelligences that Howard Gardner refers to in his book *Multiple Intelligences: Theory into Practice*.[16]

Body sculpturing and storytelling are two pedagogical techniques that tap students' bodily-kinesthetic intelligence.[17] I like these "get on your feet/get up and make it happen"[18] moments in the curriculum because they require students to become actively involved in their learning. These methods also require students to work together to negotiate meaning and achieve consensus. In the unit on Hurston's novel, we used a body-sculpturing technique to understand and name some of the important themes in *Their Eyes Were Watching God*.

Body sculpturing is a group activity that requires students to make and display meaning using their bodies in space. In that way, it is much like mime. Though there are many variations of this device, some of the standard guidelines for body sculpturing are as follows:

1. Working collaboratively, each group is assigned a quotation or passage from a text that they will interpret in the form of a body sculpture. All members of the group must be part of the sculpture.

2. Each member of the group presents her own interpretation of the quotation to the other members; the group discusses what it has heard and negotiates an interpretation.

3. Having arrived at a collective interpretation, the group creates and performs a live body sculpture that conveys the interpretation. Though at different times it may be a moving sculpture, it must end in a frozen moment. The only speech that may occur once the sculpture has begun is the pronouncement of the quotation itself.

Ten to fifteen minutes is given to the planning process. After performance, members of the class are asked to talk about what they observed. No exchange between the group and the audience is allowed until after all discussion is exhausted. The presenters may then provide clarification or further (verbal) illumination.

For *Their Eyes Were Watching God*, each group was assigned to explore a theme that gets played out in the novel, after which they were to choose a quote from the book that reflected their collective understanding. One group was asked to explore how racism gets depicted in the book. They chose the quote, "Mrs. Turner, like all other believers, had built an altar to the unattainable—Caucasian characteristics for all." [19]

This group choose to model the racist belief that light skin is better than dark skin. Their body sculpture positioned a white girl with blond hair standing on a chair, her arms extended upward, preacher-like. Standing in front of her, gazing up worshipfully, was a light-colored African American girl. The rest of the group, one Latina and two darker African American girls, lined up behind the girl standing on the chair. The last girl, whose skin was darkest of all, knelt down on the floor, her face buried in her hands. The students in the audience had no trouble identifying the hierarchy of color that the group had modeled and in the discussion that followed, we explored instances when we'd encountered this hierarchy in our lives.

Another group was assigned to explore the oppression of Janie's voice. This group used two quotations from the novel in their presentation. First, three girls lined up, one behind the other, representing three components of Janie's identity: Dream, Love, and Voice. The first girl, Dream-Janie, broke rank and danced about the room, a silk scarf fluttering behind her to suggest a bird in flight. When her dance was finished, she took the last place in line. Then a girl portraying the character of Jody walked up to Dream-Janie and said, "Ah aimed tuh be uh big voice. You oughta be glad, 'cause dat makes uh big woman outta you."[20] Then Jody crossed the room and, with another (male) character, began to build the town of Eatonville. Meanwhile Love-Janie had shriveled herself into a tuck position, as Dream-Janie wrapped her scarf around Voice-Janie's head to hide her beautiful hair. Next, the Jody character collapsed. Voice-Janie crossed over to his dead body, and, after staring at him for a few seconds, her expression blank, she crossed back to Dream-Janie, who removed the scarf from her head. Love-Janie then rose. All three, Dream-Janie and Love-Janie each looking over the shoulder of Voice-Janie into a mirror, spoke the line, "Years ago, she had told the girl self to wait for her in the looking glass . . . the young girl was gone, but a handsome woman had taken her place. She tore off the kerchief from her head and let down her hair."[21]

The students' abilities to express the complexity of conflict in the novel was impressive. "If a woman's dreams are crushed, and she is beaten in silence, then any love she had withers and dies," Michelle observed in the discussion afterward. Asked if there was anything redeeming about Jody, they were resolute in their conclusion that though they admired him as a good mayor who had built Eatonville up from nothing, his sexist and overbearing treatment of Janie was very wrong. The mention of Jody's achievements in establishing Eatonville, however, provided a segue into some historical background about this first black township and about Hurston herself, integrating received knowledge into the central discussion while allowing it to arise from a context relevant to their lives.[22]

The foundation for the students' insightful, sophisticated readings of *Their Eyes Were Watching God* was laid in their junior year when we read Alice Walker's *The Color Purple*.[23] Every time a class of mine has undertaken the study of Walker's novel, our understanding of oppression—and empowerment—has grown. As is true with everything I teach, the overriding goal in studying Walker's novel was freeing voice.

To put it simply, *The Color Purple* unearths the voices of my students, many of whom have been buried under a mountain of oppression during their young lives. With each teaching of this novel, I have come to understand how profoundly this text helps my students break their silence and move toward empowerment and healing. I have other goals in mind when I teach this novel, including placing it within a larger context of African American women in literature, exploring sources of oppression and identifying sources of empowerment, and considering the criticisms of this novel. Each time I teach this unit, I am amazed by the number of issues raised and the complexity of the students' readings.

I rarely begin a unit by lecturing. As I've said throughout this article, subjective knowledge rather than received knowledge is my usual starting point. But I like to begin *The Color Purple* with a presentation that lays the groundwork for two things: 1) locating voice in the novel and 2) the concept of triple consciousness. The second idea was outlined in a lecture Trudier Harris gave at an NEH Institute on African American Literature at Northeastern University in Boston in July 1993.

Harris provided an overview of traditional depictions of black women in literature prior to the 1960s and 1970s that critiqued the trope of the long-suffering, self-sacrificing, ever-patient, church-going black woman who offers hope and emotional strength to others. This classic depiction of the "good" African American woman was an attempt to counter negative myths about African American women. Forbidden to this "sacred cow" image were thematic depictions of lesbianism, incest, abortion, or active, pleasurable sex, and the depiction of mothers who failed to live up to their responsibilities; for example, mothers were not allowed to escape oppression by abandoning their children or even by going insane. The 1960s and 1970s saw a shift from this sanctified image. Writers such as Maya Angelou, Toni Morrison, Alice Walker, Paule Marshall, and many others began to give voice to real black women in real contexts. These writers challenged patriarchal constructs of femininity by creating multiple images and myriad stories of and about African American women. Also included were criticisms of black men, something previously taboo.

The idea of triple consciousness was not entirely unfamiliar to the students. Earlier in the semester, we had looked at Paul Laurence Dunbar's poem "We Wear the Mask" and had explored what W.E.B. Du Bois in *The Souls of Black Folk* called "double consciousness," or the dual awareness that many African Americans experience being both black and American in a racist America. Students were able to name many reasons for the wearing of masks in public. For many African American women, however, this dualism of being both black and American is compounded by sexism, or "triple consciousness," as Harris tells us.

That semester, after I finished my lecture, Juceyna was the first to respond and asked, "What's wrong with strong, patient women?" Juceyna's question indicated the great value that many of my students place on enduring with quiet dignity the many forms of oppression that they face. I quoted a line from one of their classmates' journals where Jessica had written, "She gives too much of herself to others, she is slipping away quickly from within. Was she supposed to be hurt? Was she supposed to stand by and let others walk all over her? Was she

Was she supposed to do for others and never receive anything in return?" I responded by saying that her thinking parallels the kind of questioning that lead contemporary women writers to create characters who challenge stereotypes.

I was beginning to recognize this as an epiphanal conversation for these students. Christina responded with insights that were reflected in the following journal entry:

> She learned to be strong, so strong she pushed people away even when she was hurting the most. But, strength is a disease which she learned when she was young. She never asked to be strong. She just asked to be loved and no one could give of their heart. Strength is a curse to her.

Later this conversation would serve as a basis for critically examining the strength of the women characters in *The Color Purple*. During this class, the students themselves began to think about what was taboo— what they had forbidden themselves to question. A newly constructed definition of strength emerged from this conversation, grounded in an authentic and connected voice.

As we turned from the lecture material to the text, we used a group storytelling device. Introduced to a form of this device by Michael Cremonini at the Shakespeare and Company Summer Institute in 1991, I opt for this challenging activity because it requires students to know more than "the facts." Like body sculpturing, it asks the students to employ multiple intelligences and, because each storyteller must pick up where the last left off, negotiate meaning making with others.

Some guidelines for storytelling are as follows:

1. At one point or another during a round, each student will rise out of her seat and take the storytelling scarf. She may use this scarf as a prop, a symbol, or a storyteller's "shawl." As each student takes the scarf, she may be a character in the story, the author, an imagined witness, an object in the story, and so on; but she may not be herself.[24]

2. Each student tells a part of her character's story and speaks once

87

before a new round begins. When the storyteller is finished, she has ten seconds to pass the scarf to the next storyteller before sitting down.

3. The story does not have be told sequentially, but a student may only repeat information already given only if she adds something new to it. I encourage the students to tell us about metaphoric details of the experience both imagined and textual. I encourage them to be especially interpretative, emotional, and dramatic.

4. If a student's version contradicts the text, another student may clarify by using such transition phrases as "That's not the way I saw it." If contradictions are not addressed by the students, I clarify by taking up the scarf myself or during discussion afterward.

5. When one round ends, students are allowed to take the scarf a second time and finish the story. When the story's essential facts are told, then questions, comments, and discussions begin.

When last year's storytelling round on *The Color Purple* began, I expected the usual mix of enthusiasm, insight, and voice from those who read it and silence and hesitation from those who had not. I was taken aback, however, by the students' deep understanding of theme and character; about their attention to form as employed in the novel (epistolary), and the ways the novel seemed resonant with their own lives. The following came out of this session:

DIXIE: My name is Shug, and I use my beauty to gain power over men.
WENDY: My name is Celie, and you may think I am not worth much because I poor, black, ugly, and a woman. For a long time I thought that too, but I no longer believe that. . . . I have power to curse those who try to keep me down and the power to free myself.
GEORGIA: The god of the white man never did anything for me. It did not protect me from my father, or rather the man that I thought was my father. He did not keep my children with me. . . . I thank God for the color purple, my sister, and Shug. . . . My happiness is complete, my children came home today.
ROSE: My name is Nettie, and I have lived in Africa for several years, and though my ancestors came from here, I realize more and more that, though I love many here, I cannot accept all the African ways.

NATASHA: My name is Sophia, and I have had to fight my father, my brothers, and now my Harpo, but I never expected to fight a woman in my own house.

EUNICE: My name is Miss Eleanor Jane. I went to visit Sophia, who I thought loved me like a daughter. She said that the world would not allow my baby son to love her. She said that colored women who said they loved the white children they raise are just lying. I can't accept this. Is there family across color lines? Sophia was more family to me than my own. . . . Where in this world do I go now?

KIM: . . . and when I went to help, I was raped. Maybe I do smoke weed a lot . . . but I have my dreams. I want to sing. . . . Now get this right, my name is not Squeak. My name is Mary Agnes!

These were just a few of the comments in a session that took four rounds to complete. While the full dramatic quality of their story-telling might not translate well here, their fusion of observation and interpretation, of the critical and the creative, does, I think. Let me also suggest that issues that otherwise might have taken weeks to surface were voiced in about thirty minutes.

During followup, I asked them to draw a comparison to the slave narratives and to name sources of oppression seen in the novel. The students cited Mr.____'s line that Wendy had paraphrased ("You can't curse nobody. Look at you. You black, you pore, you ugly, you a woman. Goddam, he say, you nothing at all.")[25] Her race and social class, her looks, and her gender are all used to convince Celie (and other characters in *The Color Purple*, but especially Celie) that she is worthless. Not surprisingly, "low self-esteem" became the girls' catch phrase to describe the condition of the oppressed. The students were able to name from the text and their lives how society's hierarchical structure empowers white over black, men over women, beauty over ugliness, wealth over poverty. When focused on racism, the students had no difficulty recognizing its insidious nature as seen in the novel. The attitude of the Miss Millie, her husband, and most of the whites in the town, which fuels the fear and fire that led to Sophia's beating and imprisonment, is the most evident example of racism cited by the students. Others pointed out that Celie's image of God as a bearded white man reflected a less violent but equally corrosive form of racism. And some suggested that the value placed on Mary Agnes's light complexion was a reflection of a racist society that defines whiteness as a requirement for beauty and power, something they would bring up a year later in *Their Eyes Were Watching God*.

The discussion of Mary Agnes's coloring served as starting point for exploring the power of beauty and led the class to coin of the term "beautyism." Beautyism, we decided, is when society conveys systematically the idea that women should meet certain standards of physical beauty, standards drawn from a narrow definition of beauty. Overnight, the students produced several examples from print media advertising promoting image after glossy image of women with light silken hair, flawless white or light skin, large eyes—usually blue—long limbs, thin, well-proportioned bodies, high cheekbones, straight, small noses, and symmetrical faces. We concluded that the ads implied that the more a woman resembles this definition, the more power and opportunity she has.

We came to an understanding that the systematic transmission of this standard of beauty had led many of us to adopt it as our own, to measure ourselves against it, and to commit a large portion of our financial resources to achieve it. I had the students fill out a simple worksheet that asked them to record their income from the previous year and estimate the percentages of income spent on facial beauty, on hair/nail beauty, on attaining a well-proportioned body, on maintaining the "right" wardrobe, and on accessories. Much discussion ensued about the term "right," and some general discussion took place about the cost differential between the basic brand versus designer brands, and the buying of clothing not out of need, but out of a desire to be beautiful. Through the evidence gathered based on our worksheets, the preponderance of ads we'd collected, and our discussions, we realized how subtle beautyism is as a form of oppression. The students were surprised at how unquestioningly they buy into (pun intended) Madison Avenue and Hollywood notions of beauty and how willingly they devote a major portion of their limited resources to achieve them.

Connecting this seemingly tangential line of reasoning to *The Color Purple* revealed personal as well as textual insights. "Celie views herself as ugly and worthless. Her stepfather, her husband, even Shug call her ugly, and put her down for it," Dixie commented. Nia built on this: "Her low self esteem is for many reasons, but if all your life you hear how ugly you are, then you don't have much of a chance to believe in yourself. How can anyone believe in themselves if they never know love?" Marilyn's metacognitive comment challenged her own tendency toward beautyism: "I am the first to judge someone for the way they dress . . . like, if they're not Nike's, don't be in public; but I realize how judgmental this is, how I'm putting other women down . . . there'd be no Celie in my life."

These comments reflected a shift in the students' thinking during this unit. Many of them began to realize that Celie's movement from oppression to freedom did not occur because the system changed and empowered her. Rather, Celie herself changed. Celie's personal growth over the course of the novel and the discovery of her voice leads to agency and empowerment over the oppressive forces in her life. I would venture to say that with these realizations, the possibility of personal epiphany and empowerment became more real for the girls.

When I asked the students about the sources of empowerment that help Celie overcome oppression, the students pointed to education and sisterhood. An examination of sisterhood enabled students to reevaluate their own thinking as they examined the transformation of Celie's own conceptual framework. When Sophia confronts Celie and asks why Celie advised Harpo to beat her, Celie replies, "cause I'm jealous of you . . . cause you do what I can't . . . Fight."[26] Sophia possesses a strength different from that of the saintly African American women Professor Harris outlined and a sense of worth that Celie admires. Through her relationship with Sophia, Celie begins to realize her self-worth. "If Sophia ignored her or beat her then it's saying that Celie is worth nothing. But because Sophia yells at her, talks to her, then listens to her, Celie realizes that somebody cares about what she thinks," observed Marsha. Natasha added, "It's like Maya Angelou said to Oprah, 'You did what you knew, and when you knew better you did better.' Sophia helps Celie know better, to know that she is worth something to someone other than her sister."

In *The Color Purple*, the arrival of Shug raises Celie up in many ways, for beauty and love and a free female voice arrive along with her, despite their dubious beginning when, upon introduction, Shug declares to Celie, "You sure *is* ugly. . . ."[27] Marsha said, "Shug changes her mind about Celie as she gets to know her. She saw how good she [Celie] was and how badly she was treated. Shug," Marsha continued, "helps Celie believe in her right to be herself," suggesting that sisterhood is indeed powerful.

It is Shug, as the girls pointed out in the storytelling round, who helps Celie reclaim her relationship with God.

> I been so busy thinking bout him I never truly notice nothing God make. Not a blade of corn (how it do that?) not the color purple (where it come from?). Not the little wildflowers. Nothing. Now that my eyes opening, I feels like a fool. Next to any little scrub of a bush in my yard, Mr. _____'s evil sort of shrink.[28]

Celie's words drew a powerful reaction from the students, many of whom claim a deep and sustaining religious faith. Christina drew a parallel between Celie and the Transcendentalists: "Emerson wrote about how the connection to Nature is a connection to God, and how there is no calamity that Nature cannot repair. Well, that's happening with Celie." Le, reflecting on Celie's part in repairing her own calamities, added, "But it's not just Nature or God or Shug—Celie's changing herself, the ways she thinks." Georgia, who struggles with the imposition of her mother's strict, religious beliefs, said, "Even though Celie doesn't see God as the old white man, she finds him in small things and this helps her overcome the evil. At the end, after every evil that happened to her she says, 'Dear God. Dear stars, dear trees, dear sky, dear peoples. Dear Everything. Dear God.'"[29]

It is in the letter recounting Celie and Shug's conversation about God that Shug says, "Man corrupt everything."[30] At this point, I raised one of the strongest criticisms leveled at Walker's novel, namely its perceived anti-black-male bias. I did so with three things in mind. First, I wanted to make sure that the students would be able to make a well-constructed argument whenever they want to take a position on an issue, personal, textual, or otherwise. Second, I wanted to sound a strong call for empathy—for stepping into the other gender's shoes.

Third, I wanted to help the students realize the sexism in some of their own conceptual frameworks.

After a round of refuting unqualified generalizations about men and rage against the patriarchy, I asked my students to think about Mr. Daniels, a religion teacher at our school whom the students admire and respect tremendously and also other men they know and admire. I pressed them to justify their consensus that Walker isn't male bashing. Why, I wondered aloud, isn't Walker's treatment of men in *The Color Purple* simply sexism in reverse, seeing that nearly every male character in the novel easily could be construed as evil?

I wanted this question to help to move their meaning making from subjectivist to procedural and constructed. Without any prompting from me, the students cited two strong points of consideration for constructing a defense of the novel against charges of sexism. One was about point of view. Most of the story is told through the voice of Celie, they said. It is the story of a woman who suffered terrible things at the hands of her stepfather, her husband, and her husband's children. Given this as her life experience, her attitude toward men is not unjustified, but a defensive posture that helps her survive. Their second point focused on her reconciliation with Albert at the end.

They pointed out that after Celie leaves Albert, he changes for the better too. They sensed that Albert had somehow healed. I pointed out that Celie's experiences at the hands of men were a product of author's imagination, and that she chose to have Albert's heinous actions appear on the page but his transformation off the page, and I asked again if the novel was male bashing. "Yeah, but Ms. Borab, sometimes life is that bad. Celie's life . . . I mean it happens. Her character is real," one student said. Looking into the faces of those students who were nodding in agreement, I realized that to refute this would be to deny some of my students' pain.

Over the course of the unit, my students added one more condition of oppression—sexual abuse, and this brings me to the second point of criticism and a word about the nature of the teacher who chooses to privilege students' voices in the classroom. In our classroom, the students and I deliberately have created an atmosphere of trust and respect in which they have a safe place to speak the truths of their lives,

93

to examine those truths, and to recognize the strengths and weaknesses of their thinking; to find the words to express what they know in conversations, in creative work, and in critical essays; to begin the work of transformation if they so choose. Some of my students, including the student who said, "Her character is real," are survivors of sexual abuse. As I work to free their voices, I must listen with an ear attentive to the subtext of their comments.

Invariably, one student will ask, "How come Celie is so lacking in emotions in the letters at the beginning? If I were her, I'd write letters filled with hate for what my father did to me." Invariably, one student will answer as a student answered last year, "Celie cannot get emotional in the beginning. She's got to shut down to survive. If she felt the pain, she'd kill herself. If she felt the rage, she'd kill someone else. And it's got to be letters, because you just can't write about it too long or you'll go crazy. " I recognize that the student who gives this answer and the heads that nod in agreement are often revealing their personal stories. And every student who has answered this way has later identified herself, either in her journal or in a personal conversation, as a survivor of sexual abuse. I have learned to come prepared to this class, ready to give information about sexual abuse, its effects, and, importantly, the possibility of healing. Giving voice to the topic in the class encourages those who have been abused to have a private conversation with me later if they want to. It means I can steer them in the direction of healing. One of the reasons I choose *The Color Purple*, in fact, is that Celie and the women in the book provide each other hope for empowerment, and this novel, though it awakens pain in my students, also calls them to healing.

One of the most cherished sources of empowerment and healing is the relationship of Celie to her biological sister, Nettie. This relationship was central to the students' argument that sisterhood is key to Celie's movement to freedom. Juceyna's insight struck to the heart of this freeing force:

> Nettie was the first to love Celie, just because she was Celie. She believed in her sister. She educated her—that gave Celie power. But Nettie was Celie's heart. Even when separated, each of them was so linked to the other—I mean they even think alike about nature, and

God, and disappointments. A whole continent and culture apart they are in each other's souls. Nettie and Celie love each other unconditionally—separation, abuse, hardships, continents, time could not stop this. That's power. Everything Celie faced, every change she made, every time she loved was possible because Nettie believed in her. That lives in your heart forever.

To this Dawna added,

Celie is kinda like us. When her sister left, she still had sisters. Some of us have been through a lot. Three of us, our mothers have died. Some of us face homelessness, some of us abuse, we all have the burden to carry. . . . But we come here every day. Yeah, we educate ourselves because we believe that will help our dreams come true, but this is family to us. Sure we fight sometimes, kinda of like Sophia and Shug. We get lost like Squeak. We feel deserted like when Shug finds a new love and has no time for Celie. . . . But we are there for each other. If it weren't for mah sistahs in this room, I would have given up long ago.

It is not difference which immobizes us, but silence. And there are so many silences to be broken.[31]

Audre Lorde's words direct me in my teaching as I invite my students to break the silences that preserve oppression, silences that bury intelligence, silences that sever words from true voice. Teaching African American literature by and about women helps me shatter these silences and build bridges between the differences and divisions that silences create, thus empowering my students to learn and to grow and to heal—and to speak the truths of their lives.

Notes

1. Except for Donna's remark here, which is completely a product of my memory because she was a student of mine so long ago, all student comments that are punctuated by quotation marks have been reconstructed by myself and the speaker, and often have been corroborated by others in the class.

2. Carol Gilligan, *In a Different Voice: Psychological Theory and Women's Development* (Cambridge, MA: Harvard University Press, 1982).

3. Karen J. Warren, "Critical Thinking and Feminism," in *Re-thinking Reason,*

ed. Kerry S. Walters (Albany: SUNY Press, 1994). Warren uses the term "patriarchal" because "male gender identified beliefs, values, attitudes and assumptions are taken as the only, or the standard, or more highly valued one than female gender identified one." p. 157.

4. Ibid. Warren explains her terms. Value-hierarchical thinking categorizes things as differences and distinctions and ranks them on an up-and-down scale; the higher the ranking, the more value it has, and the lower the ranking, the less value it has. For example, reason is ranked higher and has more value than emotion, which is ranked lower and often put "down." Value dualism emphasizes grouping things in either-or, oppositional pairs, e.g., reason versus emotion. Logic of domination is a structure of "argumentation which explains, justifies and maintains the subordination of an 'inferior' group by a 'superior' group on the grounds of the (alleged) superiority and inferiority of the respective groups." p. 157.

5. Ibid., p. 158.

6. Carol Gilligan et al., eds., *Women, Girls and Psychotherapy: Reframing Resistance* (New York: Harrington Press, 1991), p. 1.

7. Tracy Robinson, and Janie Victoria Ward, "'A Belief in Self Far Greater than Anyone's Disbelief': Cultivating Resistance Among African American Female Adolescents," in Gilligan, et al., ibid.

8. The usual rules of freewriting apply here. That is, students are instructed not to worry about the rules of grammar, spelling, and syntax. The journal entries in this paper are unedited and unrevised.

9. Audre Lorde, "The Transformation of Silence into Language and Action," in *Sister Outsider* (Trumansburg, NY: Crossing Press, 1984), p. 43.

10. Ibid.

11. Mary B. Belensky, et al., *Women's Ways of Knowing* (New York: Basic Books, 1986). This work theorizes five stages of knowing for women: silence, received knowledge, subjective knowledge, procedural knowledge, constructed knowledge. With subjective knowledge, the student's orientation to authority shifts from externals to internals, from acceptance of dichotomous definitions of knowledge to knowledge that arises from intuition, inner voice, and personal experiences. With procedural knowledge comes integration of critical thinking, adoption or adaption of standards, objectivity and the search for external support and evidence with the inner voice. Procedural knowledge accesses other people's knowledge and conceptual frameworks—and this leads to constructed knowledge.

12. Zora Neale Hurston, *Their Eyes Were Watching God.* (New York: Harper & Row, 1937), p. 156.

13. Ibid., p. 183.

14. Cf. Belensky, et al., *Women's Ways of Knowing.*

15. Delores Gallo, "Educating for Empathy, Reason, and Imagination," in *Rethinking Reason*, ed. Kery Walters (Albany: SUNY Press, 1994).

16. Howard Gardner, *Multiple Intelligences: Theory into Practice* (New York: Basic Books, 1993). Gardner, in this much-quoted work, expands our understanding of intelligence from the two intelligences traditionally recognized, i.e. verbal/linguistic and logical/mathematical, to include five others: spatial, musical, bodily-kinesthetic, interpersonal, and intrapersonal.

17. Ibid.

18. As sung not too long ago by Gloria Estefan.

19. Hurston, *Their Eyes Were Watching God,* p. 139.

20. Ibid., p. 43.

21. Ibid., p. 83.

22. Cf. Belensky, et al.,*Women's Ways of Knowing.*

23. Alice Walker, *The Color Purple* (New York: Washington Square Press, 1982).

24. This activity relies on empathy, imagination, and bodily-kinesthetic intelligence to lead to cognitive insights.

25. Walker, *The Color Purple,* p. 187.

26. Ibid., p. 46.

27. Ibid., p. 50.

28. Ibid., p. 179.

29. Ibid., p. 249.

30. Ibid., p. 179.

31. Lorde, *The Transformation of Silence,* p. 44.

⊟ 6 ⊟

A FEMALE FACE

Or, Masking the Masculine
in African American Fiction Before Richard Wright

Thadious M. Davis
Vanderbilt University

I

For a number of years in the 1980s, I collected materials for a book on Wright and Faulkner. I had to put the project aside, but in the process of thinking about Wright's commercial success and his "shock value," I began looking more closely at the racial texts published in the decade or so before his fiction of the late 1930s. What I noticed was a simple point that had previously escaped me: in many cases both male and female African American novelists placed women at the center of their texts. In thinking about the sociocultural reasons for an emphasis on representations of the female or the feminine in African American literature, I observed what may be the obvious to many historians of African American life: that a hostile political climate repeatedly shaped a deemphasis of masculinity in African American life and not only in the decade of the 1920s, when constructions of American masculinity flourished in response to those of the new femininity, but particularly in the period at the end of the nineteenth century when constructions of American manhood issued from the rhetoric of imperialism. As a result of this observation and also of several recent provocative examinations of American masculinity, most of which are silent on African

American men,[1] I decided that attention to the implications of female protagonists in texts by African American men might lead to an understanding of Wright's success.

This essay takes as a project an explanation of Wright's impact on African American fiction, what I term his masculinization of African American fiction. It does so not by a direct examination of his texts, but rather by presenting one formulation of a female face and an unmasking the masking of the male in selected texts before the advent of Wright, who, despite writing entirely external to the South, retains what I term a "Black-Southern-Male-in-the-Age-of-Jim-Crow writerly perspective." There is perhaps an unavoidable irony in the situation of Wright—Southern and émigré to the North and ultimately Europe—carrying with him the baggage and the legacy of a prevalent early-twentieth-century white racist construction of black maleness, the baggage and legacy that, inevitably, he refocused to include both the aggressive participation of white Southern communities and the pathetic complicity of black Southern communities in the construction and destruction of black males. While this essay may run the risk of essentializing African American male authors and totalizing African American fiction, it intends to further the possibilities for exploring the literary production of African Americans and the rhetoric of racial self-representation. It acknowledges that both female and male gender constructions within fiction are based on constructions of the social roles of women and men, and that neither male/masculine nor female/feminine has a stable meaning over time. However, it suggests that African American male/female constructions in the fictions of African American men may not necessarily follow the prevailing, contemporaneous paradigms of dominant American culture, and that the production of male characters by African American men has been more complicated than current concepts allow.

The construction of the subject is a central project of African American fiction from its beginnings. Conceptions of a necessary black subject clearly occur in response to the objectification of blacks under slavery and perhaps specifically to the vocality of Southern slave owners in defending slavery by denying subject status to blacks. The construction of the black subject is especially prominent during the period from the turn of the century, when emancipated status allowed for the assumption of literary production and created a racial audience for that production, through World War II, when expatriate experience for African American males reconfigured their raciality, as in the case of Chester Himes and Richard Wright, whereas within the United States their race functioned to divide them from a white masculine subject and classified them as Other, as object in legal, ideological, cultural, and moral discourses.

In Europe, though the concept of race did not inhibit the construction of subject or of subjectivity, it could not a provide a solution to the problem of the racialized artist in relation to nation, nationality, nationhood, or nationalism. In effect, the freedom to obtain subject position in Europe for Wright and other males of his generation ultimately alienated not them, but their American male counterparts who were left behind and could not share in that freedom. Some of the anger and the frustration apparent in the criticism of Wright's European textual production can, in fact, be read as a disappointment not with his losing touch with the racial scene in America, as was and has been claimed, but rather with his abandoning the representation of a masculine African American in fiction, and his retreat from directly challenging the codified vision of and ideological bias against African American men functioning within the masculine paradigms of American culture and society.[2]

Although Margaret Walker's *Richard Wright, Daemonic Genius* (1988) was not well received, particularly by Wright's official biographer, Michel Fabre, her text observed the aggressive masculinity of Wright despite its subtextual purpose of calling into question his sexuality.[3] Walker, I would argue, was on to something significant, but the legacy of her personal interaction with Wright in the making of his 1940s fiction obscured the potential value of her vision of Wright's struggle against the female or the feminine in his fiction.

II

But I want to historicize and speculate here about one of the ways in which African American fiction arrived at Richard Wright, and an emergence from the female and the South. From the beginnings of the African American novel in the 1850s with the appearance of William Wells Brown's *Clotel: or The President's Daughter: A Narrative of Slave Life in the United States* (1853), the figure at the center of the fiction is the female. The struggle for control of her body and its issue which, according to accepted legal codes, carried her status as enslaved, signaled the moral struggle against slavery in terms understandable to the dominant culture and its elevated vision of women as mothers and motherhood as sacred within the cult of domesticity. In the case of *Clotel*, three central women, Currer and her two daughters, Clotel and Althesa, dominate the narrative and its emancipatory strategies, which begin in a discourse on marriage: "The marriage relation, the oldest and most sacred institution given to man by his Creator, is unknown and unrecognized in the slave laws of the United States. Would that we could say, that the moral and religious teaching in the slave states were better than the laws; but alas! we cannot" (37).

Brown, of course, takes several cues from Harriet Beecher Stowe's representation of enslaved women, so that sexual servitude and sexual violation fuel the necessity for both the Christian resistance of women (mothers) and the legal abolition of slavery. But his choice of a woman-centered text rejects Stowe's use of Uncle Tom as a pivotal figure. Brown's family narrative produces an argument for the humanity of enslaved women and, by extension, their issue or the larger race, and in so doing it answers the differentiational species basis for justifying slavery. Although Brown embeds his own story, "Narrative of the Life and Escape of William Wells Brown," within his novel, he reconfigures his story, in part that of a male child torn from his mother, as the story of a mother torn from her female child. As Bernard Bell posits, "The memoir seeks to establish the unimpeachable historicity of most of the details of the narrative proper by using a third-person rather than a first-person narrator" (38). However, it is also apparent that Brown well comprehends the political and moral implications of distancing a male-driven narrative from a female-driven one.

Clotel becomes an Ur-text in a specific expressive discourse: the obliquely articulated desires and the controlling emancipatory objectives of an African American man in an antislavery fiction. That discourse depends upon the reformation of appearance, not merely in terms of humanity (that is, reforming the debasing image of the inhumanity or subhumanity of the slave) but also in terms of the gender identity of the slave (that is, reforming the image of the slave as male). The body of the slave, then, in *Clotel* is ostensibly marked female, but in several moves underscoring the fluidity of the enslaved body and undermining the presumption of a male gender identification for the one who is enslaved, Brown masks or veils the female slave body, which is already always also his own male body given his embedding of his own subject position and experiential reality within his female characters. These moves are most apparent not in the coincidences of plot details, but in the prominent positioning of cross-dressing and gender disguises in resolving the plot complications. It may, therefore, be more than coincidental that Clotel effects her escape by disguising herself as a white Southern male, and later as an Italian male, or that her daughter Mary, equally effective in assuming male disguises, changes places with her beloved, George Green, who has been imprisoned for his part in Nat Turner's revolt. The female disguised as a male becomes a trope for the potentiality of freedom through personal agency, but the female, exposed in Brown's own extended slave narrative of escape, is, in effect, a textual veiling of the male.

This textual veiling is related to, but different from the use of the frequently observed mask positioned by African Americans for subversive purposes, because Brown's public, political agenda is not hidden in the text, but presented in straightforward didactic terms. However, his draping of the male in female form functions to distract and disrupt an expectation of the consequences of slavery upon the individual. The female is at once an individual, but also unavoidably linked biologically with reproduction and progeny, and she becomes therefore emblematic of the larger race in a way not immediately accessible to the male figure or the male body. Reading Brown's placement of women at the center of *Clotel* removes the critical emphasis away from the white-skinned mulatta character as a point of self-identification or source of empathy for white readers. It sites the struggle over ownership (of the slave as commodity and of the person as capital) directly within the body of the enslaved female for, in the aftermath of the laws against the importation of slaves, only the body of the female is capable of continuing the production of slaves and the increase of the slave economy.

III

Yet to backtrack momentarily from 1853 to 1845 in order to refrain from oversimplifying early African American fiction to fit my project, I cite the now-classic *Narrative of the Life of Frederick Douglass* (1845) which looms large as a slave narrative as much about defining manhood and masculinity as about strategies for emancipation or literacy, as Robert Stepto has observed in *From Behind the Veil* (1979). Although Wilson Moses conflates sexual and gender identities in arguing that Douglass "as a black male . . . was expected to desexualize his writing," but that "he found ways of introducing sexual issues into his writing indirectly" (639), he does observe Douglass's empowerment in masculinizing himself. The example Moses uses, Douglass's description of the whipping of his Aunt Hester "to illustrate not only the sexual brutalization of black females but also the related function of psychically castrating black males," leads him to conclude: "One of the many debasing aspects of beating a black woman was that it was done in the presence of black men and boys, for whom the female became depersonalized, transformed, against her will, into an instrument for emasculating black men" (639). However, that conclusion assumes the perspective of the white slave owners and their desired outcome for such beatings.[4] It may also be that, from the perspective of the male slave observers, such performances of physical brutality against their women kin inscribed not their inadequacy to protect females, but the necessity of inverting the power structure so that protection would become a possibility.

In Frederick Douglass's case, clearly he must assume the physical power ascribed to white men within the slave economy if he is to become a man. Witnessing the beating of Aunt Hester may be read as one of the factors influencing his definition of manhood and placing his emphasis on masculinity within the power dynamics of his society.

His fight with the white overseer Covey is an example. However, at a climactic moment Douglass also names his social condition and rearticulates manhood, which he had previously represented as the physical ability and courage to fight in hand-to-hand combat with Covey, as the psychological wedge between his subjective position and enslavement:

> I've observed this in my experience of slavery,—that whenever my condition was improved instead of it increasing my contentment, it only increased my desire to be free, and set me to thinking of plans to gain my freedom. I have found that, to make a contented slave, it is necessary to make a thoughtless one. It is necessary to darken his moral and mental vision, and, as far as possible, to annihilate the power of reason. He must be able to feel that slavery is right; and he can be brought to that only when he ceases to be a man. (135)

By the time Brown wrote *Clotel*, then, Douglass's text, with its nuanced definition of man hinged upon physicality had already introduced an impulse in African American–authored texts to centralize man as a rational agent and manhood as a mental liberation. And though Brown initially remarks that "the present system of chattel slavery in America undermines the entire social condition of man" (39), he does not follow Douglass's valorization of manhood as a behavioral code and cultural value in both *Narrative of the Life* and his novella *The Heroic Slave* (1835), in which Madison Washington, leader of a successful slave mutiny, mentally and physically outmaneuvers the ship's captain who acknowledges: "I felt myself in the presence of a superior man; one who, had he been a white man, I would have followed willingly and gladly in any honorable enterprise. Our difference of color was the only ground for difference of action" (68).

However, Martin R. Delany dramatically positions racialized manhood as central to the construction of subject in his novel *Blake: or The Huts of America* (1859). A radical in political and racial vision, Delany was an abolitionist unafraid to name racism within the antislavery movement. Frederick Douglass once remarked: "I thank God for making me a man simply, but Delany always thanks Him for making him a black man."[5] *Blake*, with its emphasis on the psychological liberation of enslaved African Americans and its activist revolutionary subject, is one of the few fictional extensions of Douglass's articulation of manhood.

The novel concludes with two calls to action in racial solidarity against white oppression. The first is issued by Ambrosina, a young black woman beaten in public for accidentally brushing against a white woman. "I wish I was a man, I'd lay the city in ashes this night, so I would," she states. "One thing I do know, if our men do not decide on something in our favor, they will soon be called to look upon us in a state of concubinage" (313). She represents manhood as both protection of womanhood and compensatory action against racism. In response to Ambrosina's evocation of a necessary code of manly conduct on the parts of black men, Montego, her father and community elder, commits himself to action: "By yonder blue heavens, I'll avenge this outrage!" (313). His individual readiness for action and confrontation is extended into the larger community of men by the youth Gondolier, who has already declared: "[W]e have a race of devils to deal with that would make an angel swear. Educated devils that's capable of everything hellish under the name of religion, law, politics, social regulations, and the higher civilization; so that the helpless victim be of the black race. . . . Let me into the streets and give me but half a chance and I'll unjoin them faster then ever I did a roast pig for the palace dinner table" (312). Although initially restrained from rash action by the tempered mediation of Ambrosina's mother, Gondolier speaks the final words of the text and, catalyzed by Ambrosina, issues the second call to action. He "rejoic[ed] as he left the room to spread among the blacks an authentic statement of the outrage: 'Woe be unto those devils of white, I say!'" (313). Gondolier's departure is an entrance onto a communal stage of direct confrontational action prefigured elsewhere in the novel, and it portends a redress of offenses against black women. With very few exceptions, however, this vigorous activist stance of the male does not reemerge as a prominent legacy for African American fiction until well into the twentieth century,[6] despite the conflation of masculinity and nationalism within novels by white American authors in the 1890s.[7]

In the mid-nineteenth century, as Carla Peterson has observed of African American fiction, "African American writers produced their narratives under pressure from compelling social and economic agendas, and sought to sell their books for profit on the literary marketplace" (566).[8] That dual concern precluded certain kinds of representations of African American males throughout the nineteenth century and well into the twentieth century. Although Peterson suggests that African American writers in the 1850s "adapted conventional figures from the dominant literary culture—the tragic mulatta and picaro—to complicate and contextualize essentialized notions of black selfhood" (579), these writers also severely circumscribed the struggle for control of the larger image of the race. Fictional portraits in texts such as Frank Webb's *Garies and Their Friends* (1857) sanitize the appearance of African American men and linger over their bodily attributes in a manner comparable to that of females in the romance fictions of the period.[9] Mr. Walters in *The Garies* is exemplary and, as Blyden Jackson observes, "a beau ideal for Negro manhood."[10] Webb describes his physical attractiveness in detail:

> Mr. Walters was above six feet in height, and exceedingly well-proportioned of jet-black complexion, and smooth glossy skin. His head was covered with a quantity of wooly hair, which was combed back from a broad but not very high forehead. His eyes were small, black, and piercing, and set deep in his head. His aquiline nose, thin lips, and broad chin, were the reverse of African in their shape and gave his face a very singular appearance. (50)

Webb focuses both on the man's body and on his clothing: "The neatness and care with which he was dressed added to the attractiveness of his appearance. His linen was the perfection of whiteness, and his snowy vest lost nothing by its contact therewith. A long black frock coat, black pants, and highly polished boots, completed his attire" (121–22). The attention to Walters's physicality is primarily in terms of reconfiguring the African American male body as attractive, so that standards of beauty/handsomeness are extended to one who is "jet black," though his sartorial elegance mimics a racial contrast between black and white ("snowy," "the perfection of whiteness"). There is no suggestion of strength or vigor in the portrait; Walters is a passive figure, a spectacle to be observed, valued, and commodified for his taste in draping his body elegantly and expensively. His stylized presence in the text speaks to the safety and conformity of the African Americanized, and denies his mental or physical capacity to exert pressure on the power structure that enslaved and degraded blacks.

Admittedly, however, a few hints of Delany's masculinist militancy appear at the turn of the century; for example, in the situational context of *Imperium in Imperio* (1899) by Sutton Griggs and in the minor character of Josh Green in Charles Chesnutt's *Marrow of Tradition* (1901). Griggs intertwines the narrative fates of Belton Piedmont, a black who rises in an organization "to unite all Negroes in a body to do that which the whimpering government childishly but truthfully says it cannot do," and Bernard Belgrave, a mulatto who also participates in the Imperium but takes a more militant stance for defeating racism. But for the most part, late nineteenth-century and turn-of-the-century African American fictions were reluctant to posit a masculinist paradigm of either physical or psychological strength as central to racial uplift. Griggs, in fact, in both of his novels following *Imperium in Imperio*—*Overshadowed* (1901) and *Unfettered* (1902)—turns away from male protagonists and toward females (Erma Wysong and Morlene) to formulate solutions to racial problems. And in his last two novels, *The Hindred Hand* (1905) and *Pointing the Way* (1908), he returns to dual heroes, a mulatto and a black, but this time, they are conjoined to women and participate in marriage plots as metaphors for the institutions delimiting the social mobility and political power of African Americans. The reluctance to create masculine paradigms is oppositional to the cultural discourses on the development of the male body in physical exercise and military training as preparatory for a life of action.

One explanation for the reluctance resides in the social climate of the period and the group aspirations of racial writers. Dickenson Bruce in *Black American Writing from the Nadir* describes the era between the end of Reconstruction and the beginning of World War I (1877–1915) as not only a low point in American race relations but also an embattled period in which African American fictionists represented middle-class aspirations and values as a means of combating racism. Bruce observes: "What made those years so crucial—what makes labeling them as the nadir so apt—was that they were the setting for a visible deterioration of the position of black people in American society" (2). Racial violence, lynchings, and riots escalated in the 1890s along with racist ideologies supporting African American inferiority and discriminatory practices, such as Jim Crow legislation and its major ruling, *Plessy v. Ferguson* (1896), which legitimated "separate but equal" as doctrine and institutionalized segregation.

IV

If these observations of overt hostility to African Americans are combined with a literary emphasis on gentility and on middle-class ideals and Victorian culture, then the strategies for African American male representation in texts such as Chesnutt's *The House Behind the Cedars* (1900) or *The Marrow of Tradition*, Paul Laurence Dunbar's *The Sport of the Gods* (1902), and W.E.B. Du Bois's *Quest of the Silver Fleece* (1911) become clearer. The emphasis within the literature of uplift is decidedly upon class position as a means of distinguishing both the residual upper class and the emergent African American middle class from the masses of the race. Willard Gatewood identifies respectability, moral rectitude, social grace, formal education, and proper ancestry or good breeding, along with wealth and color as the characteristics necessary for admission to the African American elite (15). The shaping of attitudes and manners of polite society, issued from the performances of females as a model of behavior and ritual, is a point that Gatewood does not make, but that can be extrapolated from his research. According to Gatewood's examination of the social life of "aristocrats of color":

> The social ritual was important as a tangible manifestation of "good breeding," a term that appeared often in the musings of aristocrats of color. Blacks used it, as did other Americans of the era, to refer to certain "habitual attitudes and a knowledge of the proprieties and manners." It consisted of an amalgam of qualities inculcated and perpetuated through the family and through certain types of formal as well as social education. For aristocrats of color, their practice of the genteel performance in both private and public served as a model for the black masses to emulate as a significant factor in advancing the "progress of the race." (206)

One textual result of the bowing to quiet deportment and eschewing of loud expression as signs of gentility for advancing racial uplift was the dispensing with overt protest and the veiling of activist, political impulses that otherwise within the society would have been labeled masculine for their impact within a public sphere. This resultant indirection and concealment of both desire and motive mask not only political aspirations as social graces but also masculine conduct as gentlemanly behavior. Importantly, the African American "gentleman" is emasculated by the very set of virtues that supposedly would forward his own and his race's progress, because he cannot name racism publicly, he cannot demonstrate against injustice, he cannot declare his vigor in a public arena. Ultimately, this code of conduct, adopted to hide or shield a larger political motive, becomes only its own veneer, self-effacing, self-perpetuating, and self-destructive. That surface, however, is sustained by the formal properties of middle-class consumer culture, particularly within the private domestic sphere, where decor, furnishings, and appointments usually associated with the female in majority culture become the markers of African American manly success. [11]

In *The Marrow of Tradition,* Chesnutt creates an African American physician as protagonist of a fiction based on the Wilmington Race Riot or Massacre of 1898, when whites moved to impose their political and social supremacy on the citizens of a North Carolina town. Dr. Miller works diligently for the welfare of African Americans, but within a framework delimited by accommodation and acquiescence. Although his concerns for racial uplift and harmonious coexistence are represented within his public role as an educated man of medicine, his personal traits are figured through his interaction with his family and the domestic sphere. Family and genealogy intertwine in contextualizing the political plot and in characterizing Miller. He is reluctant to consider overt political action or to disrupt the possibility of acceptance by the white community. In fact, his story is so interconnected with that of his mulatto wife, Janet, and her struggle for the recognition of her white half-sister that the family plot takes over the narrative and subsumes the political plot in which Dr. Miller initially seems implicated. As he enters his wife's narrative of entitlement, he falls out of contact with the politicized black community and thus fails, on a very basic level, to understand the destructiveness of white hysteria over black political empowerment. Eric Sundquist states:

> [M]irroring images of male and female hysteria . . . in *The Marrow of Tradition* spring in part from the loss of economic and political power suffered by the South in the aftermath of the war and felt keenly by male leaders, and in part from the instability of gender relations that resulted. Negro domination did, in fact, threaten the manliness of the white southerner, though not in the way it was often represented. Male hysteria was not primarily about rape; it was about votes and the feared loss of white southern virility, which in turn sprang from the region's prolonged economic deterioration. . . . Rape was the mask behind which disenfranchisement was hidden, but it was part of a larger charade of plantation mythology that set out to restore southern pride and revive paradigms of white manliness that the legacy of the war and the economic and political rise of blacks during Reconstruction had called seriously into question. The post-Reconstruction discourse of southern masculinity . . . provided a particularly compelling context for Chesnutt's dramatization of the personal and sectional impotence that race hysteria sought to counteract in proliferating images of heroism and ancestral veneration. (425)

Though Chesnutt may pose a set of manly characteristics different from those assumed by the larger society and different avenues for achieving them, he does not actualize these in Dr. Miller's story. Instead, he has Miller come to accept his wife's values and virtues and to leave to her the climactic decision (whether to save the son and heir of Janet's half-sister and her husband, a leading citizen of the town and a racist complying with the violent imposition of white supremacy). Miller, then, becomes an extension of his wife and her personal code of family, responsibility, and grace. His identity is inseparable from that code, and as such no gender distinction can be determined between Miller and Janet. This fusing of male/female, particularly in the final moments of the text, may function to valorize the couple as the precursors of a new era of racial vision and gender cooperation, but it also subordinates the pair to the political prowess of white Southern manhood regaining vitality and control and positions Janet's face so that Miller can acknowledge seeing only through her eyes.

In *The House Behind the Cedars,* a novel preceding *The Marrow of Tradition* by one year, Chesnutt had created a white-skinned mulatta protagonist, Rena Walden, as the center of his narrative. His choice to center on Rena, or Rowena Warwick as she is known when she passes for white, is particularly intriguing because her brother not only passes but is a successful lawyer in South Carolina. Chesnutt himself was black by choice, and his appearance and background could have destabilized efforts to categorize him racially. Rena/Rowena may be linked to the idea of the arbitrariness of race and to the fluidity of racial designations, but she is also gendered female. What she apparently offered Chesnutt was not simply access to a tradition of mulatta heroines but a double veil behind which he could explore explosive issues such as interracial love and sexual relations and intraracial color and class complexes within the context of the safe gender traits attributed to women. Rena could be indecisive and agonize over her divided love for and loyalties to three men: one white, one mulatto, and one black. She could be critical of darker-skinned and working-class blacks; she could show preferences for white society and a white lover. And she could wander lost in a swamp and go mad. In short, she could be female as women's personalities were perceived and constructed. Her brother could not be located rationally within the same scenario; neither could any other male during this time period in texts written by this author. The line between fiction and fact in narratives of African American life, though clear, was not always imposed. To ascribe to a man the situational disasters and the emotional turmoil Rena faced would have implicated Chesnutt himself in racial ambivalences, despite his obvious self-selected racial designation. *The House Behind the Cedars* is not finally a woman's story; it is the masked story of not one man, but three. Rena's female body, then, unlike that of Brown's Clotel, is not the site of a discourse of ownership and property and reproductive rights; it is instead a medium for exploring the emotional and psychological implications of racial identity and its complexities for shaping a masculine identity in the postwar South. The triangulation of three men, all racialized and socialized differently, becomes a rigid projection of her fragmented desires, but the men also place themselves as points of tension outside of her body and outside of her control. In a sense, then, Rena is only object, but George Tryon, Jeff Wain, and Frank Fowler are subjects. Although Chesnutt constructs them through indirection, he clearly invests in them an agency that might initially seem surprising, given Rena's presence as a focal point. But Rena functions also as a camera by means of which Chesnutt can focus and capture his vision of southern men—white, black, and mulatto—at a critical historical moment and what they each portend for the future of his region and his race.

V

Perhaps it is James Weldon Johnson in *Autobiography of an Ex-Colored Man* (1912; 1927) who announces a change: a text playing against a masculinized response of fighting back—resistance to race violence, segregation, subjugation—and instead responding with emotion, feeling, and dependency ascribed to females, particularly to the narrator's mother. Johnson suggests a homoerotic attraction between the narrator and his benefactor, along with the narrator's desire to possess his father and thereby the South as socially constructed by the elite class of whites his father represents; these repressed desires are signs of the muting of gender identity in the novel.

Jean Toomer's *Cane* is dedicated to his white grandmother, and though it situates an unnamed male narrator within the sketches and stories of the first two parts of the text, it relies upon the experiences of females to convey the impact of racism and economic exploitation. The women—Fern, Ester, Karintha, Louisa, and so on—all may be read as different phases of the experiential reality of African American men in the South, and subsequently in the North, because it is by means of the guise of the female that Toomer narrates a man's story. The faces of the female become the trope for the multifaceted but veiled face of the male narrator. Toomer's choice of the female to center and carry his narrative, however, is particularly suggestive given his experience in body building and exercise to shape himself as a manly man and his admitted obsession with sexual expression during the same period. While in high school, Toomer began physical training, dieting, and weight lifting, using Bernard McFadden's *Encyclopedia of Physical Culture* as a guide, and in 1916, after a false start in an agriculture program at the University of Wisconsin, he enrolled in the American College of Physical Training in Chicago, where he pursued interests in gymnastics, basketball, and anatomy.[12] Somehow, even given these proclivities, Toomer disassociates vigorous masculinity from his text, and instead his sexually ambivalent and socially effacing narrator collapses his subjectivity with that of the women he would position as subjects but, in effect, manipulates as objects dominated by his construction of them and his articulation of their desires and needs.[13]

Only once in *Cane* does Toomer come close to unmasking the male in his text, and in that particular moment, he locates the subjectivity of his quasi-feminine narrator directly within that of a female subject:

> I traced my development from the early days to the present time, the phase in which I could understand her. I described her own nature and temperament. Told how they needed a larger life for their expression. How incapable Washington was of understanding that need. I pointed out that in lieu of proper channels, her emotions had overflowed into paths that dissipated them. I talked, beautifully I thought, about an art that would be born, an art that would open the way for women the likes of her. I asked her to hope, and build up an inner life against the coming of that day. I recited some of my own things to her. I sang, with a strange quiver in my voice, a promise-song. And then I began to wonder why her hand had not once returned a simple pressure. (48)

This discourse follows Toomer's own autobiography: his relationship to Washington and the repression of desires and ambitions within the literal space of Washington and the figurative space of his family; his belief that he had dissipated his talents in seeking proper outlets for them; his desire for an art that would open a way for Americans configured like him in racial terms. The narrator is at once speaking for the silent Avey, who is asleep at his side, and to Toomer's own formulation of his experiential reality. The culture of manhood and manliness, signified by his physical education and work as a physical trainer, does not accommodate his vocalizing his experiences in terms gendered male; he can only achieve expression through the projection of

113

his story onto Avey, through the layering of his mask onto her face. In his choice of the female face for his representation of societal and cultural tensions figured in terms of race, Toomer goes against the grain of the post–World War I white American authors such as Hemingway and Faulkner, whose male protagonists are overtly positioned as struggling with or against the prevailing notions of masculine strength, male prerogative, and patriarchal power.

VI

Despite the declarations of New Negroes during the 1920s and of Langston Hughes specifically in the manifesto "The Negro Artist and the Racial Mountain" (1926), little changes occurred in the fictional representation of African American males.[14] Walter White's *The Fire in the Flint* (1924), with a protagonist who is an African American physician working in the South, is similar to and intricately related to Chesnutt's *Marrow* in its vision of the male. Though White's *Flight* (1926) repeats the familiar use of a mulatta as heroine, and though Mimi, a New Orleans Creole of color, is often dismissed as just another heroine of the novel of passing, she is a major example of the displacement of the male from the center of a fiction that, I would argue, has much to do with the positionality of African American men and the textual strategy of responding to racial separation and oppression by assuming a female face. But because the fair-skinned female mask has already been a part of my treatment here, I will turn instead to Wallace Thurman's *The Blacker the Berry* (1929).

Though set in the contemporary period of the Harlem Renaissance and produced after Hughes's call for artistic freedom, Thurman's novel does not explore the problems of color complexes for males. Instead, Thurman, who was dark-skinned and sensitive to color hierarchy within the race, chose a woman as his protagonist. While clearly, Emma Lou is gendered female and colored black, she is also a trope for Thurman's own positioning within both his own family in the West and Harlem society in the 1920s. The biographical parallels between Emma Lou and Wallace Thurman are more than superficial; they produce the subtext and the tension of the fiction. The choice of a female dictates the possibilities for textual resolution, which must, given the accepted social roles for females, reside within the romance and marriage plots. But the marriage plot, with its latent aspect of sexual fulfillment, is also at the core of Emma Lou's responses to color, and it enables Thurman to represent his own homoerotic attractions by means of a female's conventional romantic engagements with men. The public world as a stage for action and correction is denied her, so that she can have no impact upon the attitudes of her peers regarding coloration and complexes of color. As in Toomer's case, Thurman's struggle with male and black sexual identity is transfigured in the woman's struggle. While Thurman is not Emma Lou, just as Toomer is not any one of his female characters, he can speak of the experiences closest to his own subjectivity only through the narrative double distance of Emma Lou.

VII

I would like to turn by way of concluding to a text appearing after Richard Wright's male protagonists explode the codes for depicting African American men and introduce a powerful revisioning of the impact of oppression and racism on African American men in particular and American society in general. That text is *The Sweet Flypaper of Life*, Langston Hughes's 1955 collaboration with photographer Roy De Carava, which has not received critical attention, though it was, as Arnold Rampersad points out, one of his critical successes: "No book by Hughes was ever greeted so rhapsodically"; "its own kind of art"; "a delicate and lovely fiction-document"; "astonishing verisimilitude" (249). The small, cheaply printed yet beautiful book is somewhat of an anomaly in the scholarship on Hughes's fiction; it immediately met a small but enthusiastic audience, but disappeared almost as quickly from view.

In examining the small volume, I have been struck by its similarity to an earlier effort, *Twelve Million Black Voices: A Folk History of the Negro in the United States* (1941) by Richard Wright with photographic

115

direction by Edwin Rosskam. The conjunction of visual representation of the lives of African Americans with literary text is another way of bringing art into the lives of ordinary people, of showing the faces of the people within the contexts of daily experience, and of telling the stories of their human relationships in contradistinction to the stereotypical constructions of their lives. In the introduction to the Thunder's Mouth Press edition of *Twelve Million Black Voices* (1988), David Bradley calls attention to the "lyrical power" of Wright's text, "an impressionistic rather than logical structure, . . . a fluid power of a clarity of expression that [Wright] would not achieve again until the midfifties" (xvi–xvii).

More recently, Houston Baker concludes from his reading of *Twelve Million Black Voices* and from Wright's textual emphasis on "a determined connection between relations of production and states of human consciousness": "The result is an essentially Afro-American male vision of the world. That vision projects a merger of Afro-American males and the progressive forces of Western industrial technology, a merger that, by its very nature, excludes black women and their domestic consciousness and calling" (115). Though Baker's reading of *Twelve Million Black Voices* is decidedly in the service of his larger effort to enter the realm of black feminist criticism, it observes a "ruthless portrayal of Afro-American women" (116) explicit in Wright's claim that "more than even that of the American Indian, the consciousness of vast sections of our black women lies beyond the boundaries of the modern world, though they live and work in that world daily" (147). This portrayal of African American women, according to Baker, "is a function of a desperately felt necessity for the black male [sic] narrative voice to come into 'conscious history'" (116).[15]

Though Wright's effort is a racial history, perhaps masculinized as Baker suggests, Hughes's is a communal history. The difference is that between a story told by an observer, external though clearly empathetic and identified with the subject, and the story told by a participant whose observations begin with the immediate, the sensory accessible, and by extension involve the larger whole. And though Wright may have figured himself into the faces in the photographs, and into the racialized "we" subjectifying his narrative, he also abstracts himself from the historicizing process, as his foreword to *Twelve Million Black Voices* implies:

> This text assumes that those few Negroes who have lifted themselves
> ... above the lives of their fellow-blacks—like single fishes that leap
> and flash for a split second above the surface of the sea—are but fleet-
> ing exceptions to that vast, tragic school that swims below in the
> depth, against the current, silently and heavily, struggling against the
> waves of vicissitudes that spell a common fate. It is not, however, to
> celebrate or exalt the plight of humble folk who swim in the depths
> that I select the conditions of their lives as examples of normality, but
> rather to seize upon that which is qualitative and abiding in Negro
> experience, to place within full and constant view the collective
> humanity whose triumphs and defeats are shared by the majority,
> whose gains in security mark an advance in the level of consciousness
> attained by the broad masses in their costly and tortuous upstream
> journey. (xix–xx)

This abstraction from inclusion in the subjectivity of the text is, I believe, one of the dominant characteristics of Wright's fiction, though ironically that fiction maintains a consistently masculinized perspective that persistently configures racial awareness and historical consciousness by refusing female participation and therefore refuting female textual dominance.

Hughes's text, on the other hand, collapses the authorial identity into the autobiographical construction of one African American woman, Mary Bradley. The distinction between fiction, history, and autobiography are intentionally blurred, and Hughes's own autobiography is transfigured into the fictional Mary Bradley's historicization of her life within contemporary Harlem. Hughes's project is fiction, then, in a way that Wright's is not. The site of narrative reality is the invented female subject who initially enters the text as voice and vision, and who on the final page leaves as image and reality.

Sweet Flypaper offers other points of difference between Wright and Hughes. Ultimately pragmatic, Hughes's writing in *Sweet Flypaper* uni-fies the speech act with its visual framing texts, the photographs of De Carava, a painter and photographer by training. While on a Guggen-heim Fellowship in 1952, De Carava angled his camera on the Harlem community and completed more than two thousand photographs, which, until he contacted Hughes, simply sat on a shelf (Rampersad, 242). After seeing a selection of about three hundred, Hughes responded: "We have to get these published!" (Rampersad, 242–43). De Carava's photographs struck a personal chord evoking Hughes's own connections to Harlem life; Rampersad reveals that within days of the meeting with De Carava, Hughes put a group of the photographs in his study "as inspiration," and started writing, almost nonstop, his second autobiography, *I Wonder as I Wander* (242). The urgency of that writing was certainly nothing new for Hughes, who in the mid-1950s churned out historical books as fast as he could to keep the "wolf from his door." But the urgency suggests the power of De Carava's visual images to galvanize Hughes into a self-reflective mode. From the hundreds of photographs, Hughes chose the figure of a woman as the focal point of the text. Though he had numerous possibilities for a protagonist or for a connecting narrative, he chose Sister Mary Bradley. Let me suggest a possible explanation.

The "image of the Black woman," according to R. Baxter Miller, "signified the rise and fall of [Hughes's] literary imagination. What made the Black woman central to Hughes' world was her role as griot and keeper of memories. . . . [S]he sought to keep alive the rites that facilitated the passage from slavery to freedom. Hers was often the lyrical imagination . . . a rite of celebration shared with the audience" (121). Miller's observation seems applicable to Hughes in his creative interaction with the voice of the elderly African American female, Mary Bradley a persona and a projection emanating from Hughes's observation of and empathy with older women of color. However, his interaction with Mary Bradley's voice is an impersonal, and yet completely imbricated, projection of his own experiences, vocalized in his participation in the lives of the people of Harlem from an unthreatening, grandmotherly locus of being. His choice of Mary Bradley as the central subjectivity of *Sweet Flypaper* is grounded in Hughes's own social history and experiences: his sense of the female at the center of discourse on African American life, community, and thought. For Hughes, socialized in the first part of the century and coming to maturity as a writer before the groundbreaking vision of Wright, no comparable figure existed for imagining the strongly communal and slowly transforming world in which urban African Americans functioned. In his dual recognition of the existence and the deterioration of community, Hughes chose a female presence as an elegy for what was both always already present, and therefore changing, and always already dying, and therefore passing in the euphemistic term African Americans frequently use for death.

Written in the voice of Sister Mary Bradley, 113 West 134th Street, New York City, *The Sweet Flypaper of Life* takes as its project the fitting of narrative to images. In a stream of consciousness provoked by a brush with death, the "bicycle of the Lord bearing His messenger," Sister Mary talks through the reasons she cannot acquiesce to the call: "Boy, take that wire right on back to St. Peter because I am not prepared to go. I might be a little sick, but as yet I ain't no ways tired" (7). Humorous and poignant, she is unprepared to untangle herself from life or the living: from family ("I got to look after Ronnie Belle"); and from race ("I want to stay here and see what this integration the Supreme Court has done decreed is going to be like."). (7). In refusing to sign her name to the telegram, she not only puts death in abeyance, but she also initiates the process of articulating an identity beyond a single textual referent. And between the first and last pages of the text, she poses her own elegy and her community's.

The construction of Mary Bradley's social, familial, cultural contexts is both an act of memory and an act of invention. It is, too, an instance of what Miller labels Hughes's "task of recording cultural history," in which "the autobiographical imagination . . . expresses the bond between history and self as well as that between fact and interpretation" (121). In *Sweet Flypaper*, Hughes displaces his own signature with the photograph of Mary Bradley, signed on the last page of the text: "Here I am" (96). The signing of the text in the end as hers—that is, as female, mother, grandmother, elderly, African American, urban, struggling, surviving, loving, and smiling from under the brim of her best hat and looking directly into the camera while holding onto an iron fence— also displaces the shaping act of De Carava, the photographer. Mary Bradley's reality becomes the subject of her own iconography or subjectivity, not of Hughes's autograph or of De Carava's camera. Though she does not write of or photograph herself, she does narrate, tell, portray, and render events and people and the emotions connecting the two within a spatial context that is at once the Harlem she describes, and therefore invents, and the photographs she issues from. At the end, she stands, seemingly larger in size than any of the other photographic images, though there is no difference in the actual dimensions.

The dual communicative nature of the enterprise aims at both a verbally oriented access and a visually oriented one. The sentences, strung across the pages, introduce and depart from the photographic images. The conjoined effort is a performance of communication as the stored and restored contextual realities of both the individual behind the camera and the individual behind the words. The impact is an emotional, sensory, and intellectual response to the linked representations of the photographer and the writer.

The interpretative imagination that Sister Mary displays foregrounds the necessity of priorities, or of ordering one's life, and therefore a hierarchical significance of generations and transformations emerges from Sister Mary's interpretive ordering, which places self at the center but, at the same time, at the lower end of priorities. In prioritizing her grandchildren, especially Rodney, and her children, particularly her youngest daughter Melinda, and her community, and only then herself, Sister Mary orders a world that could otherwise seem chaotic, without pattern.

The written communication, however, is markedly political. It argues for the possibility of a better life, within the "sweet flypaper," within the lived and varied experiences of the subjects. The sameness of the language, dovetailed to the pictures, is the sameness of difference. The argument hinges upon comprehension of the momentous possibility of the Supreme Court's striking down of "separate but equal"; on the potential of Rodney and Mary's other grandchildren; on the people-driven activities of "Picket lines picketing" (79); "And at night the street meetings on the corner—" (80); "talking about 'Buy black'" (81); "Africa for the Africans" (82); "and 'Ethiopia shall stretch forth her hand'" (83), and in all the voice of racial reality: "And some joker in the crowd always says, 'And draw back a nub!'" (83). In this sequence Hughes writes into the photographs the undercurrent of emergent political expression and a sense of the static disappointment already always interpolated into any racially aware present, but neither can occupy the textual center, because both articulate the racial and economic power of nationalism and its vocal public residency outside of spheres of domesticity, reticence, and privacy. Though briefly figured, the vocality, autonomy, and agency of an activist nationalism suggest the culturally configured social roles of men, which Hughes does not or cannot pursue, given the centrality of Sister Mary's female subjectivity and family plot.

Without despair and without bitterness, the voice inscribes at once the slyly veiled, politically subdued writerly Hughes, distrusting established institutions but unwilling to dismiss the agency of grass-roots efforts; and the voice inscribes the articulate folk speaker Mary Bradley, the unseen yet iconic maternal presence whose personal politics are staunchly based on uncompromising love and direct intervention and faith in coalitions of whoever shares her beliefs and participates in her fight.

The brief, unregulated survey of a community through the multifaceted members of Sister Mary's family positions the class stratification becoming more pronounced on the eve of integration in the mid-1950s at the center of a discourse on maternity, family, familial responsibility, children, parental duty, and the social institutions beginning to fail African American people. Instructive and educative by its very ordering, the narrative patterning deemphasizes a single conventional middle-class paradigm for racial and familial survival. Mary's litany of the "good stock in her family," those following the way of marriage, work, houses, and upward mobility is swift and short, buried a third of the way through her narrative: Chickasaw, Mary's "most up-and-coming grandchild, declares soon as he gets married, he's gonna get [a car] too, so he won't have to ride the bus to work" (20); "I got some fine grandchildren, like my son Fred's three that lives up by the Harlem River" (34); "Or like my daughter Ellen's daughter whose name is Ellen, too" (35); "Oh, there is some good stock in my family. Like Ellen's mother who really takes care of her house. And my middle boy is well married, to a girl who is a real pretty typewriter" (36). The gesture is toward the genteel and the socially proper.

121

The static objectifying image of "good stock," "fine children" is subverted, however, by Melinda, the daughter with whom Mary lives, Melinda's husband, Jerry, and their four children. In a sustained development that is uncharacteristically long in this short text—twenty pages—Melinda's family emerges as functional: four children, including a set of twins, in five years of marriage, as well as a party every Saturday night (45–46); "can't nobody say when [Jerry's] home he ain't a family man. Crazy about his children—and his children are crazy about him" (51). It is functional yet flawed: "This world is like a crossword puzzle in the *Daily News*" (45); one son "wants a gun that shoot both ways at once" (58); the father sometimes forgets to come home (61). It is flawed but central to Mary's recognition of a subjectified unit only partly controlled by her gaze. Not without a hint of irony, Mary prefaces her bittersweet portrait of Melinda's family by observing: "Me, I always been all tangled up in life—which ain't always so sanitary as we might like it to be" (43). Her words signal a correspondence between her own and her daughter's relationship with life.

However, it is not Mary's rendering of Melinda's household but rather her positioning of her grandson Rodney and his slow, easy movement at the beginning of her monologue that serves as a catalyst for the narrative of the unraveling of myths of mobility and of the persistent social constructions of race:

That Rodney! That street's done got Rodney! How his father and his mother can wash their hands of Rodney, I do not know, when he is the spitting image of them both. But they done put him out, so's they can keep on good-timing themselves, I reckon: [photo of man and woman embracing, 10]

So I told him, "Come here and live with your grandma," And he come.

Now, Lord, I don't know—why did I want to take Rodney? But since I did, do you reckon my prayers will reach down in all them king-kong basements, and sing with the juke boxes, and walk in the midnight streets with Rodney? . . . Because there is something in that boy. You know and I know there's something in that boy. If he got lost in his youthhood, it just might not be his fault, Lord. I were wild myself when I were young—and to tell the truth, ever so once in a while, I still feels the urge. But sometimes, I wonder why the only time that boy moves fast is when he's dancing. When there's music playing, girls have to just keep looking to see where he's at, he dances so fast. Where's he at? Where's he at? [photo of a girl dancing with head to one side, 11]

Mary's prayer for Rodney is the longest sustained piece of narrative uninterrupted by photographs in *Sweet Flypaper*. Its encoded revelation, however, is that Rodney is beyond the control of Mary's gaze and that he signals Mary's position as a spectator, though one involved in attempting to construct a logic of Harlem life out of its images of contradiction. Ambivalently, Mary herself typecasts both the Rodney she sees and his relationship to music and good times. She acknowledges his faults: "But when he's talking or listening, or lounging, he just looks sleepy—drinking beer down in the basement with them boys" (12); "Rodney has to come up here to me to borrow subway fare to take [his girlfriend out]" (13); "Had a baby by Surgarlee before he was even seventeen . . . he did not pay that baby no mind—not even to walk it like other young fathers do" (27); "Rodney's child growed up like that little boy down the street, sad. He don't never smile" (28). Unaggressive, "laid back," and largely inactive, Rodney is decidedly no threat to the economic and political powers subjugating African Americans. But Rodney's fate is not simply the focal point of disintegration of the family and intergenerational confusion about the courses of corrective action, but also the point of Mary's narrative strategies for coherence, textual and experimental cohesion, though qualified because as a masculine racial construction Rodney seems vulnerable to a fetishing of the ambiguous black male.

Rodney recurs throughout, and perhaps had Richard Wright constructed a narrative from De Carava's photographs, Rodney would have been the central presence, authoritative consciousness, and potentially explosive powerful masculinity. Instead in Hughes's production, he is the subordinate grandson, though as one dominant component of Mary's present condition and extended family, he figures at the center of *her* narrative and shares the center with racial progeny as her cumulative reason for living. Situated as the entry and the exit from the communal habits and ethics, behavior and values, Rodney grounds Mary's function in reflecting life and in resisting death. "He never moves fast—not even to reach out his hand for a dollar—except when he is dancing. And crazy about music. Can tell you every horn that ever blowed on every juke-box in the neighborhood" (13) serves as the entrance to the discourse on the activities of young people and their differences from Mary's generation in terms of their tastes in music and their desire for cars, which then leads to Mary's poignant differentiation between contemporary subway riders and domestic workers, who are women of Mary's generation.

Although typecast as lethargic, Rodney is a controlling and deflecting trope for the class difference and the material sameness of conditions in Harlem; he connects Mary back to her past and poses a complicated argument for her future, both of which by extension signify the Harlem community: "And then we got Rodney—and he's my boy: [photo of men grouped indoors.] They say in the neighborhood sometimes Rodney can say things that makes everybody set up and take notice—even if he don't wake up till night. I used to be that kind of sleepyhead myself, so I understands him" (41). Her strategy for decoding the mystery of Rodney's difference is to read the values of her own past into his present and future.

But looking ahead is complicated by the uncertain future not of Mary, but of Rodney, the youth with music and dance and ideas moving him only in a nocturnal world that is at odds with both the backdrop of the Supreme Court decision and eminent change, and with the foreground of the racially connected, familial, responsible community that Mary produces in visioning Harlem.

What is especially striking is the elegiac tone that contradicts Sister Mary's refusal to answer St. Peter's call. "Some have been where they are going. And some can't seem to make up their minds which way to go; And some ain't got no place at all" (67–68). "But it's sad if you ain't invited"; [followed by a photograph of a lone man facing away from the camera and toward a four-columned entry to a building]. "It's too bad there's no front porches in Harlem" [followed by a photograph of an apartment building presenting the camera two stories and ten windows of its facade] (70). And the question punctuating all: "What do you reckon's out there in them streets for that boy?" (85). The parade of people "beat up by life" offers no answers: Mazie (one of Rodney's girlfriends); Ada (another girlfriend, whose life is work and sleep and tiredness and waiting for Rodney); Miss Mary's first husband from Carolina "[H]e were cut up by life, too. But it never got him down. I never knowed him to go to sleep neither" (91). With the mention of the Carolinian grandfather, Hughes reinscribes into his narrative the migration of Southern blacks to Harlem and the underlying Southern matrix. The imposition of unwanted but inevitable change onto life is the message of the refused telegram initiating Mary's monologue, and it is the message of her reiterated statement of entanglement with life that ultimately prefigures her death.

The Sweet Flypaper of Life functions as a prelude to change: the deterioration of Harlem, the emptiness of youth, the passing of the up-from-the-South racial and social matrix, the increasing dependency on a matriarchy for several generations of child care and child rearing, and the death of Mary. Without climax or resolution, the elegiac text suspends itself in the exchange of gazes: the reader-spectator's of Sister Mary; Mary's of the camera and the out-of-focus beyond. In exchange, death as the primary transformation is also momentarily suspended. *Sweet Flypaper* thus may be read not only as a narrative of process, a chronicle of change, but also as a production occurring between the moment of the announcement of change and the moment of recognition of subject named in the actualization of change. It unites the familiarities of voice and image, self-representation, and communal representation in a final moment before fictional vision confronts the unknown and the unthinkable thereafter.

I would argue that if Hughes had followed Wright's lead in 1955, as James Baldwin would do in concentrating on the versions of masculinity even while challenging Wright's representations, *The Sweet Flypaper of Life* would have been received by a wider audience and with sustained critical attention, perhaps praised as an important contribution to African American fiction and to representation of the post–World

War II condition of African Americans. But because the text was anachronistic in the mid-1950s, as I have suggested here, it has remained largely obscure, buried in its choice of the female face as a racial subject and urban trope.

VIII

The consequence of Wright's success, then, is evident in the fiction of the late 1940s through the early 1970s (largely male-driven and mainly Northern). The expectation of both publishers and audiences, in the aftermath of Wright's aggressively masculine subjects, is that subsequent writers of African American fiction would follow his lead and thereby his commercial success. Wright's Richard in *Black Boy*, Bigger in *Native Son*, Cross in *The Outsider*, and so on, all become one norm for African American fiction: the urban male migrant to the North whose migration narrative is submerged in the text. Ann Petry's Lutie in *The Street* (1946) thus becomes in the criticism of the 1940s a female *Native Son*, even though close examination belies such easy elisions of the distinctiveness of her text. Paule Marshall's *Brown Girl, Brownstones* (1961), primarily contextualized in terms of Wright's urban ghetto, thus fails to reach a wide audience in the 1960s, perhaps because its subject construction of Selina Boyce argues against similarities to Bigger Thomas. And the blues solo of Rosie Fleming in Kristin Hunter's *God Bless the Child* (1964) falls on deaf ears, in part because it references in narrative strategy and gender construction Billie Holiday and a heritage of women whom Wright and his critics would not have recognized. Not until a decade after the death of Wright do women return to prominence in African American fiction. The reemergence of the female as subject in the 1970s and 1980s, then, may be read as redressing an erasure of the female/feminine from a prominent place in African American fiction. In sheer numbers alone, the literary production by African American women convinced readers and publishers that women's narrative, those un-Wrightlike fictions, have their own stories to tell and frames of reference to present.

Yet even in the 1970s, two of the now major African American women writers, Toni Morrison and Alice Walker, deployed men as their central protagonists. In Morrison's *Song of Solomon* and Walker's *Third Life of Grange Copeland*, women certainly figure, but they do so as subordinates and perhaps objects in the subject construction of men. Though neither Morrison nor Walker celebrates a masculinist domination or victimization of women, each is timid in these early fictions to claim and revise the territory long occupied by males after Wright's literary arrival. Still, both Morrison and Walker necessitate a subject construction that is inextricably linked to the South and the position of African American women in that landscape. Obviously, that is not the case with these authors today, and African American fiction is, despite the anti-feminist protests of some male authors, healthier, more diverse in gender representation of women *and men* than at any other point in its literary history.

Notes

1. See, for example, the work of Edward Anthony Rotundo, David Leverenz, Joe Dubbert, and Elliott Gorn on white American Manhood and masculinity and the shifting cultural definitions of both.

2. See Wright's spate of international texts which, through significant discourses on the condition of people of color in a global context, did not forward the enormous revisioning of African American men that he had begun in the late 1930s and early 1940s.

3. The Richard Wright special issue of *Mississippi Quarterly* (Fall 1989) contains Fabre's long essay-review "Margaret Walker's Richard Wright: A Wrong Righted or Wright Wronged?" in which he takes Walker to task for her representation of Wright, his life, and career. See especially the section, "Wright's Sexuality and Emotional Life" (431–33) in which Fabre attacks Walker's assertion that Wright was bisexual.

4. For example, there is no way of knowing whether enslaved men responded differently to the beating of women and other men; to presume that they did and that they shared their enslavers' assignment of meaning to the effect of beating is to impose further the ideologies of the white masters upon them. In another context, Leverenz makes another observation that is related to this point of dominant perspective: "Like and conception of manhood, and emphasis on honor functions ideologically, which is to say, as a social fiction constructed by empowered con-

stituencies to further their power, yet felt as a natural and universal law" ("The Last Real Man," 756). If his suggestion that "rituals of honoring and shaming depend upon a long-term knowable audience for their effectiveness" (757) is applied to the situation of enslavers and enslaved, then the issue of "knowable audience" becomes more complicated than Moses allows.

5. Lerone Bennett, Jr., quotes Douglass on Delany in *Before the Mayflower* (162); see also Bell (50).

6. Wilson Jeremiah Moses argues, for instance, that "*Blake* never attained any popularity and consequently had no influence. *Blake* was, however, the first novel written as a deliberate expression of black nationalist ideals" (154).

7. Amy Kaplan reads late nineteenth-century American romance novels as expressions of the political context of American imperialism and representations of the relationship between masculinity and nationality. "More than neat political allegories that transpose international conflict into chivalric heroism, the novels refigure the relation between masculinity and nationality in a changing international context" (661).

8. Peterson concludes, "African American writers in the 1850s resorted to techniques of fiction in order to open up the enunciatory gap between the narrating and narrated Is of autobiography and freely experiment with the construction of narrators and characters. . . . Although these writers perceived of fiction writing as a vehicle to freedom, they could not always escape the commodification of their literary productions and became in some instances contained by fictional and novelistic techniques. Yet the novel enabled them to meditate upon the notion of an 'economics of freedom,' explore the heterogeneity of African-American communities, and probe the tensions between the ideologies of individualism and those of collectivity, which both worked to overcome black underdevelopment" (579–80).

9. See especially the description of heroines in E.D.E.N. Southworth, Susan Warner, Caroline Lee Hentz, and Augusta Jane Evans, and compare the descriptions of white women and men in Harriet Beecher Stowe.

10. See Jackson on Walter's role as the exemplar of Negro manhood (345–47).

11. The major place and conspicuous consumption of men's clubs, boules, and fraternities in African American cultural life at the beginning of the twentieth century may be an extension of this phenomenon into a slightly larger area than the home, but nonetheless still a private rather than public area.

12. See McKay (22–23) and Kerman and Eldridge (50, 65) on Toomer's interests in body building, anatomy, and sports. According to Kerman and Eldridge, "He turned his room into a gymnasium where he worked out privately. He took so many cold baths, his grandfather complained about his using too much water. He filled scrapbooks with pictures of Greek statues and men in body-building poses. He devoted himself totally to physical combat against what he considered a destructive, evil practice, 'that practice which more than any other bleeds away the body and soul of growing beings on earth'" (50). The evil practice was sex and masturbation, which had been a "powerful force in Jean's life from his earliest days," and which he described as a "final match between the kingdoms of Good and Evil" (50).

13. Interpretations of *Cane* usually depend upon a recognition of the unnamed narrator's identification with the spirituality rather than the physicality of the women characters. But I would argue that the physical identification is significant and encoded throughout the text.

14. I believe that poetry and drama, along with the essay, were the signature genres of the Harlem Renaissance, and that fiction produced by male writers during this period does not revision possibilities for representation of African American men.

15. Cecil Brown challenges Baker's "disguise as a feminist" and a reading of *Twelve Million Black Voices* as an "aggressively masculine" text in his review of *The Workings of the Spirit*. See "The Black Literary Critic as Melville's 'Confidence Man'" (*American Review of Books*, February–March 1993, 14, 15, 31).

Works Cited

Baker, Houston A., Jr. *Workings of the Spirit: The Poetics of Afro-American Women's Writing.* Chicago: University of Chicago Press, 1991.

Bell, Bernard. *The Afro-American Novel and Its Tradition.* Amherst: U of Massachusetts P, 1987.

Bradley, David. Introduction to *Twelve Million Black Voices.* New York: Thunder's Mouth, 1988.

Brown, Cecil. "The Black Literary Critic as Melville's 'Confidence Man.'" *American Review of Books,* February–March 1993: 14, 15, 31.

Brown, William Wells. *Clotel; or, The President's Daughter: A Narrative of Slave Life in the United States.* New York: Collier 1970.

Bruce, Dickson D., Jr. *Black American Writing from the Nadir: The Evolution of a Literary Tradition, 1877–1915.* Baton Rouge: Louisiana State University Press, 1989.

Chesnutt, Charles. *The House Behind the Cedars.* Athens: Univeristy of Georgia Press, 1988.

Chesnutt, Charles. *The Marrow of Tradition.* 1901; Ann Arbor: University of Michigan Press, 1969.

Delany, Martin R. *Blake; or The Huts of America.* Ed. Floyd J. Miller, Boston: Beacon 1959.

Douglass, Frederick. *The Heroic Slave.* 1853; rpt. in *Three Classic African-American Novels.* Ed. William Andrews. New York: Mentor, 1990.

Douglass, Frederick. *Narrative of the Life of Frederick Douglass, An American Slave.* Ed. Houston A. Baker. New York: Penguin, 1986.

Dubbert, Joe. *A Man's Place: Masculinity in Transition.* Englewood Cliffs, N.J.: Prentice-Hall, 1979.

Du Bois, W. E. B. *The Souls of Black Folk.* In *Three Negro Classics.* New York: Avon, 1965.

Dunbar, Paul Laurence. *The Sport of the Gods.* 1902; rpt. in *The African American Novel in the Age of Reaction: Three Classics.* Ed. William L. Andrews. New York: Mentor, 1992.

Fabre, Michel. "Margaret Walker's Richard Wright: A Wrong Righted or a Wright Wronged?" *Mississippi Quarterly* 42 (Fall 1989): 429–50.

Gatewood, Willard. *Aristocrats of Color: The Black Elite, 1880–1920*. Bloomington, Indiana University Press, 1990.

Gorn, Elliott. *The Manly Art: Bare Knuckle Prize Fighting in America*. Ithaca, NY: Cornell University Press, 1986.

Griggs, Sutton E. *The Hindred Hand*. Nashville: Orion, 1905.

Griggs, Sutton E. *Imperium in Imperio*. Cincinnati: Editon Publishing, 1899.

Griggs, Sutton E. *Unfettered*. Nashville: Orion, 1902.

Hughes, Langston. "The Negro Artist and the Racial Mountain." *Nation*, CXXII (June 28, 1926) 692–714.

Hughes, Langston and Roy De Carava. *The Sweet Flypaper of Life*. 1955; rpt. New York: Hill and Wang, 1967.

Hunter, Kristin. *God Bless the Child*. New York: Bantam, 1967.

Jackson, Blyden. *A History of Afro-American Literature; Vol. 1: The Long Beginning, 1746–1895*. Baton Rouge: Louisiana State University Press, 1989.

Johnson, James Weldon. *The Autobiography of an Ex-Colored Man*. In *Three Negro Classics*. New York: Avon, 1965.

Kaplan, Amy. "Romancing the Empire: The Embodiment of American Masculinity in the Popular Historical Novel of the 1890s." *American Literary History* 2 (Winter 1990): 659–90.

Kerman, Cynthia Earl, and Richard Eldridge. *The Lives of Jean Toomer: A Hunger for Wholeness*. Baton Rouge: Louisiana State University Press, 1987.

Leverenz, David. "The Last Real Man in America: From Natty Bumppo to Batman." *American Literary History* 3 (Winter 1991): 753–781.

———. *Manhood and the American Renaissance*. Ithaca, NY: Cornell University Press, 1989.

Marshall, Paule. *Brown Girl, Brownstones*. Old Westbury, NY: The Feminist Press, 1981.

McKay, Nellie Y. *Jean Toomer, Artist: A Study of His Literary Life and Work, 1894–1936*. Chapel Hill: University of North Carolina Press, 1984.

———. *The Golden Age of Black Nationalism, 1850–1925*. New York: Oxford University Press, 1978.

Miller, R. Baxter. *The Art and Imagination of Langston Hughes*. Lexington: University Press of Kentucky. 1988.

Moses, Wilson Jeremiah. *The Golden Age of Black Nationalism, 1850–1925*. New York: Oxford University Press, 1978.

Peterson, Carla L. "Capitalism, Black (Under)development, and the Production of the African-American Novel in the 1850s," *American Literary History* 4 (Winter 1992).

Petry, Ann. *The Street*. Boston: Beacon, 1985.

Rampersad, Arnold. *The Life of Langston Hughes; Volume II: 1941–1967: I Dream a World*. New York: Oxford University Press, 1988.

Rotundo, Edward Anthony. "Body and Soul: Changing Ideals of American Middle-Class Manhood, 1770–1920," *Journal of Social History* 16 (1983): 28–33.

Stepto, Robert. *From Behind the Veil: A Study of Afro-American Narrative.* Urbana: University of Illinois Press, 1979.

Sundquist, Eric J. *To Wake the Nations: Race in the Making of American Literature.* Cambridge, MA: Harvard University Press, 1993.

Thurman, Wallace. *The Blacker the Berry . . . A Novel of Negro Life.* 1929; New York: Macmillan/Collier Books, 1970.

Toomer, Jean. *Cane: An Authoritative Text, Backgrounds, Criticism.* 1923. Ed. Darwin T. Turner. New York: Norton, 1988.

Walker, Margaret. *Richard Wright, Daemonic Genius: A Portrait of the Man, A Critical Look at His Work.* New York:Warner Books, 1988.

Webb, Frank J. *The Garies and Their Friends.* London: Routledge, 1857.

White, Walter. *The Fire in the Flint.* New York:Alfred A. Knopf, 1924.

White, Walter. *Flight.* New York:Alfred A. Knopf, 1926.

Wright, Richard. *Twelve Million Black Voices: A Folk History of the Negro in the United States.* Photo Direction by Edwin Rosskam. 1941; rpt. New York: Thunder's Mouth, 1988.

⧓ 7 ⧓

VOICES OF DOUBLE CONSCIOUSNESS
IN AFRICAN AMERICAN FICTION

Charles W. Chesnutt, Zora Neale Hurston, Dorothy West, and Richard Wright

Bernard W. Bell
Pennsylvania State University

Contrary to the arguments of many postmodern, poststructural, and postcolonial critics, most African American theorists and critics, especially proponents of African American double consciousness, do not claim that black Americans are biologically or culturally pure. African Americans are a biracial and bicultural people. It should be self-evident, therefore, that like its mixed European American stepbrother, the African American novel is a hybrid form. Rather than the culmination of an evolutionary process in the narrative tradition, it is the product of social and cultural forces that shape the author's attitude toward life and that fuel the dialectical process between romantic and mimetic narrative impulses. In contrast to the European American novel, however, the African American novel has its roots in the combined oral and literary tradition of African American culture. It is one of the symbolic literary forms of discourse that black Americans have borrowed from Western culture and adapted in their quest for status, power, and identity in a racist, white, patriarchal North American social arena. The African American novel, in other words, is not a solipsistic, self-referential linguistic system, but a symbolic sociocultural act.

"Precisely because successive Western cultures have privileged written art over oral or musical forms," Henry Louis Gates reminds us, "the writing of black people in Western language has, at all points, remained political, implicitly or explicitly, regardless of its intent or its subject."[1] In this sense, the nineteenth-century romances and novels of William Wells Brown, Martin Delany, Francis E. W. Harper, Harriet Wilson, and Sutton Griggs were both private and public linguistic enactments of human relationships reflecting ethical as well as aesthetic decisions inside and outside of the text. As texts they bear witness to and are weapons in the individual and collective struggle for the freedom, literacy, justice, and integrity of black Americans.

Such twentieth-century novelists as Richard Wright, Zora Neale Hurston, Ralph Ellison, James Baldwin, John A. Williams, William Melvin Kelley, Ernest Gaines, Toni Morrison, Alice Walker, John Edgar Wideman, and Ishmael Reed also use the novel and romance as symbolic acts to explore the disparity between European American myths and African American reality. But they do not approach the narrative tradition from the same ideological perspective as their white contemporaries, black predecessors, or each other. Among other things, radical social and cultural change has encouraged the movement toward more individualism in the novelists and their aesthetics. Most modern and postmodern African American novelists nevertheless share in a common tradition. As members of the largest nonwhite ethnic group in the United States, African American novelists—except those who have been estranged from African American communities and culture by birth or acculturation, circumstances or choice—develop their personal and national identities within and against the distinctive pattern of values, orientations to life, and shared ancestral memories they acquired from and contribute to African American culture.

As much as, if not more than, their white contemporaries, nineteenth-century black novelists tapped the roots of their indigenous ethnic culture for matter and method, as I demonstrate in *The Afro-American Novel and Its Tradition* (1987).[2] But the world view of the politically and economically oppressed is not the same as that of those who dominate and exploit them. Because each group's distinctive historical experience creates a different cultural frame of reference within which it views, interprets, and seeks to transform reality, corresponding differences inevitably emerge in the meaning of the archetypal

133

patterns and master narratives that they use to reconstruct their individual and collective experiences. Both white and black novelists of the nineteenth century and twentieth century, for example, draw on aspects of the Judeo-Christian tradition—especially messianic and jeremiadic themes, symbols, and rituals—for terms to order their experiences. But since, more often than not, the white man's heaven is the black man's hell, black writers generally construct a counter discourse that expresses strong ambivalence toward its values, whether by symbolic acts of silence or speech, submission or rebellion. Also, in contrast to the search for innocence and Adamic vision that informs the European American novel, we usually find embedded in the texts of nineteenth- and twentieth-century African American novels the Manichean drama of white versus black, an apocalyptic vision of new world order, and the quest to reconcile the double consciousness of African American identity.

William Wells Brown, for instance, was certainly aware of his debt to the abolitionist tradition, oral and written, as his antislavery allusions in the first chapter, epigraphs, and conclusion of his novel *Clotel* reveal. But his reconstruction of the legend of Thomas Jefferson's Creole mistress and illegitimate interracial children is different from the use of the tragic mulatto and quest-for-freedom motifs by his white contemporaries. Similarly, Dunbar and Chesnutt continue to use some of the conventions of the local color tradition of writing while simultaneously changing others, like the power and authority of the blues in *The Sport of the Gods* (1902) and of a transplanted syncretic African belief system in *The Conjure Woman* (1899), to provide more complex truths about nineteenth-century black culture and character.

In the twentieth century, Hurston's rewriting of the sentimental romance in *Their Eyes Were Watching God* (1937) celebrates the liberating possibilities of love, storytelling, and autonomy for black women. Wright's rewriting of the legends and myths of the "bad nigger" and the American Dream in *Native Son* (1940) continues to overwhelm readers with the dramatic and narrative power of its naturalistic truth. Reed's rediscovery and revitalization of such traditional forms as the Western and cowboy narrative in *Yellow Back Radio Broke-Down* (1969), the detective and mystery novel in *Mumbo-Jumbo* (1972), and the slave narrative in *Flight to Canada* (1976), intrigue us by their bold experimentation with and celebration of his neo-Hoodoo aesthetic. We are also intrigued by Alice Walker's adaptation of the epistolary method in the Pulitzer Prize–winning *The Color Purple* (1982), whose theme is a rewriting of Janie Crawford's dreams in Hurston's romance of what a liberated black woman ought to be. And we are left spellbound by Toni Morrison's Pulitzer Prize–winning *Beloved* (1987): a Gothic neo-slave narrative and postmodern romance that speaks in many compelling voices of the historical rape of black women through the concord of sensibilities that African American people share.

Thematically and structurally, therefore, from Brown and Wilson to Reed and Morrison, the hybrid tradition of the African American novel is dominated by the struggle for freedom from all forms of oppression and by the personal odyssey to realize the full potential of one's complex bicultural identity as an African American. This prototypical journey—deriving its sociocultural consciousness from the group experience of black Americans and its mythopeic force from the interplay of Eurocentric and Afrocentric symbolic systems—begins in physical or psychological bondage and ends in some ambivalent or open-ended form of deliverance or vision of a new world of mutual respect and justice for peoples of color. In short, the African American canonical story is the quest, frequently with apocalyptic undertones, for freedom, literacy, and wholeness—personal and communal—grounded in social reality and ritualized in symbolic acts of African American speech, music, and religion.

Before looking at the short stories by Chesnutt, Hurston, Wright, and West, let us examine briefly the question of the appropriateness and adequacy of the Du Boisian trope of double consciousness for interpreting African American culture and character. Du Bois's theory of double-consciousness receives a mixed reception from critics both black and white. As we are reminded by the responses of twenty black intellectuals and artists in Gerald Early's *Lure and Loathing* (1993), some argue that it is neither valid nor viable any longer because it oversimplifies and reduces the complexity and diversity of African American culture and character to a schizoid male construct that reinforces racial stereotypes. For Stanley Crouch, the former black cultural nationalist

135

Village Voice journalist, acerbic, self-designated "hanging judge," and MacArthur award–winner, for example, "the idea [of double-consciousness] is no more than another aspect of anarchic wildness overgrowing intellectual clarity." [3] Molefi Asante, the Georgia-born and Tennessee-raised leading contemporary theorist of Afrocentrism, says he "was never affected by the Du Boisian double-consciousness."[4] If when younger he "had gone to school and church with whites," he states, "I might have suffered confusion, double-consciousness, but I did not."[5] Despite the fragmenting of his ancestral African identity as a result of the transatlantic slave trade, and despite the tenacious, pervasive, and multifaceted influence of white racism, he affirms a "unitary and holistic" consciousness derived from his "tightly knit community of Africans who lived on the dirt roads of Valdosta," especially his family.[6] For Kristin Hunter Lattany, the novelist who was raised to be a "race woman" and saved "from the confusion of assimilationism" even though she attended integrated schools, "Du Bois' double-consciousness implies duality, an unhealthy state for the individual and for the group," which her parents' generation was the last to experience.[7] "To believe my consciousness double," she argues, "would be to label myself sick, schizoid."[8]

Some contemporary historians, sociologists, and literary critics have noted that the most obvious weakness in Du Bois's dialectical model is the omission of gender and class. They propose triple-, quadruple-, or even quintuple-consciousness as a necessary corrective. Historian Darlene Clark Hine contends, for example, that had Du Bois considered gender and class, "he would have mused about how one ever feels her 'fiveness': Negro, American, woman, poor, black woman. . . . As African American men and women of all classes . . . confront the twenty-first century there is a need for new thinking, and more inclusive and varied metaphors about black identity and the process of assimilation. "The history of the American Negro," she continues, "is more than the history of efforts . . . 'to attain self-conscious manhood,' of a dynamic, multiconscious black womanhood."[9] From the first edition in 1947 of John Hope Franklin's classic *From Slavery to Freedom* to the ninth edition in 1988 as well as the 1981 publication of Vincent Harding's *There Is a River*, black historians have adapted a dialectical model of black resistance to the dominance of white power, which some readers narrowly and rigidly classify as social protest, to shape their stories of the struggle of blacks for freedom, literacy, justice, and wholeness in the United States.

More specifically, such literary historians and critics as Henry Louis Gates Jr., Houston Baker Jr., Robert Stepto, Keith Beyerman, and I affirm in different ways and degrees the validity and viability of Du Boisian double consciousness as a metaphor "to depict the quest of the black speaking subject to find his or her voice. . . . As theme, as revised trope, as a double-voiced narrative strategy, the representation of character and texts finding a voice has functioned as a sign both of the formal unity of the African American literary tradition and of the integrity of the black subjects depicted in this literature."[10]

In my own work over the past twenty years, I have tried to revise and refine Du Boisian double consciousness to signify the biracial, bicultural identities of African Americans, and not necessarily a pathological or schizophrenic way of being-in-the-world with others. As socialized ambivalence, it is the dancing attitudes and movement of Americans of sub-Saharan African ancestry and acculturation, over time, space, gender, and class between integration and separation, a shifting identification between the beliefs and values of the dominant white and subordinate black cultural systems as a result of institutional racism. As double vision, it is an ambivalent, laughing-to-keep-from-crying perspective toward life as expressed in the use of irony and parody in African American folklore and formal art. I use folklore here in the contemporary sense of the artistic forms and communicative process, especially oral, by which the beliefs and values of a people are transmitted primarily among members of the same reference group: national, ethnic, regional, sexual, age, or professional. Contemporary research in anthropology, sociology, history, folklore, musicology, and sociolinguistics not only challenges the validity of pathological and deficit models for interpreting African American culture and character, but also convincingly supports the beliefs long held by many African Americans that the conflicts between black culture and white society have resulted in creative as well as destructive tensions in black people in their communities. As sociologist Robert Blauner notes, "the black cultural experience more resembles an alternating current than it does a direct current. The movement toward ethnicity and distinctive consciousness has been paralleled by one inducing more 'Americanization' and identity."[11] At the same time, of course, white American culture was becoming first Africanized and then American Africanized, especially by black music.

Like race, gender, and class, Du Boisian double consciousness has the capacity to illuminate the relation of individuals and groups to power. Power may be defined as the ability, either active or potential, to control or influence the self, situation, or others in the face of resistance. Social power relations—such as parent over child, male over female, and master over slave—use various resources, such as tangible goods (e.g., material possessions and organizational members) or intangible assets (e.g., skills and organizational unity) to exert dominance, authority, and force.[12]

Let us now test the viability of Du Boisian double consciousness in understanding the importance of race, gender, and class in the quest for the freedom and power of self-definition and self-determination in Charles Chesnutt's "The Goophered Grapevine" (1899), Zora Neale Hurston's "The Gilded Six Bits" (1933), Richard Wright's "Bright and Morning Star" (1938), and Dorothy West's "Jack and the Pot" (1940). Although all four stories have black protagonists and characters who use black dialect, even a cursory reading of them reveals that race, gender, and class, as filtered through the prism of double consciousness, are weighted very differently in each story. In an ironic and parodic rewrite of the pro-slavery genre of plantation school fiction, Chesnutt's story-within-a-story privileges a dialectic of race and class as Uncle Julius, a cunning former slave, empowers himself by spinning a series of conjure (Goopher) tales to outwit a white, postbellum, carpetbagging grape grower into becoming his employer. Readers are challenged by the style and structure of the narrative to identify and interrogate the different types of voices in the frame and interior stories. They are also invited to examine the relationship among the voices as well as how and what they constitute as a just and fulfilling postbellum life of racial, class, and cultural difference and coexistence.

Rather than ironically undercutting pro-slavery literature and the commodification of black people, Hurston's romantic story of poor but proud, married, rural protagonists of all-black Eatonville, Florida, thematically and symbolically stresses race, class, and gender. Joe Banks's gullibility and envy of a black urban confidence man's fake gold watch chain and tie pin are the catalysts for his wife's infidelity and the dramatic irony of the amused contempt for the white community, the reunion of the couple, and the renewed marital ritual of tossing silver dollars at his wife's door after the birth of their son. Here readers are encouraged by the style and structure of the story to examine and explain how the different voices dramatize intraracial domestic and regional tensions of gender and class difference in a rural post–World War I historically black Southern community.

In contrast, West situates her story in an urban environment during the Depression years and employs dramatic irony to highlight gender and class in rendering the anxiety and ambivalence of the protagonist, Mrs. Edmunds. She has mixed emotions about how to spend her jackpot winnings, which she conceals from her unemployed husband, without jeopardizing their qualifications for government relief assistance, without sacrificing her remaining dignity, and without violating the moral imperative to help a neighbor in greater economic and personal crisis than herself. Once again readers are engaged by the sound and sense of voices that struggle to retain their compassion and dignity in the face of economic depression, physical death, and spiritual despair.

It is in Wright's *Bright and Morning Star*, however, that the voices of race, gender, and class are most dramatically and dialectically balanced. The black Christian faith and hope of the aging female protagonist, Sue, is in dialectic tension with the communist dedication and hope of her sons: Sugs, who is in jail as a communist organizer, and Johnny-Boy, who follows in his brother's footsteps. Their dedication and sacrifice to the Marxist "terrible vision" of class struggle moves Sue to adopt a surface commitment to their cause. But, in the marrow of her bones and the depths of her soul, she is sure that "nona our folks" betrayed to the sheriff the Communist Party meeting planned for that night.

139

night. Johnny-Boy's firm response is: "Ma, Ah done tol yuh a hundred times. Ah cant see white n Ah cant see black. . . . Ah sees rich men n Ah sees po men." It is Sue's grounding in her Christian faith, however—as voiced in the recurring spirituals, especially "He's the Lily of the Valley, the Bright and Morning Star," prayers—invocations of the name of the Lord and of the symbol of the cross—that sustain her in the ultimate sacrifice of herself and her son to prevent the white Judas informer from identifying the names of the Communist Party members.

Double consciousness, in other words, is most apparent in the ironic and parodic voices of the stories as the protagonists seek to free themselves from the ascribed identities that frustrate and stifle the realization of their full potential as Americans of African descent. I suggest that readers, and especially students and educators, explore the usefulness of Du Boisian double consciousness in their approach to understanding, appreciating, and teaching African American fiction.

Notes

1. Henry Louis Gates, Jr., *The Signifying Monkey: A Theory of Afro-American Literary Criticism* (New York: Oxford University Press, 1988), p. 132.

2. Bernard W. Bell, *The Afro-American Novel and Its Tradition* (Amherst, MA: University of Massachusetts Press, 1987).

3. Stanley Crouch, "Who Are We? Where Did We Come From? Where Are We Going?" in *Lure and Loathing: Essays on Race, Identity, and the Ambivalence of Assimilation,* ed. Gerald Early (New York: A. Land/Penguin Press, 1993), p. 83.

4. Molefi Kete Asante, "Racism, Consciousness, and Afrocentricity," in ibid., p. 136.

5. Ibid., p. 137.

6. Ibid., p. 133.

7. Kristin Hunter Lattany, "Off-Timing: Stepping to the Different Drummer," in ibid., p. 167–68.

8. Ibid., p. 171.

9. Darlene Clark Hine, "In the Kingdom of Cultures: Black Women in the Intersection of Race, Gender, and Class," in ibid., p. 338.

10. Henry Louis Gates, Jr. *The Signifying Monkey,* p. 239.

11. Robert Blauner, "Black Culture: Myth or Reality?" in *Afro-American Anthropology: Contemporary Perspectives,* ed. Norman E. Whitten, Jr. and John F. Szwed (New York: The Free Press, 1970), p. 351.

12. Marvin E. Olsen, ed., "Power as a Social Process," in *Power in Societies* (New York: Macmillan, 1970), pp. 3, 6–8.

▣ 8 ▣

TO SHATTER INNOCENCE
Teaching African American Poetry

Jerry W. Ward
Tougaloo College

I

Teaching African American poetry in public schools, particularly in those exceptionally conscious of "multiculturalism" and "political correctness," may prove a difficult task. Imagine that you are in a tenth-grade classroom, teaching American literature to a group of students who come from diverse ethnic backgrounds. In the poetry unit, you have been discussing the sonnet. It has been an uphill struggle to get these students interested in form, imagery, and figurative language. You begin the unit with Frost's "Stopping by Woods on a Snowy Evening." Thanks to John Ciardi's formal explanation of what that poem means (or another commentary on aesthetic distance you excavated from your college notes), you have succeeded in deflecting some questions about Frost's message. Indeed, you boldly informed these lively students of the MTV/ hip-hop/ crossover generation that a poem may have no message at all. It is sufficient unto itself. The purpose of literature is to provide intellectual delight, not pragmatic directions.

Your guardian angel reminds you there is another side to the Horatian formulation. And you politely ignore the angel and the subtle bud of a question from the student who said he found more delight in the music of Arrested Development than in snow, a horse, and the woods. You ignored another question about how and whence delight comes to be. But you did tell the student that Frost's craft was to be admired (the musical swoop of noun and verb) and reminded him that Frost, like Maya Angelou, had read at a presidential inauguration. As the period bell rang, you added, "Culturally literate Americans need to know Frost."

After the class, you began to have second thoughts about tomorrow's lesson. You chose to have the students read Claude McKay's "America" rather than Cullen's "Yet do I Marvel" or Gwendolyn Brooks's "First Fight. Then Fiddle." Despite the technical superiority of the sonnets by Cullen and Brooks, you wanted to illustrate a point about literary heritage with McKay's poem. You required students to compare it with Shelley's "Ozymandias." Your hope to focus on difference in tone and structure and to note how the shifting personifications used by McKay's persona are distracting and the irony is heavy-handed. Given your love affair with the Romantic period, you want to make a point about the British past in the twentieth century. But suppose, you worry, that tomorrow a student will contend that McKay's poem is not all that flawed, that it does make aesthetic sense. Did you not tell her that a poem must not mean but be? And isn't the imperfection an objective correlative to the arrogance that Shelley addresses with judicious irony? Already this young woman has begun to sound like a certain college classmate you remember none too favorably. What if she asks how many African American poets have written sonnets? What if she should ask about the historical matrix out of which Frost and McKay created poems? You cannot back off from these potential problems without compromising your integrity.

This hypothetical, minor crisis may tell us a great deal about American pluralism, our cultural literacy, and our roles as teachers. Permit me to put aside the day-to-day problems of the public school classroom, including the crucial matter of who these students are, in order to focus on *teaching* African American poetry. There never was, nor is there now, a magic melting pot in the United States that enables normalization and consensus about *what* is to be taught in our schools and *how* students are to respond to what is taught. The only normalizing instruments we can use are locally constructed tests or standardized examination. The myth or social fiction that influenced the teaching of literature in our schools and colleges up to the latter part of the twentieth century was blinding. What is slowly coming into view is an image of American literature as a national treasure. And no matter how dim our vision of a national literature might be, the new possibilities are both frightening and challenging.

We are frightened because we are beginning to know that the official literary history of the United States was exclusionary, concealing its ideology behind aestheticism and some discourse about merit, about greatness. The challenge is to reconceptualize literary history and to rethink pedagogical strategies. Indeed, the task is to reconstruct instruction.

When A. LaVonne Brown Ruoff and I edited *Redefining American Literary History*, we had in mind the implications of setting new boundaries for teachers at all levels. We were aware that our position was also ideological, but we were not tendentious. As I urge that teaching of black poetry be an act of shattering innocence, it is sobering (at least for me) to revisit what we wrote in 1990:

> Anyone teaching American literature must at some point confront the issue of a canon. Not surprisingly, growing numbers of teachers have begun to question the works to be included in a literary history of America, the place of works in languages other than English, and the intellectual, cultural, and political implications of selecting certain works and rejecting or ignoring others. Such questions suggest that the study of American literature, the inquiries made about it, and the methods of teaching it warrant thorough reconsideration. In fact, many literature teachers and American writers believe that the history of American literature must be reconstructed. The Committee on the Literatures and Languages of America of the Modern Language Association shares this belief.[1]

However noble, democratic, well-meaning, and genuine our beliefs, they mean little until they are transformed by the art of teaching.

For the teaching of African American poetry in the public schools to be even moderately successful, certain things are essential. Among them is how teachers begin to have any discussion about teaching subject matter that seems new but is in reality very old. Because we sought to address issues within a *national* rather than a *nationalist* frame, Ruoff and I did not mention the impact of slavery, Reconstruction, civil rights struggles, desegregation of schools, the phenomena of the Black Arts/Black Aesthetic, the use of "Harlem Renaissance" as both an historical trope and as a body of works to be reexamined, the scholarly efforts to rescue "forgotten" texts from oblivion, the seminal importance of *The New Negro* (1925), *The Negro Caravan* (1941), *Black Fire* (1968), and Steven E. Henderson's *Understanding the New Black Poetry* (1973) and the ensuing debates about an African American canon. We did not say anything either about the rumblings that made it necessary to argue for the study of Asian American, Chicano, Puerto Rican, and American Indian literatures as elements of national literature. We were silent about the other ethnic contributions because the Modern Language Association had already published *Ethnic Perspectives in American Literature: Selected Essays on the European Contribution* (1983).

We could not be silent, of course, about a national discourse that pertains rather directly to American education, the rich arguments begot by Allan Bloom's *The Closing of the American Mind* (1987) and E. D. Hirsch's *Dictionary of Cultural Literacy* (1987). Bloom and Hirsch were to be taken seriously because they addressed the matters of language, value, teaching, cultural politics, and so forth, that are crucial in the study of a national literature and its constituent parts.

From our vantage, it was more productive to engage Hirsch than Bloom, because he spoke more directly to our enterprise. He was convinced that we should abandon efforts to implement multicultural education and we should get on with ensuring "our children's mastery of American literate culture."[2] We also wanted "our children" to be literate, to think historically and critically, to be intelligent in the face of difference. Thus, our penultimate introductory paragraph was a mild retort:

> Concerned with the kinds of cultural literacy transmitted by the study and teaching of American literatures, *Redefining American Literary History* sketches out opposition to Hirsch's ideas. The redefining project eschews traditional, patriarchal thought about culture and literature, seeking instead explanatory models that account for the

144

multiple voices and experiences that constitute the literature and literary history of the United States. In contrast to Hirsch, and to the traditional Americanists for whom he could be a spokesman, those committed to a redefinition emphasize the idea that American literature is not mainstream, and that what everyone needs to know about it may be quite beyond the creation of canon. (4)

What this might mean for the teaching of African American poetry as one of several American poetries is remarkable. Phillis Wheatley should not be taught as if her neoclassical verse is merely "imitative" of Alexander Pope and other eighteenth-century figures. Her imitating must be contextualized.

What a very young child needs to know is the joy of creating sound and sense in language, the delight of participating in the first stages of making poetry. At the upper end of public education, where African American poetry is most likely to be taught, adolescent students need to know the historical placement of speech acts in tradition. One's success or failure in teaching the poetry has to do with attitude and learning to deal with semiotic features of literature that New Critical education did not address well. Success requires also what I would call a shattering of *innocence*, or the liberal vision of art as a privileged and universal object. Our hypothetical teacher would have entertained less anxiety in teaching African American poetry (or any poetry for that matter) had s/he thought more deeply about poetry as a stylized or specially angled speech, and of the sonnet as an instance of singular communication poised to become operative. Preparing to teach African American poetry begins with reflection on speaking and singing.

II

Like the origins of poetry throughout the world, the beginnings of African American poetry are in speech and song. This fact is of no small consequence. Primacy of the oral and aural forces us to be active in imagining just how it is that peoples displaced from one part of the world and reassembled in another created a distinctive body of poetry. What is primal about its origins and strongly marked in its continuity

145

as a tradition suggests the value of listening to the poetry as carefully as we read it silently. Listen to the intonations of the spirituals. The beginning of African American poetry is the sound of Africans in the complex process of becoming Americans. Those historical moments of transformation are inflected with resistance, the trauma of loss, adaptation, cross-fertilization, and synthesis. Without the sound the words remain mute marks on a page.

An African American poetics emerges from the detente of African languages and cultures with themselves first, then with encountered European languages and cultures. The initial New World points of becoming (which includes the Afro-Asiatic) remain in deep waters beyond salvage. Nevertheless, the links of African American poetry to its mixed ancestry recur in the black American oral traditions, in the early inscriptions of Lucy Terry, Jupiter Hammon, Phillis Wheatley, and George Moses Horton; it is to be heard in the sorrow songs, sacred musics, blues, and jazz, and in the penchant for return to African sources among some early- and late-twentieth-century poets. You hear the ancient links in rap's musical levels. As Eugene Redmond reminds us in *Drumvoices: The Mission of Afro-American Poetry* (1976), we obviously do not know the precise time "when the first African sounds or movements were incorporated into 'white' or Western frames of reference or vice versa; but we do know that it did happen."[3] The conceptual difference implicit in the results requires that we try to teach them as complements to the work of Anne Bradstreet, Edward Taylor, Philip Freneau, William Cullen Bryant, Emily Dickinson, and Walt Whitman, themselves modifiers of referential frames.

Poetry is one of the gifts of African Americans who have made a tradition of sound and uncommon sense. Early and late these Americans insist that musicality and speech be fused into a literature for exploring, acquiring knowledge, creating delight and instruction, praising and criticizing, remembering and transforming, and meeting, in the early years of this century, an odd demand: proof of civilization. African American poetry moves into the new public spheres of the twenty-first century. It absorbs the pre-future of now. We are called to rediscover how it evolved. We are also called to remember it comes

146

from a tradition that, in the words of Margaret Walker, has "remained singularly faithful to the living truth of the human spirit."

Truth of the human spirit in poetry is not something mystical, beyond human grasp. It is a property that language yields when we read and teach others to read with an inquiring attitude about words. We certainly should have civil disputes about how to read, how to read a poem, and how to theorize about literary works as items of cultures. None of us has the answer. We have answers and responses, many of them won from experience in the classroom; others may come to us by way of conversations with other teachers, from what we hear at conferences, from intense discussions of the historical use of literary devices in an institution or seminar. However we have gained our knowledge about kinds of poetry, our teaching of poetry must always be done with heightened respect for language in action, respect for multiple connotative dimensions.

To provide one telling example from African American poetry at the beginning of the century, consider Paul Laurence Dunbar's poetry in standard English and that in dialect. Dunbar provides his own gloss on the humor and pathos of his dialect work in such poems as "We Wear the Mask" and "Sympathy." But we should not simply dismiss his work in dialect as too demeaning or embarrassing to be discussed in the insult-sensitive public classroom. One should discuss with students why exaggerated dialect from any sector of the English language community provokes laughter or shame or both. In such an instance, one should certainly use sociolinguistics and reliable sources on American minstrelsy in the late nineteenth century to help students understand why Dunbar's work is double-voiced at several levels. If the claim that poetry delights and instructs is to be taken seriously by students, we must demonstrate that Dunbar's formation of standard English is akin to contemporary experiments in language but very differently motivated. One of the great values of teaching African American poetry is the opportunity to open American minds.

To encourage richer creative and critical responses to the African American poetic tradition, we should emphasize fruitful tensions between poets and history or among individual poets who treat the same themes. No matter how little or how much time one has in the classroom to deal with African American poetry, it is crucial that it be taught as an ongoing tradition, not as randomly selected poems. If one were compelled to teach only five poems, I would argue that the first should be an example of oral poetry to mark off a time when works were most often anonymous, when the texts chosen can represent only the "spirit" of a time prior to their being recorded. The second poem should be chosen from the period 1746–1865 to draw attention to the poets as enslaved people or free people of color, the acceptance of prevailing modes of writing poetry or some effort to be innovative within accepted forms. The past does impinge upon the present. Readers should compare the oral example with the self-consciously formal work that may yearn for emancipation in language and form consonant with prevailing poetic tastes. The third poem might be chosen from the period 1865–1910, thus emphasizing the poetic voice as a bridge between the late-nineteenth-century obligation to deal with an immediate slave past in the same moment it wishes to address the promises of a twentieth-century future. The problem of finding the "right" language for poetry complements Du Bois's famed "problem of the color line." It is most poignantly "represented" in the work of Paul Laurence Dunbar and finds temporary resolution in the works of James Weldon Johnson. Indeed, it would be worthwhile to summarize Johnson's magisterial introduction to *The Book of American Negro Poetry* (1921) which still deserves study for what it says about poetic language and emotion, turn of thought, and the demands of conventions. Johnson sets forth the possibility of creating new forms "which will still hold the racial flavor."

The forms that embody the intellectual, artistic, and social concerns of African Americans from the 1920s to the present are stunning in magnitude, variety, and quality. William Stanley Braithwaite and Countee Cullen use language to register ambivalence about the "rightness" of modernist experimentation. Jean Toomer, Claude McKay, Melvin B. Tolson, and especially Langston Hughes experiment daringly; indeed, Hughes's use of blues and jazz to inform poetic sites of memory is prototypical for the later activity of Bob Kaufman, Ted Joans, and the Beat poets. Anne Spenser, Arna Bontemps, May Miller,

Naomi Long Madgett, and Pinkie Gordon Lane revitalize the expressive potential of lyric. Sterling Brown, Margaret Walker, Gwendolyn Brooks, Robert Hayden, Alvin Aubert, Sterling D. Plumpp, Brenda Marie Osbey, Angela Jackson, and others demonstrate that modernist poetic techniques as well as respect for folk heritage and history are essential in creating art from the raw complexities of African American life. The pool from which the fourth poem might be chosen is immense.

The fifth and final poem should be chosen from one of the younger poets, let us say Charlie Braxton, who celebrates the necessity of "iambic trochaic pentameter" to evoke anguish and beauty for those

> just a few generations removed
> from the chains that bind the flesh
> but not the spirit[4]

or from the splendidly controlled nuances of Rita Dove, Cornelius Eady, and Elizabeth Alexander, or from the urban sensibility of Kevin Powell or Paul Beatty. The final poem should enable students to circle back to the poetic work of oral creation, back to Toomer's observation that "one seed becomes/ An everlasting song" for the new age and its future-oriented voices.

Teaching African American poetry in the public school may be difficult, but the challenge of showing how this poetry complements other poetries is worth doing. Imagine yourself in the classroom teaching our national poetry of the twentieth century, works by William Carlos Williams, Arna Bontemps, Anne Sexton, Robert Frost, Adrienne Rich, Janice Mirikitani, e. e. cummings, Wendy Rose, Amiri Baraka, Richard Wilbur, Tato Laviera, Hart Cane, Joy Harjo, and dozens more. Imagine the cacophony, the conflict, the concurrent honesty. But imagine more than anything else the fulfillment to come from knowing that you are guiding your students through the national poetic conversation, from knowing you are guiding them into the knowledge to be gained as language exercises its potency among the poet, the poem, the reader, and the American world of becoming. You are enabling them to taste again the joy of poetry as human speech.

Notes

1. A. LaVonne Brown Ruoff and Jerry W. Ward, eds., *Redefining American Literary History* (New York: Modern Language Association of America, 1990), p. 1.

2. E. D. Hirsch Jr., *Cultural Literacy: What Every American Needs to Know* (Boston: Houghton Mifflin, 1987), 18–19.

3. Eugene Redmond, *Drumvoices: The Mission of Afro-American Poetry: A Critical History* (Garden City, NY: Anchor Press, 1976), 19.

4. Charlie Braxton, "Say Hey Homeboy." *Trouble the Water: 250 Years of African American Poetry.* Ed. Jerry W. Ward, Jr. (New York: Mentor, 1997), p. 537.

THE WAY WE DO THE THINGS WE DO

Enunciation and Effect
in the Multicultural Classroom

Elizabeth Swanson Goldberg
Miami University of Ohio

The small auditorium was close to full: sixty first-year students at a largely white, upper-middle-class, Midwest university watching the film version of John Guare's play *Six Degrees of Separation* for English 111, a composition course. The auditorium was close to silent—excepting the crunch of popcorn and the rustle of students getting comfortable in their seats—as the screen filled with images of the hysterical Kittredges, a wealthy white Manhattan couple whose home has been invaded by an intruder, describing for each other and the audience the mere hairsbreadth by which they escaped having their throats slashed and their possessions stolen. The auditorium remains comfortable, relaxed even—legs up, bodies settled—as the film flashes back to a scene depicting a young, well-dressed, well-spoken black man, a friend of the Kittredges' children from boarding school, presumably the victim of a mugging in Central Park, asking the Kittredges for help. After bandaging his wound, the Kittredges listen in fascination as Paul regales them with stories of their kids at their posh boarding school; they are so taken with him that they invite him to stay for dinner. Although the Kittredges experience moments of noticeable discomfort at Paul's presence, these moments are represented as a kind of controlled tension, an undercurrent, far from the hysteria of the previously mentioned scene. This tension is demonstrated most pointedly in a scene during dinner when Paul disappears into the kitchen to get more wine; the white people practically suspend their breathing, apprehension flashing among their questioning eyes until Paul reappears, wine in hand, putting their fear that he has made off with the silver momentarily to rest. At this point in the film, the tension is constructed solely in relation to Paul's blackness—which has, for the moment, been mediated by his voice, dress, education, and, not least, his status as the son of actor Sidney Poitier. Back in the auditorium, comfort still reigns; my students crunch relaxedly on their popcorn. It is not until much later, after Paul has been comfortably tucked into the Kittredges' cushy spare room, and after Ouisa Kittredge has discovered him in bed with a white male hustler, that the auditorium full of students erupts into a chorus of disgusted moans, groans, and simulated retching sounds. The hysteria in the auditorium mirrors that on screen: the flashback has come full circle, back to the chaos which began the movie, the cause of which has now been revealed to the audience. Paul's difference has become too much for these students—and their counterparts in the film, the Kittredges—to bear.

Let me place this classroom incident in context with some discussion of the film. Director Fred Schepisi and Metro-Goldwyn-Mayer studios brought Guare's play to the Hollywood screen in 1993. The film stars Will Smith as Paul, a poor, gay, black confidence man attempting to make his way into the hearts and homes of white, heterosexual, upper-class, Upper East Side Manhattan families (importantly, this plot is based upon a true story). That same year, Smith received a "Sissy of the Year" Award in *The Advocate* magazine for wimping out because he refused to kiss the male characters in the film with whom his character was sexually involved. The most explicit kiss that didn't happen was shot from behind Paul's back, so that the audience is unable to see the faces of the two men, much less the meeting of their lips. Also, all three men that Paul doesn't kiss in the movie are white.

Schepisi's cinematic choices in this regard cut two ways: on the one hand, Paul's character—arguably a trope for "difference" in the film—is made hypervisible when the audience discovers that his blackness (up until now warily tolerated in the white households he enters) and his poverty (hidden beneath the stock blue blazer, loafers, and affected dialect Paul has adopted to ease his passing) are accompanied by homosexuality. At the same time, this visibility is erased by the film's unwillingness to develop gay as a real identity characteristic (in other words, a point of self-identification with emotional and material significance), choosing instead to use it as an undeveloped marker of Paul's alienation and difference or, simply as a sign of negation; i.e., *not* heterosexual. This contradiction is further complicated by the fact that the film's purpose, proclaimed in its title, seems to be to reveal identity difference as falsely constructed and illusory, asking audiences—in this case, my students—to question their own presumably natural tendency to pass judgment on others based upon identity characteristics rather than upon "real" (individual) character. If all people on the planet ("a native in a rain forest . . . A Tierra del Fuegan . . . An Eskimo . . .") are psychically separated by only six other people, then presumably we ought to be able "to get over" (smoothly, like water passing over stones) things like racial, class, gender, geographical, and yes, even sexual, difference as we get to the heart of what connects us all as humans: imagination, creativity, sympathy, pain.[1] Yet Ouisa Kittredge's revelation at the end of the film that it is dehumanizing to reduce Paul in all his glorified difference to a titillating anecdote ultimately falls flat on top of the film's one-dimensional construction of Paul as an empty vessel for prevailing cultural stereotypes.

At the moment when Flan and Ouisa Kittridge learn that Paul is gay, the Kittredges' own presumption of Paul's heterosexuality is not questioned; rather, Paul's heterosexuality is the first domino in a long line of identity traits which, lined up in orderly, acceptable rows earlier in the evening, come crashing down when Ouisa finds Paul with the hustler. The hysteria that follows as Ouisa and Flan chase the naked hustler around their apartment culminates in a new reading of Paul as con man, hustler, burglar, murderer. Suddenly Paul's blackness reverts to its original signification, the one that the Kittredges visibly squelched earlier in the film in light of the "extenuating circumstances" of Paul's class status, presumed heterosexuality, and celebrity. These latter identity characteristics changed the sign black in the Kittredges' minds from threatening to acceptable. It is important to note here that noth-

153

ing else about Paul's identity has been revealed to be false at this point in the movie except for his heterosexuality; his presumed class and "celebrity" status are still intact as far as the Kittredges know. However, once Paul's heterosexuality has been challenged, he becomes black and gay, now a sign for black and alien, Other. The next morning, when I entered my English 111 classroom, the first question I was asked was, "Why did he have to be gay?"

I should say that, although it is written by a white author, I include *Six Degrees of Separation* in my discussion of teaching African American literature to emphasize the importance of teaching what Toni Morrison calls American Africanist texts. Morrison argues that race is an abiding (if ignored) force in all American literatures, and that it is as important to study the presence of race in texts by white European Americans (whether that presence is acknowledged or disavowed) as it is to study texts written by people of color. American Africanism is, in Morrison's words, "a term for the denotative and connotative blackness that African peoples have come to signify, as well as the entire range of views, assumptions, readings, and misreadings that accompany Eurocentric learning about these peoples." Perhaps more relevant to my discussion of the character Paul in *Six Degrees,* Morrison writes that, while studying American Africanism in literature, "What became transparent were the self-evident ways that Americans choose to talk about themselves through and within a sometimes allegorical, sometimes metaphorical, but always choked representation of an Africanist presence."[2] Guare's representation of Paul is "choked" from the start by being programmed for the robotic task of pointing up things about white folks for white folks' benefit. Paul is almost pure metaphor, a metaphor that must die at the end of the film in order to prove a point, in order that (at least one of) the rich white people in the film can finally see him, who has simply been a spot of color in otherwise pale lives—"a burst of color forced to carry the weight of the picture."[3]

I begin my essay with this analysis, then, to try to get at the problem of displacement in reading, which I believe is a central difficulty in the theory and practice of teaching all literary texts. Morrison asserts that black characters in texts by Euro-American authors carry the displaced burden of those authors' ideas about race; I would also argue that when students read African American texts that have been included in a largely European American syllabus, they may displace their feelings about the characters and plots onto the authors' and characters' racial identities. This displacement carries serious consequences as it becomes part of student's larger perceptions and understandings of difference. A text such as *Six Degrees of Separation* provides a working example of the problem of teaching with integrity the layers of difference within and among African American literatures (and characters) in the context of a world—and classrooms—still pervaded by racism, xenophobia, and homophobia, and with the dangerous tendency to organize identity characteristics in an unwritten hierarchy moving from "acceptable" to "intolerable" within the scheme of a majority white classroom which perceives its own cultural standards as a gauge of the "norm."

In the case of *Six Degrees*, for example, Paul's blackness was, in a sense, displaced by his gayness as the identity characteristic marking him most different in my students' eyes; this characteristic then became the primary container for negative audience perceptions of Paul's actions and ideas. It is this "hierarchy of hate" (to borrow Sharon Pineault-Burke's only-half-ironic term) that must be undone when teaching literature and history. Listen to the words of filmmaker and writer Marlon Riggs as he describes the changing meaning of his own blackness when considered in terms of his gayness:

> I am a Negro faggot, if I believe what movies, television, and rap music say of me. My life is a game for play. Because of my sexuality, I cannot be black. A strong, proud, "Afrocentric" black man is resolutely heterosexual, not even bisexual. Hence I remain a Negro. My sexual difference is considered of no value; indeed, it's a testament to weakness, passivity, the absence of real guts—balls. Hence I remain a sissy, punk, faggot. I cannot be a black gay man: by the tenets of black macho, black gay man is a triple negation.[4]

Compare Riggs's words with those of Will Smith discussing his difficulty playing a homosexual character (which resulted in the decision to shoot the kiss of his on-screen lover from behind so that their lips would not actually have to touch):

155

> I tried to block out the homosexual aspect . . . but psychologically, I just couldn't do it. . . . Movie actors can be whoever they want . . . but because TV audiences let me into their houses every Monday night at 8 p.m., [via his sit-com *The Fresh Prince of Bel-Air*] they think they know me. I'm not an actor to them. This wouldn't be Will Smith playing a homosexual. In the 'hood, believe me, I am who I play. I could already hear them saying, "Will, boy, watcha doing this for?"[5]

Both Riggs and Smith articulate from different perspectives the issue of homophobia within the black community, and the negation of parts of one's identity that can result from living in intolerant cultures. However, contained within Riggs's description of the sexual intolerance he experiences in the black community are the racist negations suffered by a black community situated within a dominant white culture. The deck is now stacked: how will we teachers deal an even hand to students, authors, and characters when we take up these texts in the classroom?

In light of these problems, the rest of my essay will focus on three main issues in teaching African American literatures: first, the undoing of hierarchical categorizations of identity difference; second, the necessity for establishing clear goals for teaching African American literature that will inform teachers' choices of texts and supporting materials; and third, the importance of, to borrow Homi Bhabha's term, "enunciation in teaching all literature."[6] This last imperative refers to the practice of making visible and conscious for students the institutional and historical contexts of difference within and among texts, as well as the substance of student, parent, and school board responses to those differences in terms of curricular reform and debate.

I
Why Does He Have to Be Gay?

Why, indeed. If the purpose of John Guare's play—and Fred Schepisi's film—is to ask audiences to question their own assumptions about and reactions to difference, then what are the politics and ethics of reinforcing prevailing stereotypes of gayness, and blackness, and poorness, in the process? The film uses gayness as the last brick in the construction of a character's utter, impregnable difference; when we look at the "whole" identity that has now been revealed, what audiences see is a poor, black, gay man who hates himself so much that he fashions himself into an exact reversal of his own identity in an effort to find acceptance and happiness. Perhaps a particularly thoughtful audience might consider the self-hatred that accompanies internalized racism, classism, homophobia. Such an audience might be willing to read Franz Fanon's *Black Skins, White Masks* for an analysis of the psychic damage done to people of color in a racist society (as well as the dehumanizing effect of racism on those who perpetuate it); or read Dorothy Allison's *Bastard Out of Carolina* for a fictional indictment of the rampant class bias in this country; or watch Marlon Riggs's documentary film *Tongues Untied* for a description of what it is like to be hated because you are gay. With these tools in hand, this audience might take John Guare's idea that we are all "separated" from one another by (at the most!) only six other people (of any color, sex preference, class, or nationality) to heart, questioning their own "majority" responses to difference, as it cuts in various directions. However, as I have seen happen time and again with texts that claim to ask/demand audiences to question their responses to difference—and even with those that don't overtly ask, but rather embed the questions in their narratives—many members of my student audience simply came away with their opinions about black people, white people, gay people, poor people, and rich people reinforced, tightened, fortified against further questioning and critical analysis. Perhaps this is because in this fast media age we find ourselves and our students ill-equipped to deal with complexity, with nuance, with layers of meaning, and with critical concentration. Perhaps, then, my essay is really a call to arms to all teachers to counter this flatness, this easy organizing by (stereo)type, this lack of thoughtfulness; for without thoughtfulness and concentration and complex analyses, I am afraid that "multicultural education" is doomed to reinforce the walls that keep "us" in those limited and limiting spaces marked You and Me, They and We, and never the twain shall meet.

Because I think that there is much of value in the film, both on its own merits and as a teaching tool, I have shown *Six Degrees of Separa-*

tion to several student audiences; the one described above was, as noted, an all white audience of eighteen- and nineteen-year-olds, largely upper-middle-class, largely self-described "conservatives" politically. For these students, the initial focus of discussion was Paul's gayness; we talked about the problem of openly expressed homophobia given that one's sexuality is often not "clearly marked," as one's race or ethnicity might (or, just as importantly, might not) be. How could these students be sure that the person sitting next to them, listening to them make retching noises at the sight of gay characters on screen, was not gay? We also thought about identity characteristics such as race, class, and sexual preference as social constructions, the meanings of which shift in the tides of historical and cultural change. We then attempted to address the effects that historical, cultural, and institutional pressures might have had on the ideas, choices, and actions expressed by the characters, ending with a discussion of the overarching concern of storytelling in the film (which is structured as a series of occasions wherein the Kittredges tell the story of "that boy" who came into their lives to other members of their wealthy, white social circle).

I showed this film in another English I classroom, at an urban college of nursing, which included students of different ages, races, classes, nationalities, and sexual preferences. In this room, I discovered that despite these clearly marked differences (students with different skin colors, students who were openly gay and who had spoken about being gay over the course of the semester, students who spoke English with accents), people easily expressed deeply "phobic" responses to the various markers of Paul's difference: some black and white students expressed disgust at his "gayness," certain white students remarked upon his "blackness," and many students noted the "problem" of his "lower-class" status. This is not to say that there were not a lot of insightful, thoughtful, nuanced readings of the film: there were. However, even in trying to take apart conventional notions of identity, grappling with the movie's pointed attempt to ask audiences to question these notions, some students slipped smoothly into a reinforcement of the very stereotypes they attempted to question: "The fact that [Paul] was educated and smart showed that being black doesn't mean that one is stupid," wrote one white student. Another student asserted that, "[Paul's] homosexuality is contrary to traditional cultural beliefs. Also, the fact that he is black."

In the first response, the student's analysis of the film as a critique of prevailing stereotypical notions about race contains within its own structure a firm, unquestioned reassertion of that very racist stereotype. In the second response, the student, in a stunning display of unexamined bias, describes (and conflates) blackness and homosexuality as seemingly material practices, things people do that run counter to "traditional" (read: white, middle-class) cultural beliefs. Even as these students ponder the film's attempts to question such assumptions, they reiterate and reinforce their own biases, leaving hierarchical walls of identity intact, ramparts strengthened by a couple more sandbags full of stereotype thrown into the foxhole.

I argue, then, that we teachers need to develop means and methods of adding "multicultural" texts to our curricula in ways that do not inadvertently strengthen uninformed, unquestioned, easily assumed notions of bias. I will end this section with a brief discussion of two texts that do not proclaim so loudly as *Six Degrees* does their desire for audience self-examination regarding matters of identity difference, setting that imperative into their narratives instead: Toni Morrison's *Sula* and Richard Wright's *Native Son*. In both cases, in my experience teaching in majority white classrooms, the blackness of the characters and their social milieux can easily become vessels or containers for what students perceive to be negatives (things or ideas "contrary to traditional cultural beliefs") in plot and character development. In *Sula*, for instance, I have found that many students are deeply offended and confused by Eva Peace's decision to kill her son Plum, who, deeply scarred by his experience in World War I, has become addicted to heroin. The scene wherein Eva kills Plum, dousing him with kerosene and burning him up, is a deeply complex scene of motherhood with a long history in African American women's letters: infanticide as an act of mothering, a more loving gesture than allowing your child to live in a world that will kill her, soul and body, torturously, inhumanely. As Sethe killed her daughter Beloved to recaim her from a life of slavery in Morrison's *Beloved*, so Eva killed her son Plum to save him the indignity of enslavement to drugs, the indignity of being reduced to an

159

infant again in his dependence. Eva was able to find "a way for him to die like a man"; the question of the "rightness" or "wrongness" of her act is secondary to the reasons for and results of it in the flow of the narrative. Indeed, the scene of Plum's death is radically redemptive:

> Plum on the rim of a warm light sleep was still chuckling. Mamma. She sure was somethin'. He felt twilight. Now there seemed to be some kind of wet light traveling over his legs and stomach with a deeply attractive smell. It wound itself—this wet light—all about him, splashing and running into his skin. He opened his eyes and saw what he imagined was the great wing of an eagle pouring a wet light-ness over him. Some kind of baptism, some kind of blessing, he thought. Everything is going to be all right, it said.[7]

Plum's death is figured here as a baptism into life, into freedom (repre-sented by the eagle's wing, which is also Eva's arm), into security and health in a time before detoxification programs and twelve-step plans. Given typical cultural ideas of motherhood, however, some students find it difficult to see this as anything less than a monstrous act, a crime against humanity and—perhaps more painfully for them—against their own firmly held notions of what it means to be mother and mothered. Taken in concert with the widespread media discourse (a discourse that, arguably, all students have been initiated into) made up of deeply racist rhetoric and images such as "welfare mothers," "crack babies," and "the breakdown of the black family," students have now imbibed a cocktail mix of ideas and events that, when digested unhindered, reinforces their preconceived notions of black mothers who are poor, and that can be uncritically read back onto the character of Eva Peace in Morrison's *Sula*. A careful reading of the text, however, reveals the architecture of Eva's decision: her struggle to birth Plum and to keep him alive in the face of abject poverty, a struggle that was precursor to her attempts to save him from drugs as an adult; the beginning of Plum's addiction in his combat experience in World War I, a war in which black men were conscripted to fight in the front lines overseas, dying or ruining their lives for a country that did not allow them to sit down to a meal in some public restaurants. A careful reading disallows the moralistic judgment of individual "right" or "wrong" when considering such personal and public events, placing Plum's death into the communal web of people, events, and institutions that make history.

The same analysis can be applied to the character of Bigger Thomas in Wright's *Native Son*, who kills both his black girlfriend and a wealthy white woman in the course of the narrative. All the material necessary to contextualize Bigger in terms of a history of white fear/desire of black male sexuality—a history that includes the lynching of black men for their supposed desire for white women in the U.S. antebellum and Reconstruction eras, and thereafter—is present in Wright's text.[8] Still, when studying this book, I see students walking a kind of tightrope. On one side is the difficult free-fall dive into Wright's complex representations and analyses of the institutional conditions perpetuating black male crisis, and the devastating effects of a certain brand of misplaced, patronizing, self-serving white liberalism and guilt. On the other is the more comfortable net of culturally perpetuated stereotypes of black men as sexually excessive and likely to engage in criminal activity, a net supported by widely disseminated media images. Falling into that net remains frightfully easy for students (across race, class, and gender lines, obviously with different effects), even if they never proclaim it as such. Keeping in mind that students don't say all of what is on their minds in even the safest, most open classroom spaces, clearly such "choked" misreadings of characters and events as Morrison cautions against remains a possibility. Perhaps the first step in addressing this problem practically as teachers is an examination of our current teaching philosophies and goals.

II
The Way We Do the Things We Do

In my role as teacher of literature, women's studies, and writing, I continue to struggle with the understanding and definition of my goals in the classroom for my students. What do I want them to learn? What do I want them to think about, to question, or, perhaps, to unlearn? What part do the texts I choose play in this process? What is my part

161

in this process? What is my view of the brief sceneries offered in my classroom when they are situated in the much broader landscapes of students' educations as a whole, of their family and personal lives, and of their social, cultural, and economic circumstances?

The way I see it, I'm caught in a bind. On the one hand, my most urgent goal is to ask students to engage in the act of critique, pressing against what they see around them and what they "know" in order to see beyond the status quo, to bring to the level of consciousness that which is oblique so that they may take control of their lives and their learning, and so that they may effect change. Latin American educator Paulo Freire defines such consciousness in terms of the capacity for critical reflection, which, he asserts, requires that students think both from a subjective position, imagining themselves as "in" the world, and from a position of "objective distance," visualizing themselves "with" the world. Importantly, the ability to think from these two positions, either alternately or simultaneously, is to be both body in the world and mind reflecting upon the world at once. From this critical perspective, students are able to reinterpret and resist those dominant cultural representations that they do not find useful. Freire terms this "education as the practice of freedom," describing its effects as follows:

> Education as the practice of freedom—as opposed to education as the practice of domination—denies that . . . the world exists as a reality apart from people. Authentic reflection considers . . . people in their relations with the world. In these relations consciousness and world are simultaneous: consciousness neither precedes the world nor follows it.[9]

What we must do as educators committed to honoring and teaching diversity is to reattach literary texts to their worlds, and to the people who live in those worlds. While I believe that much of Freire's theory and method is applicable to United States classrooms, we must remember that Freire is speaking from a revolutionary context, about a revolutionary pedagogy, in ways that cannot be translated wholesale to a United States context. Freire has devoted a great deal of his teaching life to working among Brazilian peasants on basic literacy, working toward revolutionary political and economic change in a context wherein individual constitutional "rights" are not "guaranteed" as they are in the United States. (I use quotes here to acknolwedge the gaps between the theory and practice of democracy in these United States.) Freire was "'invited' by the Brazilian government to leave his homeland after the military coup of 1964" precisely because of his teaching practices. Still, teaching self-awareness and awareness of the effects of institutions upon individual lives; teaching voice, critique, and action as opposed to teaching acceptance and silence, are radical practices in any context, and it is the "hows" of these practices that I would like to address.

Before I do, however, let me talk briefly about the other side of that double bind I mentioned above. If, on the one hand, my goal in the classroom is to plant seeds for the growth of critical consciousness, as Freire teaches, I am likewise faced with the equally compelling need to prepare my students to survive physically, emotionally, and economically in this rapidly changing world. In junior high, high school, and in the first and second years of college, teachers in the humanities are concerned with "basic" skills: literacy, writing, analysis, and so on. How, then, are we to simultaneously teach the basic standard English, and basic standard writing techniques (say, proper grammar and punctuation; thesis statement with supporting paragraphs) that students need to get by and get hired, while simultaneously teaching students to be critical of those institutionalized ways of thinking, speaking, learning, knowing, and to effect radical change upon narrow speaking, writing, and—perhaps most importantly—hiring practices? How can I empower students to participate skillfully in the sameness of world market employment skills while also teaching them to honor and nurture their own, and others', cultural differences? Are we training our students to be capable of radical awareness and critique, or are we training them to be good capitalist soldiers in an increasingly multicultural world, an increasingly globalized economy?

Lately I have heard some rather fascinating remarks about the contradictions of multiculturalism. Take David Reiff's deeply cynical, often misguided, but still cogent analysis of multiculturalism in *Harper's* August 1993 issue. Reiff asks, "Are the multiculturalists truly unaware of how closely their treasured catchphrases—'cultural diversity,' 'difference,' the need to 'do away with boundaries'—resemble the stock

163

phrases of the modern corporation: 'product diversification,' 'the global marketplace,' and 'the boundary-less company?'"[10] Reiff, unfortunately, makes a valid point. We teachers must think about the impossible contradiction we face in the classroom resulting from the simultaneous fragmentation and globalization of the twenty-first-century world. On the one hand, people are moving into increasingly cramped corners according to identity characteristics (and by including a text by an African American, Asian American, Native American, Hispanic American, working-class, or gay author in our still Eurocentric middle-class classrooms we inadvertently reinforce such "cornering," or fragmentation). On the other hand, traditional cultural practices and differences are being flattened, erased—or worse, commodified—as ideas, goods, monies, and peoples move across formerly firm national and cultural borders that are all but disappearing into the thin air of cyberspace and the multinational corporation. In light of the changing reality of world organization, Reiff's cynicism is not all that misplaced:

> But then campus radicalism is awfully selective anyway. Its talk is long on race and gender, short on class. And that is probably just as well, since the market economy, ready though it may be to admit blacks and women, is hardly likely to sign its own death warrant by accepting a radical revision of class relations. . . . The academic multi-culturalists' . . . program is little more than a demand for inclusion, for a piece of the capitalist pie. And capitalism is not only increasingly willing but increasingly eager to let in women, blacks, gays, and any other marginalized group. Eureka, more customers![11]

What I know I do not want to do in my classroom is to deepen the correspondence of race, gender, and sex oppression with class oppression. I do not want to help my students to participate more effectively in a system that exploits workers and consumers alike down traditional race and gender lines by teaching them to think about the world in terms of fragmented, consumable, exploitable identity characteristics. What I would like is for my teaching philosophies, goals, and practices to keep pace with the reality of the world as it shifts technologically and economically, and to teach my students to think critically about those shifts even as we study the representations of such shifts in literary and historical texts.

Perhaps part of my response to the double bind described above—the need to train students to function skillfully in the world balanced against the need not to perpetuate the oppression and exploitation that often mark encounters with various kinds of "difference" in the United States—is to work hard every day at teaching skills and teaching texts while simultaneously learning in the classroom how to critique ourselves and our institutions in constructive ways. I try to teach students the importance of being able to criticize what we love—our countries, our cultures, our ancestors—without throwing the baby out with the bath; that is, leaving room for celebration of what is working, and for hope and the energy to change what is not.

I rely upon a couple of activities to help me with this in the classroom. First, I devote some time to a discussion of the words "critical" and "critique" before even beginning the work of reading, analyzing, and writing about literary (or any other) texts. Most often, students conceptualize these terms in negative ways: to be critical is to pick, to nag—like what their mothers or fathers do when students want to go out with a certain person or wear a certain outfit. "Critique," then, is simply the verb form of this nasty adjective "critical." Our first move as a class is to distinguish between criticism as an inter-personal activity that might have negative overtones (or at least might leave the person being criticized feeling vulnerable and threatened) and criticism as an intellectual action that indicates involvement and care, even love, with the subject of critique. We care for the world we live in, care for the people living in it, care for our nations, our cultures, our institutions. We may not always agree with the way things are going in our world, our nations, our cultures, or with certain people therein, but we care enough to spend time thinking about (analyzing) and articulating responses to those things we disagree with. We might even read this "intellectual" kind of criticism back onto that personal kind that students find so annoying, talking about interpersonal criticism as an act of care, even if it does not always feel that way. The bottom line is to shift the aura of these words (and their corresponding activities) from ugly and negative to positive, responsible, and empowering; after all, if we didn't care, we wouldn't bother.

My next move in juggling this double bind is to introduce the notions of participation and complicity into analyses of texts, their historical contexts, and our relationships with them. I try to talk about the world as an infinitely complex web of people and events that is in constant motion, shifting with the movements, words, and actions of every person. We talk about the effects people have on their worlds (another deeply empowering notion referring back to Freire's pedagogy of liberation) that they may or may not even be aware of. I use the old (but, I think, still useful) metaphor of the ripples caused by throwing a stone into water: those ripples make more ripples and more effects, far-reaching effects not always known to the person who cast the stone. I try to talk about complicity in a way that is not accusatory or threatening, describing it as a "universal" effect of the interrelatedness of all people (through economic flows, if nothing else). We talk about privilege (racial, sexual, economic, national, religious, etc.) and its relativeness, and about our own places in the hierarchical organizations called cultures. I try to make clear to my students my belief that no "innocent" place exists, no place free from the enactment of (positive and negative) effects on others. If this is true, then our recourse, our action, must be to think about and take personal responsibility for our actions, our effects, our "ripples"—regardless of who we are racially, ethnically, sexually, and economically.

One text that I have found particularly useful to supplement this discussion is "Are My Hands Clean?"—a song written by Bernice Johnson Reagon and performed by the African American women's a cappella group Sweet Honey in the Rock.[12] The text serves a variety of purposes: I use it as an example of a rhetorical form of argument; I use it to talk about voice and the construction of poetic and musical texts; and I use it to illustrate the ideas of complicity and personal responsibility. The song begins with a statement: "I wear garments touched by hands from all over the world." The lyrics then trace the movement of a blouse from its birth as a roll of cotton picked in a "blood-soaked" province of El Salvador, through its marriage to polyester filament in DuPont's petro-chemical mills in New Jersey, to the sewing factories in South Carolina where the fabric is woven, and to Haiti where the blouse is assembled by factory workers who make $3 a day. The song ends: "And I go to the Sears department store where I buy my blouse/

On sale for 20% discount/Are my hands clean?" Reagon traces to its source each material used to make that shirt: the polyester filament strands from Venezuela, the oil from Trinidad and Tobago, processed by Exxon, which fuels the Cargill tankers used to ship the shirt, and so on. She also describes the conditions of the workers who complete each leg of the task. Students look at the labels of their clothes, wondering about who made them and what it cost those workers. We talk about what it means to people and events around the world each time we lay down our dollars for a cup of coffee, a blouse, a tank of gas, a computer. We talk about this in terms of complicity and participation: although we may still conceive of ourselves as local people whose lives don't have much effect on the world, we do participate and are active in world events, and our participation has effects.[13] I use the example of my own education to talk about complicity, describing the struggles of my immigrant grandparents to make it in this country, to make a better life for their children by sending them to college, and then about my father's career as a chemical engineer at a large oil corporation, which in turn helped pay for my education. This source of income, however, also had effects on the lives of people all over the globe, putting me in a certain relationship with them, and in a certain place in our cultural and economic organization. If I can help students to see these implicit hierarchies and our (shifting) places in them, then I find it more productive and comfortable when we examine our own tendencies to organize texts, authors, and characters by their respective identity characteristics (i.e., Paul in *Six Degrees of Separation*). It also becomes easier to think of ways to dismantle such negative hierarchies, to replace our judgments of narrative events—sometimes displaced onto characters' and authors' identity characteristics—back onto their sources in historical contexts and cultural organization.

There is a balance here, but it is a tricky one. In my experience, many students find it most threatening to critique the institutions that support and define them, that give them comfortable places to situate themselves socially and culturally. Undoubtedly this method of teaching implies a kind of radicalism, because whatever the critique you and your students make, it will be a comment upon entrenched institutions and principles. Critiquing the United States, for instance,

167

can be very difficult, but reading American literatures (and especially African American and other ethnic American literatures) requires such critique given the violences, oppressions, and inconsistencies marking U.S. history. Many of my students are thoroughly awash in a "super-power" mentality, a kind of nationalist patriotism that, without even the Cold War competition with the former Soviet Union to shake things up, has left the United States unquestioned in the position of "Number One": strongest, smartest, free-est, best. I want to give students room to retain their patriotism, their love of country, their love of freedom and democracy while they become patriots with critical eyes, noting and working to eradicate the limits to democracy in this country, scouting the landscape for dead foliage, looking for places to plant new seeds, grow new crops.

III
ENUNCIATE!

Let me tell you a story that my father still teases me about: apparently, when I was a small child watching the Flintstones cartoon, I once ran crying to my mother, asking, "Why is Fred so mean to Bonnie?" The simple answer to my question, I suppose, would have been "Because he can be," an answer that bespeaks the power imbalance between the characters Fred and Barney on that cartoon. The humor for my parents, though, was in my misunderstanding of Fred's New York accent, which erased the "r" from Barney's name, turning him into the girlish "Bonnie" in my childish mind. I remember vividly my mother teaching me to enunciate and to inflect. I remember being stopped midconversation and told to slow down, pronounce each word, give it its proper inflection. Don't turn statements into questions. Don't mispronounce or skip words, or miss the nuances of different accents and inflections, in order to get more quickly to the end of the story. She taught me the power of careful voice and careful articulation.

I think the same lesson can be applied to a classroom that teaches culturally diverse materials. When we teach Morrison's *Sula* in a literature classroom paying attention to plot, character, theme, technique, even authorial and historical context, but without including deep attention to the institutional imperatives informing its action, we are, in a sense, erasing the inflections, the "accent" of that particular text. What if we were to teach the historical and cultural contexts of each and every literary text we take up in the classroom—including European American texts—as well as teaching the particular debates around inclusion of that text in a shifting curriculum? In fact, let me take a step back: what if we were to carefully teach students the debates around curricular reform simultaneously with the texts themselves? I return to Paulo Freire's theories as a basis for the organization of such a classroom.

An effective multicultural pedagogy must first consider the relationship between teacher and student. Progressive educational theory is committed to decentering the power structure of teacher as ultimate authority and student as passive learner. This means that the teacher acknowledges that he or she speaks from a particular position, rather than speaking from the privileged position of abstract knowledge, which is essentially nowhere. This also means acknowledging that all components of the classroom—teacher, students, and texts—are embodied, occupying places within culture and its discourses. In my classroom, I begin by locating myself as a white woman of a certain age group, with a certain level of education, operating from within certain belief structures.[14] I do so because I want to invite students to consider the way I present materials, as well as my choices of materials, in the context of my "theoretical stance," giving them a place to locate their reflections upon and critiques of what we do in class. And I do so in the hope that this might provide students with a model of self-reflexivity applicable to their work as readers in relationship with texts. I also let them know that I have a life outside the classroom, that I am fallible, that I have anxieties and pain and joy and exhaustion. Letting down the armor of "teacher" is a process that can be undertaken over the course of the semester—in the classroom and in private conference time with students. It is informal, in some senses intangible, and of course must be subject to certain limits, but I think it is a crucial part of

169

establishing a working relationship with students. I will add that this does not mean relinquishing authority, discipline, or respect in the classroom, and it does require setting firm personal boundaries.

As the teacher cannot speak from the position of objective "knowledge," neither can knowledge itself be removed from the cultural ideals and biases that construct it. The way to establish such embodiment of knowledge in the classroom is to self-consciously and deliberately discuss it with students. For instance, in my introductory college writing courses I will often assign an essay by or interview with progressive education theorists such as Paulo Freire and black feminist teacher bell hooks next to essays expressing more conservative philosophies, such as William Bennett's or E. D. Hirsch's defenses of the traditional Western canon. In his essay "Why the West?" for instance, Bennett gives a conservative response to the multiculturalism controversy.[15] Students are intrigued to discover that the education they may have taken for granted as a fixed entity is actually open to debate. Students in my classes are well aware that something is going on with multiculturalism in their history/English/social science classrooms. But they are angered and confused to have the actual terms of the debate obscured from their view—now they're reading books by black women and homosexual men, and they still don't know why these texts that used to be "unacceptable" (or at least excluded) are now "correct." Even as educators work to change the canon and to transform power relations in the classroom, we often still present material to students as though it is a given, natural, The Curriculum. When students are given the opportunity to engage the actual debate, they become active participants in their learning, rather than simply the objects of someone else's conversation. Often they will take the critiques they are formulating, using some of the teaching theory we read, into other classrooms. On the middle and high school levels, teaching theory may not be appropriate reading, but perhaps looking at something like E. D. Hirsch's "list" for cultural literacy, which is "intended to illustrate the character and range of the knowledge literate Americans tend to share," will be a way of grounding a discussion of the changes students are encountering in their classrooms.[16]

This kind of specific positioning must be established before teachers can move on to discuss the challenges of studying culture, given the power of culture to present itself as neutral, natural, unmarked, "born, not made" (to borrow from Christian rhetoric). In the case of cultural study, messages given by the media and social institutions are so pervasive as to seem "invisible" and detached from their cultural and political origins. Such mystification leaves students alienated from themselves and their world, allowing them to rest in a comfortable zone of unquestioned canonicity wherein culture and literature pretend to a kind of mathematical fixity. Such false neutrality and stability preclude, in students' minds, the need for the messy painfulness of unstable categories and canons; such continuing mystification encourages students' sometimes fierce resistance to the changes encountered in the multicultural classroom. I will use the example of the debate about multicultural education to illustrate the effects of—and a possible counteraction to—this mystification. In one of my introductory writing courses I worked with a student who had just graduated from a conservative, all-white, all-male Catholic high school. This student was deeply confused when confronted with the university's progressive multicultural curriculum—the materials he was reading and studying did not resemble those he was accustomed to; in fact, they resembled everything he had been taught was radical and liberal in a negative sense. For Paul, this curriculum constituted a full-scale attack on his value system. After spending a semester in my Introductory Writing course, Paul signed up for my second-semester Writing About Literature course. After discussing the syllabus, which consisted of seven books, four of which were written by men, I asked if anyone had any questions, and Paul's hand immediately shot up. He asked, "Why do we have to read all books by women and only two by men?"[17] Because of the diverse national origins of the writers on the syllabus, Paul had been unable to determine their genders. Informing him that we actually would be reading "all books by men, and only three by women," led to an extraordinary classroom discussion exploring students' (not just Paul's) diverse responses to the changes in education: where did Paul's assumption come from? Why did he respond the way he did to texts that were unfamiliar to him? Why would he have felt anger if indeed we had been reading more books by women than by men? In this way we critically analyzed our learning process as a group, attaching classroom organization and materials to their historically and politically grounded contexts. I will add that I received a letter from Paul at the end of the semester in which he speculated upon his responses in the classroom, writing:

> In all my high school career I never realized that I could be wrong on an issue. . . . This class has made me realize that if I want to make my arguments understood I have to speak in a more thought-out fashion. I also never had women in my classes so the majority of the class didn't want to hear any arguments that women's liberation supports. I always thought that girls worked twice as hard for the same grades I soon realized that too was wrong [sic]. Some of the girls in our class were just as smart if not smarter than me. I guess that this has proved to be a learning experience in itself.

The reattachment of cultural and academic texts to their historical and political origins is the basic methodology of progressive teaching theory, with the goal that students will become more aware of themselves and their positions within culture. This is, I think, one way to help students to spend time in that difficult place that Freire describes as both "in" the world (moving about, surviving materially and physically) and "objectively distanced" enough from the world to enable positive critique.

In some senses, I believe that English classrooms on all levels must become places for interdisciplinary study, where literary texts are studied next to cultural texts and historical documents—all of which are examined for an understanding of the work they do in the world. One example of such a contextualized, interdisciplinary approach to teaching a literary text is the "Bedford Documentary Companion" Cultural Contexts for Ralph Ellison's *Invisible Man*, compiled by Eric J. Sundquist. To provide a contextual foundation for studying the plot and character development of Ellison's richly textured novel, Sundquist gathers excerpts from the Constitution, from Supreme Court decisions (*Brown v. Board of Education*), from oratory (Booker T. Washington's Atlanta Exposition address), from folk culture (African American folk songs and stories), and from speeches and writings by prominent African Americans at the time of the novel's publication (Marcus Garvey's speech "Africa for Africans," the Federal Writers' project "Portrait of Harlem").

According to this model, the classroom is interactive—rather than give a lecture, the teacher guides and participates in classroom discussion, the purpose of which is to link classroom materials to life experiences. Rather than exclusively doing textual analyses that ask students to think about what the text means, this pedagogy works toward contextualization, placing texts within their cultural contexts first, and then asking students to analyze how the text makes meaning for them —and why. This technique places responsibility upon students; teachers might delegate contextual materials to individuals or groups, who will be responsible for presenting them to the class as a whole in creative ways.

Another way to accomplish the kind of interdisciplinary study necessary to do justice to literary texts is to propose team-teaching experiments to school boards and administrators. Imagine a course in African American literature from the period 1865–1945 taught in conjunction with carefully coordinated history and social studies courses. Texts, lectures, and activities in all classrooms would support one another, setting up a multidirectional conversation for students to listen to and participate in.

Whatever specific strategies we develop as educators and administrators, I believe that ultimately we need to slow down and attend more carefully to each text we teach. For me, this means teaching fewer books with a greater emphasis on contextualization, close reading, and reader-response interpretation. Teachers on all levels face the problems of "coverage," of the need to fit an enormous amount of material into an inadequate amount of time; this problem must be addressed with the broad-based curricular reform and reconsideration of standardized testing criteria already in motion in many states. With the proliferation of information—printed and cyberspace texts, critical material about those texts, political and historical events and their representations— an accumulation of "essential knowledge" must be taught in order to create the "well-informed, responsible citizens" that secondary and

173

higher education strive to produce, while the time in which to present this information remains limited. This problem only reinforces my belief that education must focus on critical skills so that students will be able to selectively confront the information that will bombard them as they continue in school and in the work force, rather than attempting to introduce students to the greatest possible volume of material. It takes time to enunciate, time and great care.

I would like to conclude with a discussion of enunciation by theorist Homi Bhabha, who conceives of the enunciative process in terms of motion, of cultural instability; indeed, for Bhabha, "cultures" only articulate themselves as such at their boundaries, "where meanings and values are (mis)read or signs are misappropriated."[18] Thinking of my own discussion of displacement in reading "different" texts together in the classroom, I agree with Bhabha's formulation: a culture really only announces itself, or becomes problematic and painful, at the moment of its encounter with a different culture; these encounters, always tinged by struggles for recognition, are what has led to such controversy regarding the "multicultural" classroom. This is the problem that, I think, creates the desire in administrators, teachers, and students alike to place peoples, cultures, authors, and texts into neat categories and canons. When there was a somewhat firm, fixed, Eurocentric literary canon in this country, we were more certain about what to teach and how to teach it; teachers were less burdened by the conflict and contestation that comes from cultural contact. Shifting curriculum and canon to include texts by people of non-Eurocentric cultures living in the United States is a process marked by the accompanying politics of "real-world" cultural conflict and instability.

To bring order to chaos is a natural human desire: we feel safer and perceive our reality to be more manageable when we pretend that our ducks will stay neatly in the rows we set up for them. Imposing this false stability of canons and curricula is also a way of consolidating the power of political and economic dominance—another element in the very real struggle for cultural recognition. But this kind of falsely stable categorization leads to (mis)understandings of "different" identity characteristics in those hierarchical terms I discussed above, laid out on a scale moving from acceptable to intolerable based upon dominant cultural standards. Such misunderstandings will serve only to perpetuate cultural conflict and racial, sexual, and class oppressions.

Bhabha, then, argues that we need to locate ourselves in the (difficult, uncomfortable, uncertain) space of unstable categories, to realize that even as we teach African American (or Asian American, Hispanic American, Native American, and European American) texts in our literature classrooms, the material cultures to which those texts correspond are shifting and struggling, continually (re)articulating themselves in the terms of daily life. This argument is resonant with Freire's imperative that we attempt to live and move in the world while simultaneously watching it from a distanced perspective, allowing for positive critique that keeps pace with the rapid changes of time and history. This argument also has practical implication for teaching texts in a decentered classroom that distributes responsibility for learning among teachers and students, and works to teach texts in an enunciative fashion that accounts for the structures of the problems encountered in them: problems of events and characters in the texts, problems of student responses to those events and characters. Bhabha is critical of the fact that our discussions of culture and cultural texts are often limited to descriptions of "the effect rather than the structure of the problem."[19] While such descriptions are important steps in discussing and teaching literary texts (I like to think of them as a kind of bearing witness), enunciative teaching practice tries to articulate the structural, institutional imperatives and contexts for narrative action, for canon formation, for classroom practice, for cultural interaction in "real" life. It is a process always in motion, always, by definition, falling short of its goal, but a process that might allow students and teachers alike to follow Freire's bottom-line prescription for learning.

Notes

1. John Guare, *Six Degrees of Separation* (New York: Random House, 1994), p. 81.

2. Toni Morrison. *Playing in the Dark* (New York: Random House, 1993), pp. 6–7, 17.

3. Guare, p. 14.

4. Marlon Riggs, "Black Macho Revisited: Reflections of a Snap! Queen," in *Out in Culture: Gay, Lesbian and Queer Essays on Popular Culture*, ed. Corey K. Creekmur and Alexander Doty (Durham, NC: Duke University Press, 1995), p. 471.

5. Quoted in Richard David Story, "Six Degrees of Preparation: John Guare and Fred Schepisi Make the Ultimate New York Movie," *New York Magazine* (7 June 1993), p. 43.

6. Homi Bhabha, "The Commitment to Theory," in *The Location of Culture* (London and New York: Routledge, 1994).

7. Toni Morrison, *Sula* (New York: Penguin, 1973; 1982) p. 47.

8. See Ralph Ginzburg, *100 Years of Lynching* (Baltimore: Black Classic Press, 1962; 1988) for a thorough compilation of newspaper-reported lynching cases from 1880 to 1961, including "A Partial Listing of Approximately 5,000 Negroes Lynched in the United States since 1859." See also Winthrop D. Jordan, *White Over Black: American Attitudes Towards the Negro* (Chapel Hill: University of North Carolina Press, 1968) and Michele Wallace, *Black Macho and the Myth of the Superwoman* (New York: Verso, 1978; 1990) for in-depth analyses of the historical roots of racial mythologies in the United States; and Jan Nederveen Pieterse, *White on Black: Images of Africa and Blacks in Western Popular Culture* (New Haven, CT: Yale University Press, 1992) for an illustrated history of European and American stereotypes of black people over the last two centuries.

9. Paulo Freire, *Pedagogy of the Oppressed* (New York: Continuum Press, 1970; 1993), p. 62.

10. David Reiff, "Multiculturalism's Silent Partner: It's the newly globalized consumer economy, stupid." *Harper's Magazine* (August 1993), p. 66.

11. Ibid., p. 71.

12. Bernice Johnson Reagon, "Are My Hands Clean?" Sweet Honey in the Rock Live at Carnegie Hall (Chicago: Flying Fish Records) 1988. Liner notes to the song read: "Composed for Winterfest, Institute for Policy Studies. The lyrics are based on an article by Institute fellow John Cavanagh, 'The Journey of the Blouse: A Global Assembly.' Lyrics and music by Bernice Johnson Reagon. Songtalk Publishing Co. 1985."

13. See Cynthia Enloe, *Bananas, Beaches, and Bases: Making Feminist Sense of International Politics* (Berkeley: University of California Press, 1990) for a particularly cogent analysis of the ways in which "the personal is international."

14. I often identify my own ethnic backgrounds as well, in an attempt to undo the uncritical monolith that is "whiteness" in the United States. See Dean MacCannell, "White Culture," *Empty Meeting Grounds: The Tourist Papers* (New York: Routledge, 1992), pp. 121–46.

15. William Bennett, "Why the West?" *National Review* (27 May 1988).

16. E. D. Hirsch, *Cultural Literacy: What Every American Needs to Know* (New York: Houghton Mifflin, 1987).

17. Note the diction of Paul's question: If we were reading "all" books by women, there could not be two written by men; Paul's illogical hyperbole reveals the threat he feels at the possibility of having to read any texts written by women. The texts listed on the syllabus were: Italo Calvino's *If on a winter's night a traveler;* Ernest Hemingway's *The Old Man and the Sea;* Dolores Kendrick's *Women of Plums;* Milan Kundera's *The Unbearable Lightness of Being;* Toni Morrison's *Sula;* Art Spiegelman's *Maus;* and Jeanette Winterson's *Written on the Body.*

18. Homi Bhabha, "The Commitment to Theory," p.34.

19. Ibid.

TEACHING AGAINST THE ODDS

Marianna White Davis
Benedict College

Selena was a mature, robust, medium-height, dark-skinned girl, who sat near the back of the room in my eleventh-grade English class at a large, inner-city, senior high school in the Deep South. She was often inattentive and lazy, for she came to class without homework assignments, books, and writing paper. Usually, she had to borrow a pencil. Around school, she had the reputation of antagonizing both male and female students. Here I was, in my second year as a teacher in the public school system in South Carolina, trying desperately to impress both my colleagues and my principal that I was a very capable English teacher. The setting was familiar to me: an all-black high school with an all-black faculty, a large, industrial upstate city, a large and conservative black community, a middle- and upper-class white community that was separated from all of the components of the city, including the black neighborhoods. My challenge, therefore, was very clear to me: to teach students like Selena how to read, write, talk, think, and listen with critical skills. To meet my challenge, I also had to guide them gingerly through the mine field of racism, pointing out the familiar hidden mines of hate and destruction. I decided to use literature as my detector.

To conform to the school district's curriculum guide, I designed my literature units around several of the selections from African American literature in each of my units or series of lessons. In the beginning, however, I had to develop a very strong personal philosophy of teaching and learning. This would become my daily guide, my critical appraisal of my worth as a teacher.

Realizing that in education there was a negative and debilitating philosophy which assumes that because of the presence of some theoretical statistical equation, there must be in every group a certain number of students who must fail because they lack ability or come from inferior environments, I decided that every one of my students could learn and that I had to find ways to reach them, to encourage them to achieve beyond even their expectations. Later, I was happy to read an article by Alione Diop that now undergirds my beliefs: "[We must] teach the rising generations the art, history, literature, customs, and techniques of Black civilizations through books, exhibitions, cultural manifestations, the cinema, and the radio." [1]

As an English teacher, I knew that I had to find ways to bring into my classroom names such as Frances E. W. Harper, Alain Locke, W.E.B. Du Bois, Carter G. Woodson, Sterling Brown, Countee Cullen, Margaret Walker, Phillis Wheatley, and Gwendolyn Brooks.[2] I suppose Betty Parker's guide for teachers of black literature was a revelation for me because her list fit into what I had earlier established for my eleventh-grade classes:

1. From a black perspective, thoroughly investigate each piece of literature taught.

2. Discontinue reliance on European critics to get through an hour, lecture or a course.

3. Examine the historical, dominant world view of the European. Demonstrate how it is woven through the literature.

4. Examine the definitions of a hero and a villain from both the European and the black point of view. Expose the villains who have been proclaimed heroes in European literature and the heroes who have been proclaimed villains in black literature.

5. Teach Egyptian mythology.

179

6. Expose Greek and Roman mythology.

7. Examine slave narratives and rely on them for both literary value and historical accuracy. Beware of alterations.

8. Become familiar with black historians and literary critics.

9. Expose students to local and national literary and historical events.

10. Discuss the migratory element in black literature. Help students place in proper perspective their own geographical locations.

11. Discourage "objectivity" where black literature is concerned; all literature is political and subjective.

12. Make research and research projects meaningful so that students can form a more positive perspective.[3]

I truly liked Selena, although she was a problem student. I learned that she had an interest in music, so I decided to "connect" her to a song that would include research on her part in order to meet the requirement of the assignment. I always spent a part of each literature class period reading two or three poems to my students. Using the music in my voice, I would emphasize the "beat" so that my students could feel the movement of the words. And they did!

I assigned Selena to study the lyrics and music to "God Bless the Child," as sung by Billie Holiday. Several days later, with poster in hand, showing pictures of Billie Holiday, Selena brought light to our classroom with her well-researched report. At the end, she sang "God Bless the Child." As I looked around my classroom at the faces of my students, I knew that Selena was feeling the warmth of success—perhaps for the first time.

Following this experience of student involvement, I returned to lecturing through a kind of show-and-tell posture. All of the intellectual materials were in my mind and in my notes, but I had to work out a method of sharing a number of important ideas about black literature to these eleventh-grade students. Today, a number of articles and reports underline the theoretical concepts through which I worked years ago in attempting to reach my students in that inner-city high school. This means, I believe, that *truth* always finds a way to the hearts and minds of those teachers who sincerely want to "do the right thing."

To begin, music and language have been at the heart of a great number of pieces of black literature. For example, Paula Gallant Eckard tells us that "by title and by presence, jazz takes center stage in Toni Morrison's novel *Jazz* and winds its way through the lives of Joe Trace, his wife Violet, the murdered girl Dorcas, and indeed through the lives of everyone in the City in 1926. Like a jazz performance, it creates a montage effect in its storytelling."[4] Of course other black writers have used music as a tradition in literature, including James Baldwin, Zora Neale Hurston, Jean Toomer, and Langston Hughes. Houston Baker, in his *Blues, Ideology, and Afro-American Literature* (1984), sees this blues matrix as "a vernacular trope . . . an amalgam that seems always to have been in motion in America—always becoming, shaping, transforming, displacing the peculiar experiences of Africans in the New World." Henry Louis Gates calls "the black trope of the tropes the peculiar language of the Signifying Monkey, which is the musical subject matter and the strategies and techniques for performing the music."[5] In jazz, therefore, signifying plays an integral role as musicians improvise and signify upon each other.

In further inspecting the place of music in black literature, one also finds references to the private codes of gossip, humor, and stories. Berret tells us that Toni Morrison describes her writing as "village literature, fiction that is really for the village, for the tribe." Morrison believes, says Berret, that "today, music is no longer enough because people are being devoured by cultural symbols that do not treat them seriously or measure up to the original power of their spoken traditions."[6]

In teaching my eleventh-graders, I clearly understood my responsibility to help them identify the traditions of "home" and "place" in black literature. Since a number of them lived in substandard housing and others lived in well-built brick houses, I had to find a way to move them away mentally from physical structures to a kind of philosophical and spiritual mind-set of "home" and "place."

Although I now understand the connotation of "home" as Harriet Jacobs defined it in her autobiography, *Incidents in the Life of a Slave Girl,* I was not interested in teaching my students "home" as a domestic entity—a place where black women cooked and scrubbed and cleaned,

181

and washed, and tended babies. Just as a second reading of Jacobs's book reveals that her definition of "home" is beyond the domestic meaning, I would have to lead my students to a very clear understanding of a "home" beyond domestic borders in black literature.

In black literature, "place" is also an important element. One might suggest that Gloria Naylor's *The Women of Brewster Place* allows the reader to identify place as a literary entity that is important to the continuity of the lives of the women living within it. However, on a closer reading, one discovers that this novel is a political comment on the American Dream. For the women of Brewster Place, the dream of place is deferred! The "place" is a dungeon that eats away at the dreams and aspirations of its inhabitants. Of significance is the church in the "place" (a traditional image of solace and tranquillity) described as "a brooding ashen giant." With music, home, and place structured into my lessons on black literature, I now faced the awesome task of putting into my lectures the role of black women in society. This would be the challenge.

My show-and-tell lectures included pictures of Mary McLeod Bethune, Mary Church Terrell, Sojourner Truth, Ida Wells Barnett, Harriet Tubman, Lena Horne, Eartha Kitt, and Mahalia Jackson. To help me get through this phase of the unit, I asked students to volunteer to bring in a photograph, and asked each student to share with us something about the role that the relative shown had played in their lives. *Everyone* was attentive during this activity, and we all learned a lot about each student in my classes. Following this, I talked about the role of black women in literature and in our American society.

Roger Abrahams wrote that "how women assert their image and values as women is seldom found in folklore literature. We know even less about the verbal traditions of black women in particular."[7] Pearlie M. Peters tells us, and this is one reason why I include Hurston's work in the courses I teach, that "Zora Neale Hurston was very concerned about the African American oral tradition and the place of the Southern folk women in its verbal hierarchy. The power of the narrative and assertive voice of women in black storytelling, preaching rituals, and in intrafamilial dialogue is a recurring element in Hurston's art." Peters goes on to say that in Hurston's works, women talk with the voice of authority and power, and that they are real and essential storytellers of the race because they possess an honesty and clarity of expression that bring forth truth and stability.[8]

In the conclusion of Gloria Naylor's study of twelve novels by black women, Larry R. Andrews wrote that "even when the women understand that they share a sisterhood of oppression, they often do not act on the belief that sisterhood is powerful. They do not come together to talk about their common history and their common reality. When they do attempt to communicate as women, they fail to sustain the sisterhood."[9] The cultural problem, even for teachers of black literature, is how to move female students beyond the competitiveness, betrayal, and socioeconomic separation that black women portray in much of the literature and even in the publications of current events—newspapers and magazines.

Now, to return to Selena. After she completed her report on the Holiday song and research, I listened to the reports of other students as I continued to lecture through a show-and-tell format between reports. One day, much to my surprise, I found an assignment in my mail box from the principal that required me to visit the homes of each of the thirty students in my eleventh-grade homeroom. I did not drive, nor did I own an automobile. Another teacher and I borrowed a chauffeur-driven, old Packard of a local dentist, and off we went to visit our students on Sunday afternoons. One Sunday, when I found myself riding into an alley, I knew that I was headed toward the home of Selena. The roadway was narrow, with children playing in the yards. I had to walk several yards to the front steps of her home, where I was expected. I met her mother, father, and her six brothers and sisters. In their home, teachers were highly regarded, as I learned. As I sipped a cool glass of lemonade in their clean living room, with the children scattered outside playing, I learned from Selena's expression that she was proud of her hardworking parents. The problem was that she had to take care of her siblings because she was the oldest child. Believing that she had to be overly protective, she felt that fisticuffs would solve all problems. There was not enough money to go around to buy pencils and paper, so she always gave her share to the younger ones. Burdened with care-giving responsibilities, she truly believed that her dreams—to finish school and pursue a career in nursing—would never materialize.

After this Sunday visit, I arranged to give Selena another research project on Billie Holiday. This one was titled "Strange Fruit." I had learned from Selena's history teacher that she was failing history, so I believed that this assignment would help her in both English and in history. "Strange Fruit" is a song about lynching in the United States (Southern trees bear a strange fruit/Blood on the leaves and blood at the root/Black body swinging in the southern breeze/Strange fruit hanging from the poplar trees).[10] The lyrics tempered Selena to the extent that she became inquisitive about a number of topics in American history, and she became an avid reader in American literature for the remainder of the school year.

Selena spent considerable time researching the lynching laws in the United States. Her history teacher allowed her to give a report on this topic in her class, and in my class she used the same report as background to the song "Strange Fruit." Given that literature is closely tied to history, and that literature is a reflection of political activities in a society, I was able to help Selena see the connections and to include these major ideas in my lectures.

Eventually in the unit, I was able to return to my three major topics: music, home, and place in black literature. And, these three elements were used in the report on "Strange Fruit" as both Selena and I showed how these three entities helped the reader to understand the role of black literature, including black music, in knowing one's place in American society.

When a student asked what was the meaning of the term "gallant South" in the song "Strange Fruit," I discussed the Civil War as context for this expression. When another student asked about "Black body swinging in the southern breeze," Selena rushed to tell her classmates that not all lynching was done in the South, and she gave facts of the occurrence of lynching elsewhere in the United States. Of course, all of the class joined in on their definition of the word "fruit" as seen in the song.

My unit included other personalities such as Frances E. W. Harper, Phillis Wheatley, Charles Chesnutt, Langston Hughes, Countee Cullen,

Frederick Douglass, W.E.B. Du Bois, Gwendolyn Brooks, and Mary McLeod Bethune. As always, I included the five critical skill areas as adopted from the National Council of Teachers of English: reading, writing, thinking, speaking, and listening.

By the end of the spring quarter, Selena was both an achieving student and a calm and sensitive young woman. She passed all of her classes and entered her senior year with a determination to excel.

In conclusion, I do agree with Professor James J. Davis of Howard University, who wrote that English teachers (in fact all teachers) must consider the question of personal values and emotions in their courses, especially in literature courses. He pleads for what he calls the "pedagogy of humanism," for he believes that this is the ethical charge to all teachers. Teaching students to develop critical skills through reference of their own personal experiences is, I think, a deep investment on the part of both teachers and students. In the tumultuous beginnings of my career this method of teaching could be seen as teaching against the odds. But today, in light of a new, multicultural awareness, the odds are in our favor. We must meet this challenge.

Notes

1. Alione Diop, "Three Objectives of a Cultural Policy," in *Black World,* October 1973.

2. Charles Larson, "African-Afro-Americans Literary Relations; Basic Parallels," in *Negro Digest,* December 1969.

3. Betty Parker, "Black Literature Teachers: Torch-Bearers of European Myths?" in *Black World,* December 1975.

4. Paula Gallant Eckard, "The Interplay of Music, Language, and Narrative in Toni Morrison's *Jazz,*" in *CLA Journal,* September 1994.

5. Henry Louis Gates Jr., *The Signifying Monkey: A Theory of African-American Literary Criticism* (New York: Oxford University Press, 1988).

6. Anthony J. Berret, "Toni Morrison's Literary Jazz," in *CLA Journal,* March 1989.

7. Roger Abrahams, "Negotiating Respect," in *Journal of American Folklore* (1975): 88.

8. Pearlie M. Peters, "Ah Got The Law In My Mouth: Black Women and Assertive Voice in Hurston's Fiction and Folklore" in *CLA Journal,* March 1994.

9. Larry R. Andrews, "Black Sisterhood in Gloria Naylor's Novels" in *CLA Journal,* September 1989.

10. "Strange Fruit," words and music by Lewis Allan, copyright 1948.

INTERROGATING "WHITENESS," (DE)CONSTRUCTING "RACE"

AnnLouise Keating
Eastern New Mexico University

Race is a text (an array of discursive practices), not an essence. It must be read with painstaking care and suspicion, not imbibed.
—HENRY LOUIS GATES JR.,
Loose Canons

Race has become metaphorical—a way of referring to and disguising forces, events, classes, and expressions of social decay and economic division far more threatening to the body politic than biological "race" ever was.
—TONI MORRISON,
Playing in the Dark

Sticks and stones may break our bones, but words—words that evoke structures of oppression, exploitation, and brute physical threat—can break souls.
—KWAME ANTHONY APPIAH,
"The Conservation of 'Race'"

My title reflects several trends in contemporary cultural and literary studies. Because these trends involve exposing the hidden assumptions we make concerning racialized identities, they have far-reaching theoretical and pedagogical implications. The first phrase, "Interrogating 'Whiteness,'" refers to the recent demand for an analysis of "white" as a racialized category. Toni Morrison, for example, calls for an examination of "whiteness" in canonical U.S. literature. What, she asks, are the implications of "literary whiteness"? How does it function in the construction of an "American" identity? Arguing that a "criticism that needs to insist that literature is not only 'universal' but also 'race-free' risks lobotomizing that literature, and diminishes both the art and the artist," she urges scholars to examine the hidden racial discourse in U.S. literature.[1] Similarly, some educators have begun emphasizing the importance of developing critical pedagogies that examine how "whiteness" has (mis)shaped knowledge production in U.S. culture. According to Henry Giroux and Peter L. McLaren, the traditional Western view "of learning as a neutral or transparent process" is inaccurate and prevents us from recognizing the highly political, racialized nature of all pedagogical methods. They maintain that

> Teachers need critical categories that probe the factual status of white, Western, androcentric epistemologies that will enable schools to be interrogated as sites engaged in producing and transmitting social practices that produce the linear, profit-motivated imperatives of the dominant culture, with its attendant institutional dehumanization. [2]

bell hooks takes this demand for an interrogation of the relationship between "whiteness" and cultural dominance even further in her discussion of "white" theorists' exclusive analysis of the racial *Other*. According to hooks, "Many scholars, critics, and writers preface their work by stating that they are 'white,' as though mere acknowledgment of this fact were sufficient, as though it conveyed all we need to know of standpoint, motivation, [and] direction." Because she believes that this unquestioned acceptance of "whiteness" distorts contemporary cultural studies, she challenges "white" theorists to incorporate an analysis of their own racialized identities into their work:

> One change in direction that would be real cool would be the production of a discourse on race that interrogates whiteness. It would be just so interesting for all those white folks who are giving blacks their take on blackness to let them know what's going on with whiteness.[3]

These calls for an interrogation of "whiteness" cannot be dismissed as the latest scholarly fad in academia's publish-or-perish game. As Kobena Mercer and other contemporary theorists have argued, "whiteness" and its "violent denial of difference" serve a vital function in masking social and economic inequalities in contemporary Western cultures.[4] By negating these people—whatever the color of their skin— who do not measure up to "white" standards, "whiteness" has played a central role in maintaining and naturalizing a hierarchical social system and a dominant/subordinate world view.

However, as I began exploring recent definitions of "whiteness" and incorporating this analysis into my literature courses I encountered a number of unexpected difficulties, and this is where the second part of my title, "(De)Constructing 'Race,'" comes in. The word "(De)-Constructing"—with the prefix in parentheses—reflects my assessment of the dangers in recent interrogations of "whiteness" and other racialized identities. More specifically, it refers to the way theorists who attempt to deconstruct "race" often inadvertently reconstruct it by reinforcing the belief in permanent, separate racial categories. Although they emphasize the artificial, politically and economically motivated nature of all racial classifications, their continual analysis of racialized identities undercuts their belief that "race" is a constantly changing sociohistorical concept, not a biological fact.

In what follows, I first summarize recent theorists' explorations of "whiteness" and discuss what I see as the difficulties that can occur when we attempt to incorporate these analyses into classroom lectures and discussions. I then offer tentative suggestions for alternative approaches that investigate "whiteness" while deconstructing "race." Before I begin, however, I want briefly to describe my own pedagogy. Whenever possible, I try to integrate my scholarship with my classroom instruction. I believe that both areas can be enriched by this interchange. The classroom functions as a laboratory where the theory I read and write takes on concrete form as I attempt to translate theoretical perspectives into accessible, practical terms. Students benefit from this process; they are introduced to a variety of theoretical perspectives and become critical readers, capable of recognizing how literary canons are shaped by personal and cultural issues.

This twofold approach has played an important role in shaping the ways I began incorporating analyses of "whiteness" into my U.S. literature and composition courses. For the past several years both my scholarship and my teaching had been informed by a critical analysis of how "race," gender, and sexuality are socially constructed, but until reading Morrison's call for an interrogation of "whiteness" I had never considered including an analysis of "white" in my explorations of racialized meanings in literary texts. Yet it only made sense to do so; after all, we examine "black," Chicano/a, Native American, and Asian American literary traditions. Should we not also look at "white" literary traditions? And so, shortly after reading Morrison and several other theorists, I began to include explorations of "whiteness" in the courses I teach, which have ranged from surveys of U.S. literature to introductory composition to an upper-level/graduate elective course on "Race," Gender, and Literature. While approximately three-fourths of the students in my classes identify as "white," the remaining fourth—some of whom can easily pass for "white"—identify as "Hispanic," "Native American," and "black." But however they identify, the majority are first-generation college students from working-class backgrounds. They are motivated by their own versions of the American Dream, the belief that hard work and education will enable *anyone*—regardless of "race," gender, or economic status—to succeed. My comments in the following pages are based on these students' reactions.

Although students are often startled by the notion that language is racialized and literature can be examined for its hidden and overt racial meanings, they find it much easier to explore the racialized subtexts in works by non-"white" writers than to explore the racialized meanings in writings by "whites." When I taught Leslie Marmon Silko, Scott Momaday, or Paula Gunn Allen, for example, I described their perspectives on contemporary Native American literary and cultural conventions and asked students to consider the ways in which their poetry and prose simultaneously reflected and shaped these conventions. After an initial period of questioning, they arrived at important observations. Similarly, when I taught Nella Larsen and Paul Dunbar, I discussed W.E.B. Du Bois's theory of the "color line," described the status of African Americans in the early 1900s, and asked students to con-

189

sider how their "race" might have influenced their work. Again, they arrived at insightful comments.

However, when I suggested that "white"—like "Native American" or "African American"—is a *racialized* identity, continually reinforced and reinvented in literature, students were startled. People with pale skin are often referred to as "whites," and of course there are ethnic groups whose members have "white" skin—Italian Americans, Polish Americans, many U.S. Jews, and so on—but a white *"race"*? Although I discussed Morrison's call for and interrogation of literary "whiteness" at length, when I asked students to speculate on the contributions that Joanna Russ, John Updike, and other contemporary "white" writers have made to "white" literary tradition, they were troubled and unable to reply. Nor could they discuss Ralph Waldo Emerson's "whiteness," or analyze how Henry David Thoreau's "race" shaped *Walden*. Clearly, they had no idea what this "whiteness" entailed.

My students are not alone in their inability to comprehend "whiteness"; as Kobena Mercer states, "One of the signs of the times is that we really don't know what 'white' is." Thus he asserts that "the real challenge in the new cultural politics of difference is to make 'whiteness' visible for the first time, as a culturally constructed ethnic identity historically contingent upon the disavowal and violent denial of difference."[5] In short, "whiteness" has functioned as a pseudo-universal category that hides its specific values, epistemology, and other attributes under the guise of a nonracialized, supposedly colorless, "human nature."

Yet the hidden dimensions of this unmarked "white" culture are slowly becoming more visible as theorists in literature, cultural studies, and pedagogy embark on the first stages of an interrogation of "whiteness." Not surprisingly, though, the most commonly mentioned attribute of "whiteness" seems to be its nonpresence, its invisibility. A number of scholars associate this ubiquitous hidden "whiteness" with an unmarked superiority. As Richard Dyer suggests in his groundbreaking analysis of representations of "whiteness" in mainstream U.S. and British film, "white power secures its dominance by seeming not to be anything in particular."[6] Drawing on scientific studies of chromatics, he explains that whereas black—because it is always marked as a color—refers to particular objects and qualities, white does not: It "is not anything really, not an identity, not a particularizing quality, because it is everything—white is no color because it is all colors."[7] In literary and cultural studies this "colorless multicoloredness" gives "whiteness" an omnipresence quite difficult to analyze:

> It is the way that black people are marked as black (are not just "people") in representation that has made it relatively easy to analyze their representation, whereas white people—not there as a category and everywhere everything as a fact—are difficult, if not impossible, to analyze *qua* white.[8]

This invisible omnipresence gives "whiteness" a rarely acknowledged position of dominance and power. As Henry Giroux suggests, "whiteness," domination, and invisibility are intimately related. He asserts that although "'whiteness' functions as a historical and social construction," the dominant culture's inability or reluctance to see it as such is the source of its hidden authority; "whiteness" is an unrecognized and unacknowledged racial category "that secures its power by refusing to identify" itself.[9] Morrison makes a similar point in her analysis of canonical U.S. literature when she maintains that this unacknowledged "whiteness" has created a literary "language that can powerfully evoke and enforce hidden signs of racial superiority, cultural hegemony, and dismissive 'othering.'"[10]

By thus erasing its presence, "whiteness" operates as the unacknowledged standard or norm against which all so-called "minorities" are measured. Consider, for example, the implications of "minority and ethnic studies" in U.S. literature. Although scholars generally conceptualize the Harlem Renaissance as a "*black*" literary movement (I suppose because those identified as Harlem Renaissance writers were people of African descent), they do not conceptualize Transcendentalism as a "*white*" movement, even though—to the best of my knowledge—the transcendentalists were all people of European descent. In our "multicultural" era, we have studies of "*Chicano*" narrative, "*Asian American*" novels, "*Native American*" poetry, and so on. But imagine a course or a book devoted exclusively to white-skinned writers (as so many courses and books still are) that acknowledge this fact in its title: say, "Classics of the *White* Western World," "The *White* American Experience," or "*White* Regional Writers." In this schema, "minority" writings become deviations from the unmarked ("white") norm. As Dyer explains,

> Looking, with such passion and single-mindedness, at non-dominant groups has had the effect of reproducing the sense of oddness, differentness, exceptionality of these groups, the feeling that they are departures from the norm. Meanwhile the norm has carried on as if it is the natural, inevitable, ordinary way of being human.[11]

This invisible, omnipresent, naturalized "white" norm has lead to a highly paradoxical situation in literary and cultural studies: On the one hand, it is vital that we begin exploring the roles "whiteness" has played in shaping U.S. culture; on the other hand, its pervasive non-presence makes it difficult—if not impossible—to analyze "whiteness" as "whiteness." As Dyer asserts, "if the invisibility of whiteness colonizes the definition of other norms—class, gender, heterosexuality, nationality, and so on—it also masks whiteness as itself a category."[12] Consequently, theorists of all colors have been compelled to adopt a relational approach, where "whiteness" is examined in the context of "blackness" or other non-"white" racialized categories. In "White Woman Feminist," for example, Marilyn Frye draws on African Americans' discussions of "white" people to explore what she calls "whiteliness"—or "white" ways of thinking and acting.[13] Dyer centers his analysis of "whiteness" in mainstream cinema on instances where the narratives "are marked by the fact of ethnic difference."[14] Morrison takes a similar approach in *Playing in the Dark*, where she maintains that "blackness"—or what she terms "Africanisms"—are central to any investigation of literary "whiteness." She begins with the hypothesis that "it may be possible to discover, through a close look at literary 'blackness,' the nature—even the cause—of literary 'whiteness.'"[15] Like Dyer, she restricts her analysis to textual moments where "black" and "white" people interact, and throughout *Playing in the Dark* she explores literary "whiteness" by examining how "notions of racial hierarchy, racial exclusion, and racial vulnerability" influenced "white" writers "who held, resisted, explored, or altered these notions."[16] For instance, in her discussion of Willa Cather's *Sapphira and the Slave Girl*—

which depicts the interactions between Sapphira, a "white" slave mistress, and her female slaves—Morrison examines the ways "white" womanhood acquires its identity, as well as its power, privilege, and prestige, at the expense of "black" womanhood. And in her examination of *Huckleberry Finn* she demonstrates that the notions of independence and freedom in this novel rely on the presence of the unfree Jim.

Similarly, Aldon Lynn Nielsen focuses his analysis of literary "whiteness" on the ways "white" writers depict "blackness." In *Reading Race: White American Poets and the Racial Discourse in the Twentieth Century*, he associates "whiteness" with a racist symbolic system deeply embedded in U.S. thinking and explores how "white" identity has been constructed through racist stereotyping of the "black" other. More specifically, he examines what he terms "frozen metaphors" or stereotypes of "blacks" that reinforce "an essentially racist mode of thought," privileging people of European descent while relegating people of African descent to an inferior position.[17] In the numerous racist stereotypes he describes, representations of "blackness" take a variety of sometimes contradictory forms yet have one thing in common: in each instance, they exist to affirm the validity of the power of "whiteness." By depicting people of African descent as lazy, carefree, unsophisticated, and primitive, he argues, Hart Crane, e. e. cummings, T. S. Eliot, and many other twentieth-century "white" writers locate "blackness" outside Western cultural traditions. He emphasizes that this racist stereotyping serves an important role by reinforcing already existing beliefs in the superiority of "white" aesthetics.

As Nielsen's investigation implies, this invisible, naturalized "white" norm also seems to encompass an authoritative, hierarchical, restrictive mode of thought. Frye, for example, associates "whiteliness" with the desire for personal and collective power by asserting that "Authority seems to be central to whiteliness, as you might expect from people who are raised to run things."[18] She describes "whitely" people as "judges" and "preachers" who—because they assume that their "ethics of forms, procedures, and due process" represent the only correct standard of conduct—attempt to impose their beliefs on all others.[19] Dyer makes a related point in his discussion of *Simba*, a colonial adventure film depicting the conflict between British colonizers and the Mau

193

Mau in Kenya, in which "white" is coded as orderliness, rationality, and control, while "black" is coded as chaos, irrational violence, and total loss of control.[20] Morrison notes a similar pattern of restrictive "white" thinking which she associates with an insistence on purity, self-containment, and impenetrable borders. According to Morrison, "white" literary representations establish "fixed and major differences where the difference does not exist or is minimal." For instance, metaphoric references to "the purity of blood" have enabled writers to construct a rigid, inflexible division between "white" civilization and "black" savagery.[21] This division plays itself out in many works of U.S. literature, where false differences based on blood are used to empower "white" characters.

A number of theorists have associated "whiteness" with mystery, absence, and death. Morrison, for example, claims that although representations of "blackness" serve a variety of symbolic functions in U.S. literature, "Whiteness, alone, is mute, meaningless, unfathomable, pointless, frozen, veiled, curtained, dreaded, senseless, implacable."[22] Dyer, in his exploration of mainstream cinema, finds that on the infrequent occasions "when whiteness *qua* whiteness does come into focus, it is often revealed in emptiness, absence, denial, or even a kind of death."[23] In *Night of the Living Dead*, for instance, all "white" people are closely associated with death: "Living and dead are indistinguishable, and the zombies' sole *raison d'être*, to attack and eat the living, has resonance with the behavior of the living whites."[24] According to hooks, these literary and filmic representations of "whiteness" as mystery and death reflect a common belief in African American communities; during her own upbringing, she explains, "black folks associated whiteness with the terrible, the terrifying, the terrorizing. White people were regarded as terrorists."[25]

This shift from "whiteness" to "white *people*" concerns me, for it draws on false generalizations and implies that all human beings classified as "white" *automatically* exhibit the traits associated with "whiteness": they are, by *nature*, insidious, superior, empty, terrible, terrifying, and so on. Now, I know white folk who aren't like this, and while I would definitely agree that "white" skin and at least some of these "white" traits are often found together, I would argue that the relation between them is conditional. As Marilyn Frye suggests, "the connection between whiteliness and light-colored skin is a *contingent* connection: this character could be manifested by persons who are *not* white; it can be absent in persons who are."[26] In other words, the fact that the person is born with "white" skin does not necessarily mean that she will *not* think, act, and write in "white" ways. Leslie Marmon Silko beautifully illustrates this contingent nature of "whiteness" and skin color in *Ceremony*, where full-blood Native characters such as Emo, Harley, and Rocky think and act in "white" ways. Although she too demonizes "whiteness"—in *Ceremony* "whiteness" is associated with greed, restrictive boundaries, destruction, emptiness, absence, and death —Silko does not automatically associate "whiteness" with all "white" people. Indeed, it is the light-skinned mixed-blood protagonist, Tayo, who learns to recognize and resist this evil "whiteness."[27]

However, it's difficult not to equate the word "whiteness"—and, by extension, the negative qualities it seems to imply—with "white" people. In fact, when I first began reading about "whiteness," it became difficult for me not to make automatic assumptions about everyone who looked "white." I felt uncomfortable and distrustful around people I classified as "white"; and at this early stage in my own interrogation of "whiteness" I was tempted to draw on my African ancestry, disavow my "white" education, and entirely separate myself (intellectually, if not physically) from the so-called "white race." Interrogations of "whiteness" have had similar but far more extreme impact on my students. Despite my repeated attempts to distinguish between literary representations of "whiteness" and real-life people classified as "white," students of all colors found it extremely difficult (and at times impossible) not to blur the boundaries between them. Some became obsessed with highly negative explorations of "white" people.

Class discussion of "The School Days of an Indian Girl," an autobiographical narrative by early-twentieth-century mixed-blood writer Zitkala-Sä, illustrates this transition from "whiteness" to "white" people.[28] Although they could analyze the ways Zitkala-Sä depicted her early life in Sioux culture and her entrance into the "white" world of missionary school, students seem reluctant to take this analysis further by speculating on what these might tell us about representations of literary and cultural "whiteness." Instead, they focused their attention on the representations of "white" human beings, who, they believed, were portrayed in a highly negative light: "Whites" were emotionally and spiritually cold, overly concerned with rules and order, rude, and entirely dismissive of indigenous American cultures, peoples, and beliefs. Given the historical content of Zitkala-Sä's narrative—the U.S. government's repeated attempts to forcibly remove, assimilate, reeducate, sterilize, and Christianize Native peoples—my students' desire to demonize Zitkala-Sä's textual representations of "whiteness" is not surprising. Yet they made almost no distinction between literary "whiteness" and "white" people. Instead, they created a simplistic binary opposition between "good Indians" and "bad whites."

Classroom interrogations of "whiteness" can become even more confusing when analyzing texts by "white" writers, especially when these texts include no explicit reference to "race." Take, for example, an analysis of "whiteness" in Emerson's "Self-Reliance." Do we assume that, because Emerson was "white" his writings give insight into literary "whiteness" and should be placed in a canon of "white" U.S. literature? After all, this practice of categorizing literature according to the author's "race" has played a pivotal role in constructing African American, Native American, and other ethnic-specific canons. But this approach has problematic consequences. Should we code key themes in "Self-Reliance"—such as the desire for independence, a sense of self-confidence, a feeling of spiritual connection with nature and the divine, or a belief in the importance of creating one's own community—as "white"? To do so leads to additional problems when we encounter these "white" themes in texts by writers of color. If, for example, the quest for independence and self-trust is coded as "white," should we suggest that in his *Narrative* Frederick Douglass becomes or acts "white" when he asserts his intellectual independence from Covey, or when he resolves to "trust no one"? To my mind, such assumptions do not facilitate understanding of the literature we read.

These attempts to interrogate "whiteness" lead to other problems as well. How, for example, do we separate "whiteness" from masculinity and other forms of privilege? Is it "whiteness," masculinity, "white" masculinity, or some other combination that allows Emerson,

Douglass, and Thoreau to attain remarkable levels of confidence and self-assertiveness in their prose? In class discussions of Emerson and Thoreau, several students assumed that both writers came from wealthy backgrounds and suggested that it was class privilege, rather than "whiteness," which enabled them to achieve self-reliance. Given the financial hardships both writers experienced at various points in their lives, this suggestion, while plausible, seems too simplistic.

My brief discussion of Zitkala-Sä, Emerson, Douglass, and Thoreau illustrates a few of the difficulties that can occur in classroom interrogation of "whiteness." To begin with, "whiteness" often becomes demonized and viewed as almost entirely evil and morally bankrupt, thus creating another binary between the good non-"whites" and the bad "whites." However, like all binary oppositions this dualism oversimplifies and conflates literary representations of "whiteness" and "white" people with real-life human beings classified as "white." Perhaps most importantly for my argument in the following pages, interrogations of "whiteness" and other racialized categories seem to confirm static concepts of identity which reinforce the already existing belief in entirely separate "races."

What I discovered from these classroom investigations of "whiteness" is that students' comments are generally based on the assumption that "race" is a permanent characteristic of U.S. life. In many ways, this perspective on "race" seems like common sense. After all, in the United States categorizing people by "race" has become an accepted way of comprehending and explaining ourselves and our world. Surveys, census forms, birth certificates, and job applications often ask us to identify ourselves according to our "race." Generally, we assume that physiological differences (in skin color, hair texture, and facial features, for instance) between the various so-called "races" indicate distinct underlying biological-genetic differences, differences implying permanent, "natural" divisions between disparate groups of people.

But, this commonly accepted view of "race" is far less accurate than most people realize. To begin with, the belief that each person belongs to only one "race" ignores many "biracial" and "multiracial" people living in this country. Indeed, the implicit belief in discrete, entirely separate "races" implies a false sense of racial purity, for we could all

197

be described as multiracial. As Michael Thornton points out, "there are no such things as pure races."[29] Spaniards, for example, are a mixture of "Black Africans, Gypsies (from India), and Semites (Jews, Arabs, and Phoenicians), as well as Romans, Celts, Germans, Greeks, Berbers, Basques, and probably more."[30] Furthermore, the suggestion that we can automatically identify ourselves with others according to "race" assumes that we are fully cognizant of our ancestry. However, as one of the characters in Pauline Hopkins's *Contending Forces* asserts,

It is an incontrovertible truth that there is no such thing as an unmixed black on the American continent. Just bear in mind that we cannot tell by a person's complexion whether he be dark or light in blood. . . . I will venture to say that out of a hundred apparently pure black men not one of them will be able to trace an unmixed flow of African blood since landing on these shores![31]

Similar comments can be made about people identified as "Latina," "Native American," or as members of any other so-called "race." Appearances can be extremely deceptive, and not one of us is "unmixed." Perhaps most importantly, this mythical perspective on discrete, biologically separate "races" relies on nineteenth-century pseudoscientific theories. As Kwame Anthony Appiah notes, "What most people in most cultures ordinarily believe about the significance of 'racial' difference" is not supported by scientific evidence. While biologists can interpret the data in various ways, they cannot demonstrate the existence of genetically distinct "races," for "human genetic variability between the populations of Africa or Europe or Asia is not that much greater than that within those populations."[32]

"Race" is an ambiguous, constantly changing concept that has little—if anything—to do with scientific descriptions; as Michael Omi and Howard Winant persuasively demonstrate, "The meaning of race is defined and contested throughout society, in both collective action and personal practice. In the process, racial categories themselves are formed, transformed, destroyed, and re-formed."[33] Yet we often proceed in our interrogations of "whiteness" and other racialized categories as if these "races" were permanent, unchanging categories of meaning. To return to the second half of my title, although the theorists of "whiteness" attempt to deconstruct "race," all too often they inadvertently reconstruct it by reinforcing fixed categories of racialized meanings. Theorists find it difficult not to conflate literary or cultural representations of "whiteness" with "white" people, and this perpetual reconstruction of separate "races" can be even more difficult to avoid in the classroom, where "whiteness"—generally played out in the context of racialized "black," "Indian," and other "colored" bodies—is associated only with "white" people.

Yet even a brief look at a few of the many ways racial groups have been redefined in this country illustrates how *unstable* and *artificial* racialized identities are. For instance, throughout the nineteenth century many U.S. state and federal agencies recognized only three "races," which they labeled "White," "Negro," and "Indian." Given the extremely diverse mixture of people living in the United States, this three-part classification was, to say the least, confusing. How were U.S. Americans of Mexican or Chinese descent to be described? Were they "White"? "Negro"? or "Indian"? The state of California handled this dilemma in a curious way: rather than expand the number of "races," the government retained the existing categories and classified Mexican Americans as a "white" population and Chinese Americans as "Indian." According to Omi and Winant, this decision had little to do with outward appearance; it was motivated by socioeconomic and political concerns, for it allowed the state to deny the latter group the rights accorded to people classified as "white."[34]

Since then, both groups have been redefined numerous times. U.S. Americans of Chinese descent have been classified as "Orientals," "Asians," "Asian Americans," "Pan Asians," and "Asian Pacific Americans." Yet these terms are inadequate and erroneously imply a homogeneity unwarranted by the many nationalities, geographical origins, languages, dialects, and cultural traditions supposedly contained within these politically motivated categories. As Yehudi Webster notes, these monolithic labels indicate the U.S. government's attempt to group "heterogeneous populations into one category on the basis of apparent similarities in skin color, hair type, and eye shape."[35] Efforts to classify U.S. Americans of Mexican ancestry have been equally unsuccessful. Even in the last forty years, they have been redefined sev-

199

eral times: In the 1950s and 1960s the government included them in an ethnic category labeled "Persons of Spanish Mother Tongue"; in the 1970s, they were redefined as "Persons of Both Spanish Surname and Spanish Mother Tongue"; and in the 1980s, the "Hispanic" category was created. This most recent government invention is especially confusing, for so many so-called "Hispanics" reject the term's association with Spanish ancestry and thus its "white" Eurocentric implications, as well as its erasure of their cultural specificity, and name themselves "Chicano/a," "Latino/a," "Cuban American," and so on. Indeed, in the 1990 census over 96 percent of the 9.8 million people who refused to identify themselves according to a particular race would have been classified by the government as "Hispanic."[36] As Omi and Winant observe, such changes "suggest the state's inability to 'racialize' a particular group—to institutionalize it in a politically organized racial system."[37]

The status of so-called "blacks" and "whites" is, perhaps, even more problematic. To begin with, the terms themselves are almost entirely inaccurate. "White" is the color of this paper, not the color of anyone's skin. And people referred to as "black" would be more accurately described as they are in Nella Larsen's *Quicksand*: as "taupe, mahogany, bronze, copper, gold, orange, yellow, peach, ivory, pinky white" or even "pastry white."[38] Furthermore, although many "Hispanics," "Native Americans," and "Asian Americans" have lighter skin than some so-called "whites," they are not classified as such unless they are passing.

Though we generally think of "white" and "black" as permanent, transhistorical racial markers indicating distinct groups of people, they are not. In fact, Puritans and other early European colonizers didn't consider themselves "white"; they identified as "Christian," "English," or "free," for at that time the word "white" didn't represent a racial category. Again, racialization was economically and politically motivated. It was not until around 1680, with the racialization of slavery, that the term was used to describe a specific group of people. As Yehudi Webster explains, "The idea of a homogeneous white race was adopted as a means of generating cohesion among explorers, migrants, and settlers in the eighteenth-century America. Its opposite was the black race, whose nature was said to be radically different from that of the white race." [39]

200

Significantly, then, the "white race" evolved in opposition to but simultaneously with the "black race." As peoples whose specific ethnic identities were Yoruban, Ashanti, Fon, and Dahomean were forcibly removed from their homes in Africa and taken to the North American colonies, the English adopted the terms "white" and "black"—with their already existing implications of purity and evil—and developed the concept of a superior "white race" and an inferior "black race" to justify slavery. It's important to note that the Europeans did not originally label the people who lived in Africa "black"; nor did they see them as evil savages. As Abdul JanMohamed explains, "Africans were perceived in a more or less neutral and benign manner before the slave trade developed; however, once the triangular trade became established, Africans were newly characterized as the epitome of evil and barbarity." [40]

The meanings of "black" and "white" are no more stable in the twentieth century than they were in the past. "Colored," "Negro," "black," "Afro-American," "African-American" (hyphenated), and "African American" (unhyphenated) all describe U.S. Americans of African descent. But these terms are not synonymous; each indicates a different racial identity with specific sociopolitical and cultural implications.[41] Although the term "white"—which has been used since the late seventeenth century to designate an elite group of people— seems more stable, its meaning has undergone equally significant changes. Many people today considered "white"—southern Europeans, light-skinned Jews, the Irish, and Catholics of European descent, for example—were most definitely *not* "white" in the eighteenth and nineteenth centuries. Since the late 1960s, with the rise of what Steven Steinberg calls "ethnic fever,"[42] the "white race" has undergone additional changes. Once again, the redefinition of "white" corresponded to shifts in the meaning of "black." As the Black Power movement developed an oppositional ideology to challenge existing definitions of "Negro," "white" ethnics began (re)claiming their European cultural "roots." Recently, conservative self-identified "whites" have attempted to redefine themselves as the new oppressed group. As Omi and Winant explain, the Far Right attempts "to develop a new white identity, to reassert the very meaning of *whiteness* which has been rendered unstable and unclear by the minority challenges of the 1960s."[43] This rearticulation of racialized identities continues today, in essays like hooks's "Loving Blackness as Political Resistance" (in her *Black Looks)* and in recent demands for as interrogation of "whiteness."

I have misgivings about this increased emphasis on "whiteness" and other racialized identities. Literary theorists who discuss representations of "race" rarely acknowledge the fluidity and the historical changes in the U.S. discourse on "race." Instead, they refer to "white," "black," "Indian," and other supposedly separate "races" as though these categories are permanent unchanging facts. What are the effects of continually reinforcing these fictionalized identities? Whose interests does this uphold? Whose does it harm? To be sure, increased racial discourse has served an extremely important purpose by enabling people of color to gain a sense of historical and sociopolitical agency. Thus Houston Baker describes a "race" as "a recently emergent, unifying, and forceful sign of difference *in the service* of the 'Other.'" He explains that for people of color, racial identities function as "an inverse discourse—talk designed to take a bad joke of 'race' . . . and turn it into a unifying discourse."[44] Although Baker acknowledges the destructive, fictionalized aspects of "race" (it is, after all, a "bad joke"), he maintains that African Americans and other so-called "minority" groups can reverse its negative implications and use racial discourse in affirmative ways. For example, by aligning themselves with other people of African descent, self-identified African Americans attempt to challenge oppressive definitions of the so-called "black race."

Yet such oppositional tactics are problematic, for they cannot challenge the assumptions underlying *all* references to "race." Even the highly affirmative talk of a black, or Chicano/a, or Native American racial identity reinforces already existing conceptions of "race," conceptions that have functioned historically to create hierarchical divisions based on false generalizations concerning physical appearance and other arbitrary characteristics. By thus reinforcing fictionalized identities, contemporary racialized discourse creates further divisions between people. As Henry Louis Gates Jr. points out,

> The sense of difference defined in popular usage of the term "race" has both described and *inscribed* difference of language, belief system, artistic tradition, and gene pool, as well as all sorts of supposedly natural attributes such as rhythm, athletic ability, cerebration, usury, fidelity, and so forth. The relation between "racial character" and these sorts of characteristics has been inscribed through tropes of race, lending the sanction of God, biology, or the natural order to even presumably biased descriptions of cultural tendencies and differences.[45]

This naturalized use of "race" is especially insidious, for it reifies the destructive stereotypes already circulating in U.S. culture. Despite the many historic and contemporary changes in racial categories, people generally treat "race" as an unchanging biological fact. Often, they make simplistic judgments and gross overgeneralizations based primarily on appearance. You know the stereotypes: "Blacks are more athletic, and boy can they dance"; "All whites are bigots"; "All Hispanics are hot-blooded." Indeed, even social scientists (who should know better) acknowledge the politically, economically motivated nature of racial formation yet discuss the "black race," "the Hispanic race," "the white race," and so on as if these supposed "races" were God-given facts. In so doing, they reinforce oppressive social systems and erect permanent barriers between supposedly separate groups of people. One of the most striking examples I've encountered can be found in the 1992 best-seller *Two Nations: Black and White, Separate, Hostile, and Unequal*. In his introduction Andrew Hacker describes "race" as a "human creation," not a fixed biological fact, and acknowledges that because people use the word in numerous ways, clear-cut definitions are impossible.[46] Yet throughout the book he continuously refers to the "black race" and the "white race" without complicating the terms. Indeed, I would argue that by downplaying the economic, cultural, and ethnic diversity found within each of these two "races," Hacker heightens and reifies the tension between them. Moreover, by focusing almost entirely on the "black"/"white" binary, Hacker reinforces the myth of racial purity and ignores the incredible diversity found in this country.

This simplistic binary between fixed definitions of "blackness" and "whiteness" occurs in literary interrogations of "whiteness" as well. Take, for example, Nielsen's exploration of "whiteness" in *Reading Race*. Unlike Morrison—who begins blurring the artificial boundaries between "blackness" and "whiteness" by exploring what "white" representations of "blackness" tell us about literary "whiteness"—Nielsen focuses almost entirely on "white" poets' racist stereotypes of "blacks." Although he acknowledges the fictional, contradictory nature of these "white" representations of "blackness," his constant focus on the stereotypes themselves inadvertently reifies the racist imagery he tries to undercut. This approach seems especially dangerous in the classroom where, as Sharon Stockton points out, "students tend to think in terms of stereotyped binary oppositions."[47] In classroom interrogations of "whiteness," Nielsen's method leads to overly generalized discussions of racist, bigoted "whites" and lazy, ignorant, inferior blacks. Moreover, by continually emphasizing racism, we risk giving students the pessimistic belief that racism is inevitable and racialized barriers will never be overcome. As Omi and Winant argue in their discussion of 1960s theories of institutionalized racism, "An overly comprehensive view of racism . . . potentially served as a self-fulfilling prophecy."[48]

Let me emphasize: I am not saying that we should adopt a "color-blind" approach and ignore the roles racist thinking has played in constructing "whiteness." To do so simply reinforces the increasingly popular but very false belief that "race" no longer matters in twentieth-century U.S. culture. Racism is deeply embedded in U.S. society, and students of all colors must be aware of its systemic nature. Nor can we analyze racialized dimensions of texts by writers of color without also explaining "whiteness," for this partial analysis reinforces the long-standing belief in "white" invisibility. However, instructors must be aware of the impact interrogations of "whiteness" can have on our students. Although self-identified students of color find it satisfying to see the "white" gaze which has marked them as "Other" turned back on itself, I question the long-term effectiveness of this reversal. As I have argued, such reversals inadvertently support existing stereotypes. Moreover, these reversals trigger a variety of unwelcome reactions in self-identified "white" students, reactions ranging from guilt to anger to withdrawal and despair. Instructors must be prepared to deal with these responses. The point is not to encourage feelings of personal responsibility for the slavery, decimation of indigenous peoples, land theft, and so on that occurred in the past. It is, rather, to enable students of all colors more fully to comprehend how these oppressive systems that began in the historical past continue misshaping contemporary conditions. Guilt-tripping plays no role in this process. Indeed, guilt functions as a useless, debilitating state of consciousness that reinforces the boundaries between apparently separate "races." When self-identified "white" students feel guilty, they become paralyzed, deny any sense of agency, and assume that their privileged positions in contemporary U.S. culture automatically compel them to act as "the oppressor."

The compromise I've arrived at—admittedly temporary and always open to further revision—entails a twofold approach where we explore the artificial, constantly changing nature of "black," "white," and other racialized identities without ignoring their concrete material effects. I select texts by Nella Larsen, Zora Neale Hurston, and Langston Hughes, where students can clearly see these racialized identities as transitional states. In the stories collected in Hughes's *The Ways of White Folks*, for instance, we see "black" people reconstructing themselves as "white," self-identified "blacks" who act exactly like "whites," and "white" people who act just like "blacks."[49] These stories, as well as other textual representations of passing, destabilize students' "common-sense" beliefs in racial purity and ahistorical, fixed "races." Another topic I've employed is the concept of cultural *mestizaje*. I borrow this term from Cuban literary and political movements where its usage indicates a profound challenge to existing racial categories. As Nancy Morejón explains, *mestizaje* transculturation defies static notions of cultural purity by emphasizing

the constant interaction, the transmutation between two or more cultural components with the unconscious goal of creating a third cultural identity . . . that is new and independent even though rooted

205

in the preceding elements. Reciprocal influence is the determining factor here, for no single element superimposes itself on another; on the contrary, each one changes into the other so that both can be transformed into a third. Nothing seems immutable. [qtd. Lionnett 15–16][50]

This idea of constant transformation and change provides an important alternative to the well-known stereotype of the "American" melting pot. Unlike the melting pot, which works to assimilate culturally specific groups with distinct traditions into indistinguishable "whites," *mestizaje* emphasizes the mutually constituted and constantly changing nature of all racialized identities.

Yet these tactics are only temporary measures. I'm still searching for more effective ways of incorporating interrogations of "whiteness" into classroom discussions. Ironically, what began as an interrogation of "whiteness" has turned into an interrogation of "race," and I have even *more* questions than I had when I began. On the one hand, I agree with Mercer and others who call for an examination of the ways "whiteness" has been socially constructed. Because "whiteness"— *whatever* it is, and I would argue that at this point no one really knows —has functioned as an oppressive, mythical norm that negates people (whatever their skin color) who do not conform to its standard—we need to understand and deconstruct it. On the other hand, I worry that this analysis simply reifies already existing hegemonic conceptions of "race." As Gates explains, "we carelessly use language in such a way as to *will* this sense of *natural* difference into our formulations. To do so is to engage in a pernicious act of language, one which exacerbates the complex problem of cultural or ethnic difference, rather than to assuage or redress it."[51]

As I see it, the problems with discussing "whiteness" and other racial categories without historicizing the terms and demonstrating the relational nature of all racialized identities include (but aren't limited to) the following. First, our conceptions of "race" are scientifically and historically inaccurate; they transform arbitrary distinctions between people into immutable, "natural," God-given facts. Second, constant references to "race" perpetuate the belief in separate peoples, monolithic identities, and stereotypes. Third, in this country racial discourse quickly degenerates into a "black"/"white" polarization that overlooks other so-called "races" and ignores the incredible diversity among people. And fourth, racial categories are not—and never have been—benign. Racial divisions were developed to create a hierarchy that grants privilege and power to specific groups of people while simultaneously oppressing and excluding others. If, as Gates implies in the first epigraph to my paper, "race" is a text that everyone in this country unthinkingly "reads," I want to suggest that we need to begin reading—and rewriting—this text in new ways. At the very least, we should complicate existing conceptions of "race"—both by exploring the many changes that have occurred in all apparently fixed racial categories and by informing students of the political, economic, and historical facts shaping the continual reinvention of "race."

Notes

1. Toni Morrison, *Playing in the Dark: Whiteness and the American Literary Imagination* (Cambridge: Harvard University Press, 1992), p. 12.

2. Henry Giroux and Peter McLaren, "Radical Pedagogy as Cultural Politica: Beyond the Discourse of Critique and Anti-Utopianism," in *Texts for Change Theory/ Pedagogy/Politics*, ed. Donald Morton and Mas'ud Zavarzadeh (Urbana: University of Illinois Press, 1991), p.160.

3. bell hooks, *Yearning: Race, Gender, and Cultural Politics* (Boston: South End Press, 1990), p. 54.

4. Kobena Mercer, "Skin Head Sex Thing: Racial Difference and the Homoerotic Imaginary," in How Do I Look? *Queer Film and Video*, ed. Bad Object-Choices (Seattle: Bay Press, 1991), p. 206.

5. Ibid. pp. 205–206.

6. Richard Dyer, "White," in *The Matter of Images: Essays on Representations* (New York: Routledge, 1993), p. 44.

7. Ibid., p. 142.

8. Ibid., p. 143.

9. Henry Giroux, "Post-Colonial Ruptures and Democratic Possibilities: Multiculturalism as Anti-Racist Pedagogy," *Cultural Critique* 21 (1992): 15.

10. Morrison, *Playing in the Dark*, pp. x–xi.

11. Dyer, "White," p. 141.

12. Ibid., p. 143.

13. Marilyn Frye, "White Woman Feminist," in *Willful Virgin: Essays in Feminism, 1976–1992* (Freedom, CA: Crossing, 1992), pp. 147–69.

14. Dyer,"White," p. 144

207

ANNLOUISE KEATING

15. Morrison, *Playing in the Dark*, p. 9.
16. Ibid., p. 11.
17. Aldon Lynn Nielsen, *Reading Race: White American Poets and the Racial Discourse in the Twentieth Century* (Athens: University of Georgia Press, 1988), p. 3.
18. Frye, "White Woman Feminist," p. 156.
19. Ibid., p. 155.
20. Dyer, "White," p. 146–48.
21. Morrison, *Playing in the Dark*, p. 68.
22. Ibid., p. 59.
23. Dyer, "White," p. 141.
24. Ibid., p. 157.
25. bell hooks, *Black Looks: Race and Representation* (Boston: South End Press, 1992), p. 170.
26. Frye, "White Woman Feminist," pp. 151–52, her emphasis.
27. Leslie Marmon Silko, *Ceremony* (New York: Penguin, 1977).
28. Zitkala-Sä [Gertrude Simmons Bonnin], "The School Days of an Indian Girl," *Atlantic Monthly* 85 (1900): 37–45.
29. Michael C. Thornton, "Is Multiracial Status Unique? The Personal and Social Experience," in *Racially Mixed People in America*, ed. Maria P. Root (Newbury Park, CA: Sage, 1992), p. 322.
30. Carlos A. Fernandez, "La Raza and the Melting Pot: A Comparative Look at Multiethnicity," in *Racially Mixed People,* ed. Maria P. Root (Newbury Park, CA: Sage, 1992), p. 143.
31. Pauline E. Hopkins, *Contending Forces: A Romance Illustrative of Negro Life North and South* (1900; reprint, New York: Oxford University Press, 1988), p. 151.
32. Kwame Anthony Appiah, "The Uncompleted Argument: Du Bois and the Illusion of Race," in *"Race," Writing, and Difference*, ed. Henry Louis Gates, Jr. (Chicago: University of Chicago Press, 1986), p. 21.
33. Michael Omi and Howard Winant, *Racial Formation in the United States from the 1960s to the 1980s* (Rev. ed., New York: Routledge, 1993), p. 61.
34. Ibid., p. 82.
35. Yehudi O. Webster, *The Racialization of America* (New York: St. Martin's Press, 1992), pp. 132–33.
36. Ibid., p. 143.
37. Omi and Winant, *Racial Formation,* p. 82.
38. Nella Larsen, *Quicksand and Passing* (1928; edited with an introduction by Deborah McDowell; reprint, New Brunswick: Rutgers University Press, 1986), p. 59.
39. Webster, *The Racialization of America,* p. 9.
40. Abdul R. JanMohamed, "The Economy of Manichean Allegory: The Function of Racial Difference in Colonialist Literature," in Gates, *"Race," Writing, and Difference,* pp. 78–106, 80.
41. Henry Louis Gates Jr., *Loose Canons: Notes on the Culture Wars* (New York: Oxford University Press, 1982), pp. 131–51.
42. Stephen Steinberg, *The Ethnic Myth: Race, Ethnicity, and Class in America* (1982; reprint with epilogue, Boston: Beacon, 1989), p. 3.

208

43. Omi and Winant, *Racial Formation,* p. 120.

44. Houston Baker, "Caliban's Triple Play," in Gates, *"Race," Writing, and Difference,* pp. 381–95, 386; his emphasis.

45. Gates, *"Race," Writing, and Difference,* p. 5.

46. Andrew Hacker, *Two Nations: Black and White, Separate, Hostile, and Unequal* (New York: Ballantine, 1992), p. 4.

47. Sharon Stockton, "'Blacks vs. Browns': Questioning the White Ground," *College English* 57 (1995): 70.

48. Omi and Winant, *Racial Formation,* p. 70.

49. Langston Hughes, *The Ways of White Folks* (1933; reprint, New York: Vintage, 1971).

50. Francoise Lionnett, *Autobiographical Voices: Race, Gender, Self-Portraiture* (Ithaca, NY: Cornell University Press, 1989), pp. 15–16.

51. Gates, op. cit., his emphasis.

LYING THROUGH OUR TEETH?

The Quagmire of Cultural Diversity

Trudier Harris
The University of North Carolina at Chapel Hill

This is a practical commentary. It will present no highfalutin' theoretical constructs to be considered as I invite you to ponder the issue of diversifying your teaching. No day-to-day plan for what you should do in the classroom. No list of authors for you to consider including. It will present some situations that will raise questions, some questions that might encourage you to think, and a few examples that might prove helpful as reference points for your teaching.

I don't think any sensitive instructor who teaches today is unaware of the national and international impetus to pursue diversity and multiculturalism, which increasingly is being manifested as international studies. Cultural diversity is all the rage, and as we used to sing in elementary school, "The world is getting littler every day,/ Soon there won't be many places far away./ You can take a train in China and end up in Carolina/ or in London or in San Francisco Bay./ We'll soon be one world, one world, nations great and small, one world, one world, all for one and one for all." When we add to this diminishing psychological and physical distance the fact that colored peoples make up more than 70 percent of the world's population, it behooves those who are not colored to find ways of dealing with colored people—and colored people must find ways of dealing with the primarily white power brokers of the world.

When I was considering how to approach this topic, I started to use the word *myth* instead of *quagmire*. I selected quagmire because the topic is embattled enough without becoming defeatist before we begin; myth presupposes that we have an awareness that our efforts are doomed to fail before we start, and we just go about politely spinning our wheels. On the more entangled side, I can't resist asking, however, "OK, y'all, who're we kidding? Is diversity really what we want?" Now the word "quagmire" suggests that things might be muddy and difficult, but at least we're willing to work together to find ways of getting ourselves out of the quicksand of separatism and into serious discussion about what we want in culturally diverse curricula and student body populations.

We're still putting the cart in front of the horse, though, or letting the tail wag the dog. And that brings us to the "lying through our teeth" part. Are we guilty of lip service to diversity without being willing to make the necessary commitments to bring about the reality? Being fashionable is easy; far more difficult is getting into the trenches and bringing about the changes a volume like this is supposedly working toward. We can work at a polite level to achieve diversity, or at the nitty-gritty level, as folks on the streets would say. We can sit around and pontificate about the space we need to give to nonwhite, non-Western writers in our literature classes, and we can applaud ourselves when we add Ralph Ellison's *Invisible Man* or Toni Morrison's *The Bluest Eye* to a previously European American literature class, and we can pat ourselves on the back for sympathizing with the plights of the characters in Richard Wright's *Uncle Tom's Children*, but that is barely scratching the surface of what being culturally diverse means. If the compartmentalized, emotional empathy is all we can provide in the way of appreciating difference, then surely we have failed our purpose. I would assert, then, that adding works by African Americans and other people of color to our curricula is merely the dress rehearsal for what cultural diversity is all about. That is, merely emphasizing the polite level of difference.

If we add fifty black writers to English department curricula, would that really change how we perceive African Americans? Would it eliminate words such as "nigger," "buck," and "coon" from the national vocabulary? If we added fifty Hispanic or Asian American, or fifty Native American writers to the same departments, would that eliminate words such as "spic" or "gook" from our society? Would it encourage us to call the Atlanta baseball team something other than "Braves," or make the Cleveland one something other than "Indians"? Would it make us realize that we are perpetuating national stereotypes of Native Americans as warrior savages—unbeaten and unbeatable? Of course, if you follow Atlanta's fate—except for 1995—you realize that the name and the myth (or stereotype) were separated a long time ago. Nonetheless, we persist in maligning a variety of Native American peoples and cultures all in the name of our perceptions of a mythological American history.

If we would get down to the nitty-gritty of our cultural diversity, therefore, we have to begin to transform our perceptions of the world we live in and the people who share it with us. Let me take one of the so-called classic literary works to illustrate my point. In 1952, Ralph Ellison's *Invisible Man* was published. In 1965, a panel of two hundred critics, authors, and editors judged it to be the best American novel to have been published in the preceding twenty years. If any novel has made it into the canons of American literature, *Invisible Man* has done so. It's the Jackie Robinson of the literary hard hitters, having gone across the color bar into territory where no novel by a black American had ever gone. Teachers pointed proudly to the fact that they could see the structure of an Odyssean journey in the book, so therefore Ellison wasn't writing exclusively about black culture, but he had joined hands with the great international, universal adventure, whatever the heck that is. So we could talk about the wonderful Greek structure of the novel and Ellison's kinship in the use of myth and legend to T. S. Eliot. We could speak of his American (read white) kinship to Mark Twain, Ralph Waldo Emerson, and Ernest Hemingway (to whom he refers as his literary "ancestors"). And we could send our students off to do wonderful little comparative papers about how Ellison fit into traditions that were much larger than that of the black American experience. We felt good about it. We had validated Ellison in terms of white Western traditions. We could be smug about having taught a novel by a black American writer, and we were prepared to go to war against anyone who asserted that we had done less than our duty.

Well, I'd like to say that we hadn't done very much. We were presumptuous enough to think that Ellison had to be read on somebody else's cultural terms, not on the primarily African American terms that are his own. The question becomes, then, what would have been required in that teaching situation for us to appreciate the diversity that Ellison's novel brings to the landscape of American literature? How can we fully appreciate Ellison's novel, for example, without first acquiring at least a smattering of knowledge about jazz and its practitioners? The underlying theme of the novel is "What did I do to be so black and blue?" What did Louis Armstrong mean by that question? How did the song get composed? What personal and communal history did it reflect in the 1920s? And why did Ellison choose it as the thematic unifying structure for a novel written in the 1940s and published in the 1950s? Since jazz requires listening, how much time are we willing to spend listening to get a sense of the experience the narrator tries to portray in words in the prologue to the novel? And how do we move from polite understanding on the page to the nitty-gritty of black life?

If we really want to know what the jazz experience means, perhaps we would take our students to a jazz set in a black club—or a mostly black one—to allow them the opportunity to get a feel for the music in its context. There they could rub elbows with people who are not like them, but from whom the impetus for a great novel came. There the smoke is thick, the vocal interactions loud, and status is negotiated on the basis of performance, not on the basis of color. There the booze flows, and someone might look at us strangely, but ultimately no one is going to eat us alive or kill us, and we can learn a lot about the musical traditions that gave shape to Ellison's novel. For not only is the prologue saturated with jazz and blues, but the entire composition might be viewed as a blues piece. Being black and blue is also the condition of the blues, the blues that the invisible man has because he cannot return to college, the blues he has when he is jobless, the blues he has when he ends up in the hole in Harlem and realizes that his enemies and presumed friends have been one and the same. Will we allow our students to get to know the blues tradition, not only from records, but from living practitioners? True understanding of diversity can come only when we move across barriers that history and custom have put in our way.

To appreciate the cultural difference in *Invisible Man*, the reader must know the folk tradition that goes beyond the music, the tradition that goes into black churches and onto street corners where the voice is the major instrument of communication and again where status is linked to performance, not color. When we read Homer A. Barbee's sermon on the founder, or the invisible man's speech on "No more Dispossessing of the Dispossessed," or Tod Clifton's sales spiel on the street corner, we are reading material creatively drawn from vibrant verbal patterns in African American communities. We need to bring taped sermons into the classroom, or tapes of Muhammad Ali's harangues of his opponents, for what we read of in the novel is the tradition of the man- or woman-of-words in African American communities. The vibrancy of that tradition cannot be felt in those little black squiggles on the white page; students need to see and hear the living counterparts. So why don't we take our students to African American church services? It would give them the opportunity to witness the call-and-response pattern that informs all of the speeches in Ellison's novel. It would give them the opportunity to witness the relationship between the individual and the community that informs the man-of-words tradition, as well as the jazz and blues tradition.

African American churches are some of the most welcoming institutions in our society. Members love to have visitors; they usually recognize them in a grand style and pay special attention to them (with handshaking, songs, and other interaction). Encouraging your students to put themselves in such environments has important by-products. They can see an institution where black people are totally in charge. They can see a transformation between black folks who take the garbage out of hallowed halls of institutions like the ones they attend and what those same people are like in their churches. Mind you, now, I am not talking about your students going in and simply being gawking spectators. Certainly going to a black church will be a learning experience for them, but it will also give those in the church an opportunity to change their perceptions of this monolith called "white people." A word of advice if you take your students to black churches—black folks generally dress up when they go to church; they traditionally do not wear pants or casual clothing. Appreciation of diversity comes in respecting other people's traditions, and I have seen enough white folks in pants in black churches to offer this advice. Also, black church services are participatory; that is the whole purpose for understanding the call-and-response tradition. So when your students go, instead of gawking, they should sing along with the congregation (even if they sing off-key), make a genuine effort to participate, for participation is one of the ways we can begin to break down the barriers to diversity.

Now let's think about food. Cultural critic Bernard Wolfe argues that the entire Brer Rabbit series of stories is based on a search for a communal meal between blacks and whites in the South. Brer Rabbit is always coming up with schemes to take food because he is searching for a true statement of diversity, for, as Toni Cade Bambara asserts, when people can sit down and eat together across races and cultures, that is at least the beginning of a willingness to accept difference. I was in Egypt in 1980 and received an invitation to dine at the home of an army major and his wife. The woman, who was scheduled to enter the doctoral program at the University of North Carolina, must have cooked for at least two days in preparation for me and my brother and his family. Well, the first course for that meal was something green, slightly lighter in color than green peppers, that had been made into a cold soup. It was seriously slimy, sort of like a long string of mashed okra that would cling from the spoon as it went up to my mouth all the way back down to the bowl. I can't remember the taste, but I do remember the psychological experience. It was hard to get the stuff down simply because of the texture and the look of it. But when I looked at the table, which also included roast turkey—her bowing to our Western tastes—then I had no choice but to make my little gesture at diversity. I obviously survived, and I learned a bit more about Egyptian culture.

You will remember the scene in *Invisible Man* in which the narrator goes into a diner and the waiter insists that he looks like a man who will appreciate the special, which is composed of "pork chops, grits, one egg, hot biscuits and coffee."[1] Well, the narrator is offended because he thinks the waiter labels him as backward and Southern and identifies these foods as soul food. Obviously the poor narrator is deluded, but the scene does make the point about the value of appreciating diversity in food tastes across races and cultures. The yam scene is another instance of this. Perhaps one outing for your students as you are studying the novel, therefore, would be a trip to a black-owned restaurant, or at least to one that serves a preponderance of food identified as soul food. For folks who are accustomed to having orange juice, toast, and coffee for breakfast, and London broil for dinner, the experience of chitterlings will undoubtedly be strikingly different. With their taste buds as witnesses, and a bit of history on the kinds of foods that black people were routinely given during slavery and what kinds of meats were most readily available to them for decades after slavery, your students might begin to understand the significance of the invisible man's bid to humiliate Bledsoe by whipping him with chitterlings.

My examples essentially serve to support the same point. Diversity cannot simply be a classroom experience; it cannot be limited to the mixing of texts and discussions. It must be more than that. It must mean the breaking down of one of the last bastions of separatism, which is a social interaction. How can we profess to understand each other if we never socialize together? If we never shop together, or go to the movies together, or play cards together? If we never chastise each other for wrongheaded opinions we hold, or demand that we live up to the very best that we can be? How can we know each other if we never treat each other as human beings? Just think to yourself, when was the last time that you voluntarily interacted socially with a person of another race or culture? And not because that person was in a class and you were having the traditional end-of-the-semester meal, not because it was a business luncheon, or a committee meeting over breakfast or dinner, but because you *wanted* to, because you *genuinely enjoyed* that person's company and conversation?

Will we continue to travel to Kenya, Nigeria, and India for examples of the exotic, and lord it over the indigenous peoples in those countries, instead of truly getting to know the people of different races and cultures in our own backyards? I spent six years as a faculty member at the College of William and Mary in Virginia, and the first couple of years I must have gone to four or five reception/cocktail type gatherings a week. It always amazed me that not once, in all that martini consumption, did one of my hosts or hostesses think to invite another black human being. And they weren't overly interested in me; they usually resorted to what I call the "colored conversation." It goes something like this: see a black person at a cocktail party, go up to him or her and talk about something black—perhaps (these days) the Martin Lawrence show, or Harvey Gantt's bid for the U.S. Senate, or Spike Lee's *Get on the Bus*. The impetus for the "colored conversation" is either a misguided liberalism, or an "oh, here's a poor colored person by herself; I must do something to make her feel at home." I haven't decided which.

But the beyond-the-classroom interactions cut both ways with students as well. We hear tales of white students sharing rooms with black students and interacting with them perfectly fine in the privacy of their quarters. But when they cross campus or enter classrooms, the white students conveniently pretend not to know or at least not to see the black students. And African American students have been guilty of the same thing. And I heard of a case recently where black women on a predominantly white college campus forbade the women in a white sorority from stepping with the men in a black fraternity. [For those of you who don't know what stepping is, I will explain: it's an intricate, syncopated dance/ song/ rhythmic foot movement routine that brings waves of applause and approval from audiences. It requires extensive practice, and the performances, when well done, are an art. Black fraternities and sororities even have a national step competition, which has been the subject of a report on National Public Radio.] Now what do we do with something like that? If we are truly talking about effecting diversity, what do we do? Can we afford to allow black students to create their own little police station of public opinion, which will ostracize anyone who goes against the grain of what they espouse? Who are the students who will take the initiative to defy custom and tradition, to do something different? Keep in mind that if somebody hadn't defied custom and tradition, black people in this country

217

would probably still be in slavery. And I certainly wouldn't be writing this commentary.

In terms of the students as well, there's the old, old issue of who gets called on in class when material is being covered that has to do with some of the other folks, like black folks. If the class has one black student, that person is frequently made into the expert on things black. So all the "why do black people do so and so?" questions get directed at that individual. As has been pointed out by numerous observers, not only is that unfair to the student, but it excuses the teacher from assuming responsibility for expertise about the material he or she brings to the classroom.

The issue of expertise has other dimensions to it as well. Frequently when nonblack faculty members add the Ellison novel to their class, they then find a resident colored teacher (or they import one) to teach the novel for them. So why do they add the novel to their class? They haven't been transformed in any way. They haven't worked to study *Invisible Man* and let it make a difference in their intellectual experience. I cannot recount to you the number of times that I have been a guest lecturer in classes of my colleagues and watched them take notes as furiously as their students. I should have received part of their paychecks for that month, because I did double time in their classes.

A word of caution here. I am not suggesting that African Americans should not lecture for their nonblack colleagues. What I am suggesting is that those lectures should not become the excuse for the white or other nonblack teacher not doing his or her own homework on the novel. Then there can be an exchange of equals when you get to the question-and-answer session, instead of one faculty member lecturing another in addition to lecturing the class.

What I resist is this pervasive notion that black professors, teachers, and critics have some nebulous gestalt that enables them to understand African American texts infinitely better than their nonblack colleagues. Presumably any one of us who went through reputable graduate programs should have some acquaintance with analytical skills, and presumably nonblack people in the United States have some acquaintance with African American culture. I say presumably because I obviously get surprised on this a lot. Certainly I, as a black professor of folklore and literature, have been saturated with those scholarly traditions for almost twenty-five years. And certainly I grew up knowing Brer Rabbit stories that nonblacks may have read only in their adult lives, so that may give me some edge in knowing how those stories function within the culture and in discussion of that culture. But, and this is a big BUT, I did not grow up in England being saturated with the tradition of Shakespeare. Nor did I grow up in New England or Maryland being saturated with the traditions that shaped Hawthorne, Melville, and Poe. Yet, as a *trained* literature professor, I am as competent to discuss those authors and works as I am to discuss the works of Ralph Ellison, Toni Morrison, and Alice Walker. Why can't nonblack professors, then, who have achieved a book-learning response to Ellison, Morrison, and Walker, feel as competent to discuss them as I do to discuss British and New England writers?

Face it, colleagues, the numbers of black faculty who can be hired on any college or university or in any other school in America will always be minimal. Does that mean you cut all courses out of the curriculum that deal with African American culture because white folks don't have the necessary spiritual gestalt to teach them? If that's the way you feel, we're in deep, deep trouble. Simple demographics tell us that the numbers of black students going to graduate school is dismal, and those going into the humanities is even more dismal. So do we put the entire creative output of a people on hold because we don't have any of them to teach it? Obviously to do so would be absurd. The majority of the doctoral students I train at the University of North Carolina at Chapel Hill to do what I do are not black; yet, I want the work of black writers and critics to be discussed in the twenty-first and twenty-second centuries and well beyond that. So I train willing disciples. I train people with good minds to do the work that I do. And those of you who are in the process of retraining yourselves to add works and perspectives of African Americans to your classes, I wish you speed and success. We never assert that only French people can teach French, or only British folks can teach English literature; in fact, we are still so colonized over here that most of us teach in the departments where a substantial number, if not most, of our requirements for the undergraduate major are in British literature. But we Americans hap-

219

pily continue to teach it. And we never assert that only scraggly bearded, linty pants, squinty-eyed, bespectacled, absentminded people should teach mathematics. We measure such people on the basis of competence. In like fashion we have to conclude that competent non-black people are going to be treating African American materials in their classrooms for a long time to come.

I mean, let's be serious. Publishers do not go in for money-losing ventures. And a quick check of any *Books in Print* will reveal that the numbers of volumes currently available by and about black people is probably at an all-time high. Major publishers are not keeping those books in print because they expect only black teachers to use the books. So clearly the market is driven by other forces and factors. And those factors are simply that the materials have intrinsic worth, more and more black and nonblack people are discovering that worth, and they are designing their courses accordingly.

A white professor came up to me at a summer institute in 1991 and asked what I thought of his teaching African American literature. He came from a small college where there are no black faculty members, yet he felt the need to teach Langston Hughes's poetry to his students. And not only did he teach it, but, inspired by current rap trends, he decided to "perform" some of the poetry. Well, he had this image in his head of this white guy reciting the blues in this dramatic way before a class of black and white students. Was it all right, he wondered, if he did that? Well, I had to give him my spiel about French people teaching French. Then I suggested to him that if students responded negatively to his imitation of black folk speech and blues rhythm, he should use the occasion to discuss language—the value of language in society, what it means to have a prestige dialect, what it means to have a nonprestige dialect, and to get his students to understand that everyone speaks a dialect; it's just that some are more valued than others. And once he got past the language business, then perhaps he could also bring some blues records into the classroom, or some recordings of Langston Hughes discussing his poetry, or whatever other helpful aids he could identify.

Who teaches what, who has expertise, is obviously one issue. How the works gets taught is another. Even as I recognize that more and more nonblack people are going to be teaching black works, that does not give them license to be stupid. You know, where they could make all kinds of generalized assertions about black people. It certainly behooves any sane teacher to make sure that he or she is as broadminded as possible in dealing with the works. If you teach Charles W. Chesnutt's *The Conjure Woman* and conclude that all black people are superstitious, then you haven't accomplished much. If you teach Alice Walker's *The Color Purple* and indict all black men for their kinship with Albert and presume that they abuse black women, then you haven't accomplished much. Some kind of sensitivity must go with the territory, the willingness to go where the literature takes you without making egregious interpretive side roads on the journey.

More and more, too, as new generations of African American students are discovering their heritage, and as there is much discussion of schools that enroll only black males, the need will increasingly arise for an Afrocentric perspective on the works you discuss. And I would contend that that is the kind of perspective my examples bring to *Invisible Man.* The assumption is that you start with the culture that spawned the work, not with other cultures that might simply have an evaluative reaction to it. And you will be called upon to explain why black folks don't appear in some places on the American literary landscape, especially when they were (and are) so prominent on the physical landscape.

As Toni Morrison argued in the Tanner lecture she delivered at the University of Michigan in 1988 (which, in spite of a sprained ankle and an encounter with a policeman, I drove students from my seminar at Ohio State to hear), the issue is not that nineteenth-century white American authors did not include blacks prominently in their works, but how, under the circumstances of their lives, they managed that effacement. But, let Morrison speak for herself:

> We can agree, I think, that invisible things are not necessarily "not-there"; that a void may be empty, but is not a vacuum. In addition, certain absences are so stressed, so ornate, so planned, they call attention to themselves; arrest us with intentionality and purpose, like neighborhoods that are defined by the population held away from them. Looking at the scope of American literature, I can't help think-

221

ing that the question should never have been "Why am I, an Afro-American, absent from it?" It is not a particularly interesting query anyway. The spectacularly interesting question is "What intellectual feats had to be performed by the author or his critics to erase me from a society seething with my presence, and what effect has that performance had on the work?" What are the strategies of escape from knowledge? Of willful oblivion?[2]

Do we ourselves continue to escape from knowledge and encourage our students to do so, or do we welcome the diversity of the twenty-first century by preparing for it now, by dealing with the Afrocentric as well as the Eurocentric, the uncomfortable as well as the complimentary? I tell my students that my classrooms are open to practically any discussion. All I ask is that people make reasonably sane comments. That was difficult in a recent session of my folklore class, where all the black students wanted to tell the white students that they hated those McDonald's commercials where black people are rapping, singing, and dancing, and all the white folks were telling the black folks that they should be proud that somebody appreciated their culture enough to want to use it in commercials. We had to do a little eye-opening work on both sides. I'm not sure that any minds were changed, but at least the students got a chance to hear dramatically divergent viewpoints.

We cannot escape from the world in which we live. It is indeed getting littler every day. But it is a littleness with depth—for all the convolution of distance and geography, we have the depths of learning left to explore. Perhaps we can begin to come up with some interesting ways in which to achieve that objective.

Notes

1. Ralph Ellison, *Invisible Man* (New York: Random House, 1952), p. 135.
2. Toni Morrison, "Unspeakable Things Unspoken: The Afro-American Presence in American Literature," *Michigan Quarterly Review* 28:1 (Winter 1989): pp. 11–12.

❇ 13 ❇

SELECTED BIBLIOGRAPHY
FOR TEACHING
AFRICAN AMERICAN LITERATURE

Compiled by Sharon Pineault-Burke
and Jennifer R. Novak

This bibliography is far from exhaustive, but we do think it offers a good starting point for teaching African American literature and, we hope, a multitude of possibilities for the classroom. Our aim was to suggest a range of African American primary and secondary sources that would help teachers gain a sense of the rich traditions and contexts out of which the literature emerges.

I. POETRY

Individual Collections

Alexander, Elizabeth. *The Venus Hottentot.* Charlottesville, VA: University Press of Virginia, 1990.

Angelou, Maya. *The Complete Collected Poems of Maya Angelou.* New York: Random House, 1994.

———. *Phenomenal Woman: Four Poems Celebrating Women.* New York: Random House, 1994.

Aubert, Alvin. *Harlem Wrestler: and Other Poems.* East Lansing: Michigan State University Press, 1995.

———. *If Winter Come: Collected Poems, 1967–1992.* Pittsburgh: Carnegie Mellon University Press, 1994.

Baraka, Amiri Imanu. *Black Magic: Sabotage, Target Study, Black Art; Collected Poetry, 1961-1967.* Indianapolis: Bobbs-Merrill, 1969.

———. *Funklore: New Poems, 1984–1995.* Ed. by Paul Vangelisti. Los Angeles: Littoral Books, 1996.

———. *Selected Poetry of Amiri Baraka/LeRoi Jones.* New York: William Morrow, 1979.

223

Braithwaite, William Stanley. *The William Stanley Braithwaite Reader*. Ed. by Philip Butcher. Ann Arbor: University of Michigan Press, 1972.

Brooks, Gwendolyn. *To Disembark*. Chicago: Third World Press, 1981.

———. *Selected Poems*. New York: Harper & Row, 1963.

———. *A Street in Bronzeville*. New York: Harper & Brothers, 1945.

Brown, Sterling Allen. *The Collected Poems of Sterling A. Brown*. Ed. by Michael S. Harper. Evanston, IL: TriQuarterly Books, 1996.

Clifton, Lucille. *Good News About the Earth*. New York: Random House, 1972.

Cullen, Countee. *My Soul's High Song: The Collected Writings of Countee Cullen, Voice of the Harlem Renaissance*. Ed. with an introduction by Gerald L. Early. New York: Doubleday, 1991.

Dunbar, Paul Laurence. *The Collected Poetry of Paul Laurence Dunbar*. Ed. by Joanne M. Braxton. Charlottesville: University Press of Virginia, 1993.

———. *The Complete Poems of Paul Laurence Dunbar*. New York: Dodd, Mead, 1980.

Dove, Rita. *Grace Notes: Poems*. New York: Norton, 1989.

———. *Mother Love: Poems*. New York: Norton, 1995.

———. *The Yellow House on the Corner: Poems*. Pittsburgh: Carnegie Mellon University Press, 1989.

Evans, Mari. *A Dark and Splendid Mass*. New York: Harlem River Press, 1992.

———. *I Am A Black Woman*. New York: William Morrow, 1970.

Giovanni, Nikki. *Black Feeling, Black Talk, Black Judgment*. New York, William Morrow, 1970.

———. *Racism 101*. New York: William Morrow, 1994.

———. *The Selected Poems of Nikki Giovanni*. New York: William Morrow, 1996.

Hammon, Jupiter. *America's First Negro Poet; The Complete Works of Jupiter Hammon of Long Island*. Ed. with an introduction by Stanley Austin Ransom Jr. Port Washington, N. Y.: I. J. Friedman Division, Kennikat, 1983.

Harper, Frances E. W. *The Complete Poems of Frances E. W. Harper*. Ed. by Maryemma Graham. New York: Oxford University Press, 1988.

Harper, Michael S. *Dear John, Dear Coltrane: Poems*. Pittsburgh: University of Pittsburgh Press, 1970.

Hayden, Robert Earl. *Collected Poems*. Ed. by Frederick Glaysher. New York: Liveright, 1985.

———. *Selected Poems*. New York: October House, 1966.

Hughes, Langston. *The Collected Poems of Langston Hughes*. Ed. by Arnold Rampersad. New York: Knopf: dist. by Random House, 1994.

Jackson, Angela. *Dark Legs and Silk Kisses: The Beatitudes of the Spinners*. Evanston, IL: Northwestern University Press, 1993.

Johnson, Georgia Douglas. *The Heart of a Woman and Other Poems*. Freeport, NY: Books for Libraries Press, 1971.

———. *Bronze*. Boston: B. J. Brimmer, 1922.

Johnson, James Weldon. *Black Manhattan*. New York: Da Capo Press, 1991

———. *The Selected Writings of James Weldon Johnson*. Ed. by Sondra Kathryn Wilson. New York: Oxford University Press, 1995.

Jordan, June. *Things That I Do in the Dark: Selected Poems*. New York: Random House, 1977.

Kendrick, Dolores. *Women of Plums*. New York: William And Morrow, 1989.

Knight, Etheridge. *The Essential Etheridge Knight*. Pittsburgh: University of Pittsburgh Press, 1986.

Lane, Pinkie Gordon. *Girl at the Window: Poems*. Baton Rouge: Louisiana State University Press, 1991.

Lorde, Audre. *The Marvelous Arithmetics of Distance: Poems 1987–1992*. New York: Norton, 1993.

———. *Undersong: Chosen Poems Old and New*. New York: Norton, 1992.

Madgett, Naomi Cornelia Long. *Remembrances of Spring: Collected Early Poems*. East Lansing: Michigan State University Press, 1993.

Major, Clarence. *The Cotton Club; New Poems*. Detroit: Broadside Press, 1972.

———. *Symptoms and Madness; Poems*. New York: Corinth Books, 1971.

McKay, Claude. *The Dialect Poetry of Claude McKay: Two Volumes in One*. Salem, NH: Ayers, 1987.

Miller, E. Ethelbert. *First Light: New and Selected Poems*. Baltimore, MD: Black Classic Press, 1994.

———. *Where Are the Love Poems For Dictators?* Illustrated by Carlos Arrien. Washington, D.C.: Open Hand Publishing, c1986.

Osbey, Brenda Marie. *In These Houses*. Middletown, CT: Wesleyan University Press, 1988.

Reed, Ishmael. *Conjure: Selected Poems, 1963–1970*. Amherst: University of Massachusetts Press, 1972.

———. *New and Collected Poems*. New York: Atheneum, 1988.

Rodgers, Carolyn M. *Songs of a Black Bird*. Chicago: Third World Press, 1969.

Rushin, Kate. *The Black Back-Ups*. Ithaca, NY: Firebrand Books, 1993.

Sanchez, Sonia. *I've Been a Woman: New and Selected Poems*. Sausalito, CA: Black Scholar Press, 1978.

———. *Generations: Poetry, 1969–1985*. London: Karnak House, 1986.

Tolson, Melvin B. *Libretto For The Republic Of Liberia*. New York: Collier Books, 1970, c1953.

———. *A Gallery of Harlem Portraits*. Columbia: University of Missouri Press, 1979.

Toomer, Jean. *The Collected Poems of Jean Toomer*. Ed. by Robert B. Jones and Margery Toomer Latimer. Chapel Hill: University of North Carolina Press, 1988.

———. *Essentials*. Ed. by Rudolph P. Byrd. Athens, GA: University of Georgia Press, 1991.

———. *Cane*. New York: Liveright, 1975, c1923.

Walcott, Derek. *Collected Poems: 1948–1984*. New York: Farrar, Straus & Giroux, 1986.

———. *Omeros*. New York: The Noonday Press; Farrar, Straus & 1992, c1990.

———. *Rendezvous with America*. New York: Dodd, Mead, 1944.

Walker, Alice. *Good Night, Willie Lee, I'll See You in the Morning: Poems*. New York: Dial Press, c1979.

———. *Revolutionary Petunias & Other Poems*. New York: Harcourt Brace Jovanovich, 1973.

Walker, Margaret. *This Is My Century: New and Collected Poems*. Athens: University of Georgia Press, 1989.

———. *For My People*. Salem, NH: Ayer, 1990.

Wheatley, Phillis. The Collected Works of Phillis Wheatley. Ed. with an essay by John C. Shields. New York: Oxford University Press, 1988.

———. *Memoir and Poems of Phillis Wheatley*. Salem, NH: Ayer, 1988.

Williams, Sherly Anne. *The Peacock Poems*. Middletown, CT: Wesleyan University Press, 1975.

Wright, Jay. *Selected Poems of Jay Wright*. Edited with an introduction by Robert B. Stepto; afterword by Harold Bloom. Princeton, NJ: Princeton U P, c1987.

Anthologies

Adoff, Arnold, ed. *I Am the Darker Brother: An Anthology of Modern Poems by Negro Americans*. New York: Macmillan, 1968.

Bontemps, Arna Wendell, ed. *American Negro Poetry*. New York: Hill and Wang, 1974.

Cullen, Countee, ed. *Caroling Dusk; An Anthology of Verse by Negro Poets*. New York and London: Harper & Brothers, 1927.

Harper, Michael, and Anthony Walton, eds. *Every Shut Eye Ain't Asleep*. Boston: Little Brown, 1994.

Honey, Maureen, ed. *Shadowed Dreams: Women's Poetry of The Harlem Renaissance*. New Brunswick, NJ: Rutger University Press, 1989.

Jackson, Bruce. *Get Your Ass in the Water and Swim Like Me: Narrative Poetry from Black Oral Tradition*. Cambridge, MA: Harvard University Press, 1974.

Johnson, James Weldon, ed. *The Book of American Negro Poetry*. San Diego: Harcourt Brace Jovanovich, 1983, c1931.

Major, Clarence, ed. *The Garden Thrives: An Anthology of Contemporary African American Poetry*. New York: HarperPerennial, 1996.

Miller, E. Ethelbert, ed. *In Search of Color Everywhere: A Collection of African-American Poetry*. Illustrated by Terrance Cummings. New York: Stewart, Tabori & Chang, 1994.

Randall, Dudley, ed. *The Black Poets*. New York: Bantam Books, 1972, c1971.

Redmond, Eugene, ed. *Griefs of Joy: An Anthology of Contemporary Afro-American Poetry for Students*. East St. Louis, IL: Black River Writers, 1977.

Robinson, William H., ed. *Early Black American Poets: Selections with Biographical and Critical Introductions*. Dubuque, IA: William C. Brown, 1969.

Sherman, Joan R., ed. *African American Poetry of the Nineteenth Century*. Chicago: University of Illinois Press, 1992.

———. *Collected Black Women's Poetry*. 4 vols. Schomburg Library of Nineteenth Century Black Women Writers. New York: Oxford University Press, 1988.

Stetson, Erlene, ed. *Black Sister: Poetry by Black American Women, 1746–1980*. Bloomington: Indiana University Press, 1981.

Taft, Jr. Michael, comp. *Blues Lyric Poetry: An Anthology*. New York: Garland, 1983.

Ward, Jerry W., ed. *Trouble the Water: 250 Years of African American Poetry*. New York: Mentor Books, 1997.

II. OTHER ASPECTS OF THE ORAL TRADITION

Abrahams, Roger D., ed. *Afro-American Folktales: Stories From Black Traditions in the New World*. New York: Pantheon, 1985.

Brewer, J. Mason, ed. *American Negro Folklore*. Chicago: Quadrangle, 1968.

Brown, Carolyn S. *The Tall Tale in American Folklore and Literature*. Knoxville: University of Tennessee Press, 1987.

Courlander, Harold. *A Treasury of Afro-American Folklore: The Oral Literature, Traditions, Recollections, Legends, Tales, Songs, Religious Beliefs, Customs, Sayings, and Humor of Peoples of African Descent in the Americas*. New York: Crown, 1976.

Davis, Gerald L. *"I Got the Word in Me and I Can Sing It, You Know": A Study of the Performed African-American Sermon*. Philadelphia: University of Pennsylvania Press, 1985.

Foner, Philip S., ed. *The Voice of Black America: Major Speeches by Negroes in the United States, 1797–1973*. 2 vols. New York: Capricorn, 1975.

Johnson, James Weldon. *God's Trombones: Seven Negro Sermons in Verse*. New York: Penguin Books, 1976, c1927.

——— and J. Rosamond Johnson, ed. *The Books Of American Negro Spirituals: Including The Book Of American Negro Spirituals And The Second Book Of Negro Spirituals*. New York: Viking Press, 1940.

Jones, Gayl. *Liberating Voices: Oral Tradition in African American Literature*. Cambridge: Harvard University Press, 1991.

Levine, Lawrence W. *Black Culture and Black Consciousness: Afro-American Folk Thought from Slavery to Freedom*. New York: Oxford University Press, 1977.

III. DRAMA

Anthologies

Branch, William, ed. *Crosswinds: An Anthology of Black Dramatists in the Diaspora*. Terre Haute: Indiana University Press, 1993.

Brown-Guillory, Elizabeth, ed. *Wines in the Wilderness: Plays by African-American Women From the Harlem Renaissance to the Present*. New York: Praeger, 1990.

Harrison, Paul Carter, and Gus Edwards, eds. *Classic Plays from the Negro Ensemble Company*. Pittsburgh: University of Pittsburgh Press, 1995

Harrison, Paul Carter, ed. *Totem Voices: Plays From the Black World Repertory*. New York: Grove Press, 1989.

Hatch, James V., and Ted Shine, eds. *Black Theatre U. S. A.: Plays by African Americans: The Early Period: 1847–1938*. New York: The Free Press, 1996

———, eds. *Black Theatre U. S. A.: Plays by African Americans: The Recent Period: 1935–Today*. New York: The Free Press, 1996

Hatch, James V., and Leo Hamalian, eds. *The Roots of African American Drama: An Anthology of Early Plays, 1858–1938*. Detroit, MI: Wayne State University Press, 1991.

Hill, Errol. *Black Heroes: 7 Plays*. New York: Applause, 1989.

Hughes, Langston. *Five Plays*. Ed. with an introduction by Webster Smalley. Bloomington: Indiana University Press, 1968, c1963.

King, Woodie Jr, ed. *The National Black Drama Anthology: Eleven Plays from America's Leading African-American Theaters*. New York: Applause, 1995.

———, ed. *New Plays from the Black Theatre*. Chicago: Third World Press, 1989.

———, ed. *Theaters*. New York: Applause, 1995.

Mahone, Sydne. *Moon Marked and Touched by Sun: Plays by African-American Women*. New York: Theatre Communications Group, 1994.

Ostrow, Eileen Joyce. *Center Stage: An Anthology of Twenty-one Contemporary Black-American Plays*. Urbana: University of Illinois Press, 1991.

Oliver, Clinton F., and Stephanie E. Sills. *Contemporary Black Drama: From "A Raisin in the Sun" to "No Place to Be Somebody"*. New York: Scribner's, 1971.

Patterson, Lindsay, comp. *Black Theater: A 20th Century Collection of the Work of Its Best Playwrights*. New York: Dodd, Mead, 1971.

Perkins, Kathy A. *Black Female Playwrights: An Anthology of Plays before 1950*. Bloomington: Indiana University Press, 1989.

Turner, Darwin T., ed. *An Anthology of Black Drama in America: Second Edition*. Washington, D. C.: Howard University Press, 1994.

Wilkerson, Margaret B. *9 Plays by Black Women*. New York: New American Library, 1986.

Research Sources

Hatch, James V. *Black Images on the American Stage: A Bibliography of Plays and Musicals, 1770–1970*. New York: DBS Publications, 1970.

Peterson, Bernard L. *A Century of Musicals in Black and White: An Encyclopedia of Musical Stage Works By, About, or Involving African Americans*. Westport, CT: Greenwood, 1993.

———. *Early Black American Playwrights and Dramatic Writers: A Biographical Directory and Catalogue of Plays, Films, and Broadcasting Scripts*. New York: Greenwood press, 1990.

———. *Contemporary Black American Playwrights and Their Plays: A Biographical Directory and Dramatic Index*. New York: Greenwood Press, 1988.

Reardon, William R., and Thomas D. Prawley, eds. *The Black Teacher and the Dramatic Arts: A Dialogue, Bibliography, and Anthology*. Westport, CT: Negro Universities Press, 1970.

Woll, Allen L. *Dictionary of the Black Theatre: Broadway, Off-Broadway, and Selected Harlem Theatre*. Westport, CT: Greenwood, 1983.

IV. FICTION, SHORT AND LONG

Individual Texts

Ansa, Tina McElroy. *Baby of the Family*. San Diego: Harcourt, Brace, Jovanovich, c1989.

———. *Ugly Ways: A Novel*. New York: Harcourt, Brace & Co., c1993.

Attaway, William. *Blood on the Forge*. With an introduction by Nicholas Lehman. New York: Anchor Books, 1993.

Baldwin, James. *Another Country*. New York: Dell, 1988, c1962.

———. *Blues for Mister Charlie*. New York: Dell, 1964.

———. *Go Tell It on the Mountain*. New York: Grosset and Dunlap, c1953.

———. *Just Above My Head*. New York: Dial Press, 1974.

———. *If Beale Street Could Talk*. New York: Dial Press, c1979.

Bambara, Toni Cade. *Gorilla, My Love: Short Stories*. New York: Vintage, 1992.

———. *The Salt Eaters*. New York: Vintage Books, 1981, c1980.

———. *The Sea Birds Are Still Alive: Collected Stories*. New York: Vintage, 1982, c1977.

Baraka, Amiri Imanu. *Tales*. New York: Grove Press, 1968, c1967.

Beatty, Paul. *The White Boy Shuffle*. Boston: Houghton Mifflin, 1996.

Bonner, Marita. *Frye Street & Environs: The Collected Works of Marita Bonner*. Ed. with an introduction by Joyce Flynn and Joyce Occomy Stricklin. Boston: Beacon Press, 1997.

Bontemps, Arna Wendell. *Black Thunder*. Boston: Beacon Press, 1992, c1936.

Bradley, David. *The Chaneysville Incident: A Novel*. New York: Harper & Row, c1981.

Brooks, Gwendolyn. *Maude Martha*. New York: A. M. S. Press, 1974, c. 1953.

Brown, William Wells. *Clotel, Or, The President's Daughter*. Armonk, NY: M.E. Sharpe, c1996.

Butler, Octavia E. *Kindred*. With an introduction by Robert Crossly. Boston: Beacon Press, c1988.

———. *Adulthood Rites: Xenogenesis*. New York: Warner Books, 1988.

———. *Parable of the Sower*. New York: Four Walls, Eight Windows, 1993.

———. *Blood Child and Other Stories*. New York: Four Walls, Eight Windows, 1995.

———. *Your Blues Ain't Like Mine*. New York: G.P. Putnam's Sons, c1992.

Chesnutt, Charles Waddell, 1858–1932. *Collected Stories of Charles W. Chesnutt*. New York: Penguin, 1992.

———. *The Conjure Woman, and Other Conjure Tales*. Durham, NC: Duke University Press, 1993.

———. *The House Behind the Cedars*. Athens: University of Georgia Press, c1988.

———. *The Marrow of Tradition*. New York: Penguin, 1993.

Childress, Alice. *Like One of the Family: Conversations from a Domestic's Life*; with an introduction by Trudier Harris. Boston: Beacon press, 1986, c1956.

Cliff, Michelle. *Abeng*. New York: Penguin, 1991, c. 1984.

———. *No Telephone to Heaven*. New York: Vintage, 1989, c. 1987.

Cooper, J. California. *Family: A Novel*. New York: Doubleday, c1991.

229

———. *Some Soul to Keep*. New York: St. Martin's Press, c1987.

Dixon, Melvin. *Trouble the Water*. Boulder: University of Colorado: Fiction Collective Two, 1990, c1989.

Dunbar, Paul Laurence. *The Best Stories of Paul Laurence Dunbar*. Ed. by Benjamin Brawley. New York: Dodd, Mead, 1938.

———. *The Sport of the Gods*. New York: Dodd, Mead, 1902.

Ellison, Ralph. *Invisible Man*. New York: Random House, 1952.

———. *Flying Home and Other Stories*. Ed. with an introduction by John F. Callahan. New York: Random House, c1996.

Fisher, Rudolph. *The Conjure Man Dies*. Anne Arbor: University of Michigan Press, 1992.

———. *Walls of Jericho*. Ann Arbor: University of Michigan Press, 1994.

Forrest, Leon. *Two Wings to Veil My Face*. Chicago: Another Chicago Press; dist. by IL Literary Publishers Assoc., 1988.

———. *Divine Days: A Novel*. New York: Norton, 1992; Chicago: Published in conjunction with Another Chicago Press, 1992.

———. *There Is a Tree More Ancient Than Eden*. New York: Random House, 1973.

Gaines, Ernest. *Catherine Carmier*. New York: Vintage, 1993.

———. *A Gathering of Old Men*. New York: Vintage, 1983.

———. *In My Father's House*. New York: Vintage, 1992.

———. *The Autobiography of Miss Jane Pittman*. New York: Bantam Books, 1972, c1971.

Golden, Marita. *Long Distance Life*. New York: Doubleday, 1989.

———. *Migrations of the Heart*. Garden City, NY: Anchor Press, 1983.

Himes, Chester B. *Cotton Comes to Harlem*. New York: Vintage, 1988, c1965.

Hurston, Zora Neale. *Their Eyes Were Watching God*. Urbana: University of Illinois Press, 1991, c. 1937.

———. *Seraph on the Suwanee: A Novel*. New York: HarperPerennial, 1991.

Johnson, Charles R. *Faith and the Good Thing*. New York: Plume, 1991.

———. *Middle Passage*. New York: Atheneum, 1990.

Jones, Gayl. *Corregidora*. New York: Random House, c1976.

———. *Eva's Man*. New York: Random House, 1975.

Kelley, William Melvin. *A Different Drummer*. New York: Bantam Books, c1962.

Kincaid, Jamaica. *Annie John*. New York: New American Library, 1985.

———. *Lucy*. New York: Farrar, Straus & Giroux, 1990.

———. *Autobiography of My Mother*. New York: Farrar, Straus & Giroux, 1996.

Lamming, George. *In the Castle of My Skin*. New York: Schocken Books, 1983.

Larsen, Nella. *An Intimation of Things Distant: The Collected Fiction of Nella Larsen*. Ed. by Carles R. Larson. New York: Anchor Books, 1992.

Major, Clarence. *Such Was the Season*. San Francisco: Mercury House, 1987.

Marshall, Paule. *Praisesong for the Widow*. New York: Dutton, 1983.

———. *Brown Girl, Brownstones*. Old Westbury, NY: Feminist Press, 1981, c1969.

———. *The Chosen Place, The Timeless People*. New York: Vintage Books, 1984, c1969.

McCluskey, John. *Look What They Done to My Song; A Novel*. New York: Random House, 1974.

McKay, Claude. *Banjo, A Story Without a Plot*. New York: Harper & Brothers, 1929.

———. *Home to Harlem*. New York: Harper & Brothers, 1928.

McMillan, Terry. *Waiting to Exhale*. New York: Pocket Books, 1992.

Morrison, Toni. *Beloved: A Novel*. New York: New American Library, 1988, c1987.

———. *The Bluest Eye*. New York: Knopf, 1993, c1970.

———. *Song of Solomon*. New York: New American Library, 1987.

Mosely, Walter. *Devil in a Blue Dress*. New York: Norton, 1990.

Murray, Albert. *The Seven League Boots: A Novel*. New York: Pantheon Books, 1995.

———. *Train Whistle Guitar*. New York: McGraw-Hill, 1974.

Naylor, Gloria. *Bailey's Cafe*. 1st ed. New York: Harcourt Brace Jovanovich, c1992.

———. *Mama Day*. New York: Vintage, 1988.

———. *The Women of Brewster Place*. New York: Penguin, 1983, c1982.

Petry, Ann. *The Street*. Boston: Houghton Mifflin, 1946.

———. *The Narrows*. Boston: Houghton Mifflin, 1953.

Phillips, Caryl. *Crossing the River*. New York: Knopf, distributed by Random House, 1994.

Reed, Ishmael. *The Last Days of Louisiana Red*. New York: Atheneum, 1989.

———. *Mumbo Jumbo*. New York: Atheneum, 1988.

———. *Flight to Canada*. New York: Random House, c1976.

———. *The Free-Lance Pallbearers*. Garden City, NY: Doubleday, 1967.

———. *Yellow Back Radio Broke Down*. Garden City, NY: Doubleday, 1969.

Sapphire. *Push: A Novel*. New York: Alfred A. Knopf: Distributed by Random House, 1996.

Shange, Ntozake. *Betsey Brown: A Novel*. New York: St. Martin's Press, c1985.

———. *Nappy Edges*. New York: St. Martin's Press, c1978.

Thurman, Wallace. *Infants of Spring: A Novel*. Carbondale: Southern Illinois University Press, 1979, c1932.

———. *The Blacker the Berry*. New York: Collier, 1970.

Walker, Alice. *The Color Purple*. New York: Pocket Books, 1982.

———. *In Love and Trouble: Stories Of Black Women*. New York: Harcourt Brace Jovanovich, 1973.

———. *The Third Life Of Grange Copeland*. New York: Pocket Books, 1988, c.1970.

———. *You Can't Keep a Good Woman Down: Stories*. New York: Harcourt Brace Jovanovich, 1982, c1981.

Walker, Margaret. *Jubilee*. Boston: Houghton Mifflin, 1966.

———. *Meridian*. New York: Pocket Books, 1976

West, Dorothy. *The Richer, the Poorer: Stories, Sketches, and Reminiscences*. New York: Doubleday, 1995.

———. *The Wedding*. New York: Doubleday, 1995.

Wideman, John Edgar. *All Stories Are True*. New York: Vintage, 1993.

———. *The Cattle Killing*. Boston: Houghton Mifflin, 1996.

———. *Sent for You Yesterday*. New York: Vintage, 1988, c1983.

———.*The Homewood Books*. Pittsburgh: University of Pittsburgh Press, c1992.

———. *Identities: Three Novels*. New York: H. Holt, 1994.

———. *Reuban: A Novel*. New York: H. Holt, c1987.

Wilson, Harriet E. *Our Nig, Or, Sketches from the Life of a Free Black, In a Two-Story White House, North, Showing That Slavery's Shadows Fall Even There.* New York: Vintage Books, c1983.

Wright, Richard. *The Richard Wright Reader.* Ed. by Ellen Wright and Michael Fabre. New York: Harper & Row, 1978.

———. *Native Son.* With an introduction by Arnold Rampersad. New York: HarperPerennial, 1993.

———. *Outsider.* With an introduction by Maryemma Graham. New York: HarperPerennial, 1993.

———. *Uncle Tom's Children.* With an introduction by Richard Yarborough. New York: HarperPerennial, 1993.

Anthologies

Andrews, William, ed. *The African American Novel in the Age of Reaction: Three Classics.* New York: Mentor, 1992.

———. *Three Classic African American Novels.* New York: Mentor, 1990.

Gates, Henry Louis, Jr, ed. *African American Women Writers, 1910-1940.* New York: G.K. Hall & Co., 1994.

Major, Clarence, Ed. *Calling the Wind: Twentieth Century African-American Short Stories.* New York: HarperPerennial, 1993.

Reed, Ishmael, ed. *The Before Columbus Foundation Fiction Anthology: Selections from the American Book Awards, 1980–1990.* New York: Norton, 1992.

———, ed. *19 Necromancers from Now.* Garden City, NY: Anchor Books, 1970.

Washington, Mary Helen, ed. *Black-Eyed Susans, Midnight Birds: Stories by and About Black Women.* New York: Doubleday, 1990.

———. *Memory of Kin: Stories About Family by Black Writers.* New York: Doubleday, 1991.

———. *Invented Lives: Narratives of Black Women, 1860–1960.* Garden City, NY: Doubleday, 1987.

V. AUTOBIOGRAPHY

Angelou, Maya. *I Know Why the Caged Bird Sings.* New York: Bantam, 1970.

———. *Conversations with Maya Angelou.* Ed. by Jeffery M. Eliot. Jackson: University of Mississippi Press, c1988.

Baldwin, James. *Conversations with James Baldwin.* Ed. by Fred L. Standley and Louis H. Pratt. Jackson: University of Mississippi Press, c1989.

Baldwin, James. *Notes of a Native Son.* Boston: Beacon Press, c1984, c1955.

Bontemps, Arna Wendall. *Arna Bontemps-Langston Hughes Letters, 1935–1967.* Selected and edited by Charles H. Nichols. New York: Dodd, Mead, c1980.

Brooks, Gwendolyn. *Report From Part One.* Prefaces by Don L. Lee and George Kent. Detroit: Broadside Press, 1973, c1972.

Campbell, Bebe Moore. *Sweet Summer: Growing Up With & Without My Dad.* New York: Putnam, c1989.

Cooper, Anna Julia. *A Voice from the South*. The Schomburg Library of Nineteenth-Century Black Women Writers. New York: Oxford University Press, 1988.

Douglass, Frederick. *My Bondage and My Freedom*. New York: Arno, 1968.

———. *Life and Times of Frederick Douglass*. New York: Thomas Y. Crowell, 1966.

DuBois, W. E. B. *Dusk Of Dawn: An Essay Toward an Autobiography of a Race Concept*. With a new introduction by Irene Diggs. New Brunswick, NJ: Transaction Books, 1984, c1940.

Ellison, Ralph. *Conversations with Ralph Ellison*. Ed. by Maryemma Graham and Amrijit Singh. Jackon: University of Mississippi Press, c1995.

Gaines, Ernest. *Conversations With Ernest Gaines*. Ed. by John Lowe. Jackson: University of Mississippi Press, c1995.

Gates, Henry Louis, Jr., ed. *The Classic Slave Narratives*. New York: Penguin, 1987.

Giovanni, Nikki. *Conversations with Nikki Giovanni*. Ed. by Virginia C. Fowler. Jackson: University of Mississippi Press, c1992.

Himes, Chester B. *The Quality Of Hurt: The Autobiography of Chester Himes*. Garden City, NY: Doubleday, 1972.

Hughes, Langston. *The Big Sea, An Autobiography by Langston Hughes*. New York & London: Knopf, 1940.

———. *I Wonder as I Wander: An Autobiographical Journey*. New York: Hill and Wang, 1993.

Hurston, Zora Neale. *Dust Tracks on the Road: An Autobiography*. Chicago: University of Illinois Press, 1984.

Jacobs, Harriet. *Incidents in the Life of a Slave Girl. Written By Herself*. Ed. by Jean Fagen Yellin. Cambridge, MA: Harvard University Press, 1987.

Kennedy, Adrienne. *People Who Led to My Plays*. New York: Theatre Communications Group, 1987.

Lorde, Audre. *Zami: A New Spelling of My Name*. Trumansburg, NY: Crossing Press, 1983, c. 1982.

Moody, Anne. *Coming of Age in Mississippi*. New York: Dial, 1968.

Morrison, Toni. *Conversations With Toni Morrison*. Ed. by Danielle Taylor Guthrie. Jackson: University of Mississippi Press, c1994.

Northrop, Solomon. *Twelve Years a Slave*. Ed. by Sue Eakin and Joseph Logson. Baton Rouge: Louisiana State University Press, 1968.

Souljah, Sister. *No Disrespect*. New York: Vintage, 1994.

Walcott, Derek. *Conversations With Derek Walcott*. Ed. by William Baer. Jackson: University of Mississippi Press, c1996.

Walker, Alice. *The Same River Twice: Honoring the Difficult: A Meditation on Life, Spirit, Art, And The Making Of The Film, "The Color Purple" Ten Years Later*. New York: Scribner, c1996.

Walker, Margaret. *How I Wrote Jubilee and Other Essays on Life and Literature by Margaret Walker*. Ed. with an introduction by Maryemma Graham. Old Westbury, NY: Feminist Press, 1990.

Washington, Booker T. *Up From Slavery*. Williamstown, MA: Corner House Press, 1971.

Washington, Margaret, ed. *Narrative of Sojourner Truth*. New York: Vintage, 1993.

Wideman, John Edgar. *Brothers and Keepers*. New York: Holt, Rinehart & Winston, c1984.

———. *Fatheralong: A Meditation on Fathers and Sons, Race, and Society*. New York: Pantheon Books, c1994.

Wright, Richard. *Black Boy*. With an introduction by Jerry W. Ward, Jr. New York: HarperPerennial, 1993.

———. *Black Boy*. New York: Harper & Row, 1966.

———. *Conversations with Richard Wright*. Ed. by Kenneth Kinnamon and Michael Fabre. Jackson, MI: University of Mississippi Press, c1993.

———. *American Hunger*. Afterword by Michel Fabre. New York: Harper Colophon Books, 1983.

X, Malcolm. *Autobiography of Malcolm X*. New York: Ballantine Books, 1992.

VI. GENERAL ANTHOLOGIES

Baraka, Amiri Imanu, and Amina Baraka, eds. *Confirmation: An Anthology of African American Women*. New York: Quill, 1983.

Chapman, Abraham, ed. *Black Voices: An Anthology of Afro-American Literature*. New York: New American Library, c1968.

Davis, Arthur P., J. Saunders Redding, and Joyce Ann Joyce. *The New Cavalcade: African American Writing from 1760 to the Present*. Washington, D. C.: Howard University Press, 1991–92.

Gates, Henry Louis, Jr., ed. *The Shomburg Library of Nineteenth Century Black Women Writers* New York: Oxford University Press, 1988.

Gates, Henry Louis, Jr., and Nellie McKay, eds. *The Norton Anthology of African American Literature*. New York: Norton, 1997.

Jones, LeRoi, and Larry Neal, eds. *Black Fire: An Anthology of Afro-American Writing*. New York: Morrow, 1968.

Harper, Michael S., and Robert B. Stepto, eds. *Chant of Saints: A Gathering of Afro-American Literature, Art, and Scholarship*. Urbana: University of Illinois Press, 1979.

Hill, Patricia Liggins, et al., eds. *Call and Response: The Riverside Anthology of the African American Literary Tradition*. Boston: Houghton Mifflin, 1997.

Locke, Alain LeRoy, ed. *The New Negro*. With an introduction by Arnold Rampersad. New York: Antheneum, 1992.

Long, Richard A., and Eugenia W. Collier, eds. *Afro-American Writing: An Anthology of Prose and Poetry*. University Park: Pennsylvania State University Press, 1985.

Magill, Frank N., ed. *Masterpieces of African American Literature*. New York: Harper-Collins, 1992.

Powell, Kevin and Ras Baraka. *In the Tradition: An Anthology of Young Black Writers*. New York: Published for Harlem River Press by Writers and Readers Publishing, 1992.

Smith, Barbara, ed. *Home Girls: A Black Feminist Anthology*. New York: Kitchen Table, 1983.

VII. SECONDARY SOURCES

Literary Studies

Baker, Houston, A. Jr. *Afro-American Literary Study in the 1990's.* Berkeley: University of California Press, 1993.

———, ed. *Workings of the Spirit: The Poetics of Afro-American Women's Writing.* Chicago: University of Chicago Press, 1991.

———. *Afro American Poetics: Revisions of Harlem and the Black Aesthetic.* Madison: University of Wisconsin Press, c1988.

———. *Blues, Ideology, and Afro-American Literature: A Vernacular Theory.* Chicago: University of Chicago Press, c1984.

———. *Long Black Song: Essays In Black American Literature And Culture.* Charlottesvile: University Press of Virginia, 1990.

Bell, Bernard W. *The Afro-American Novel and Its Tradition.* Amherst: University of Massachusetts Press, 1987.

Bruce, Dickenson D., Jr. *Black American Writing from the Nadir: The Evolution of a Literary Tradition, 1877–1915.* Baton Rouge: Louisiana State University Press, 1989.

Carby, Hazel V. *Reconstructing Womanhood: The Emergence of the Afro-American Woman Novelist.* New York: Oxford University Press, 1987.

Christian, Barbara. *Black Women Novelists: The Development of a Tradition, 1892–1976.* Westport, CT: Greenwood Press, 1980.

Davis, Arthur P. *From The Dark Tower: Afro-American Writers 1900–1960.* Washington DC: Howard University Press, 1974.

Davis, Thadious and Trudier Harris, eds. *Afro-American Writers After 1955.* Detroit: Gale Research Co., 1985.

——- and Trudier Harris, eds. *Afro-American Fiction Writers After 1955.* Detroit: Gale Research Co., c1984.

Dixon, Melvin. *Ride Out the Wilderness: Geography and Identity in Afro-American Literature.* Urbana: University of Illinois Press, c1987.

Evans, Mari, ed. *Black Women Writers (1950–1980): A Critical Evaluation.* Garden City, NY: Anchor Press/Doubleday, 1984.

———, ed. *Reading Black, Reading Feminist: A Critical Anthology.* New York: Meridian Books, 1990.

Gates, Henry Louis, Jr., *The Signifying Monkey.* New York: Oxford University Press, 1988.

———, ed. *Figures in Black: Words, Signs and the "Racial" Self.* New York: Oxford University Press, 1987.

———. ed. *Black Literature and Literary Theory.* New York: Methuen, 1984.

Gayle, Addison, Jr. *The Way of the New World and the Black Novel In America.* Garden City, NY: Anchor Doubleday, 1975.

Harris, Trudier, ed. *Afro-American Writers Before the Harlem Renaissance.* Associate Ed. Thadious Davis. Detroit: Gale Research Co., c1986.

———. and Thadious Davis, eds. *Afro-American Poets Since 1955.* Detroit: Gale Research Co., c1985.

——. *Exorcizing Blackness: Historical and Literary Lynching and Burning Rituals.* Bloomington: Indiana University Press, c1984.

——. *Afro-American Writers From the Harlem Renaissance to 1940.* Associate ed. Thadious Davis. Detroit: Gale Research, 1987.

——. *Afro-American Writers, 1940–1955.* Asscoiate ed. Thadious Davis. Detroit: Gale Research, 1988.

——. *From Mammies to Militants: Domestics in Black American Literature.* Philadelphia: Temple University Press, 1982.

Holloway, Karla F. C. *Codes of Conduct: Race, Ethics, and the Color of Our Character.* New Brunswick, NJ: Rutgers U P, c1995.

——. *Methods And Metaphors: Figures of Culture and Gender in Black Women's Literature.* New Brunswick, NJ: Rutgers University Press, c1992.

Jackson, Blyden. *History of Afro American Literature.* Volume I. Baton Rouge: Louisiana State University Press, 1989.

McDowell, Deborah E. *"The Changing Same": Black Women's Literature, Criticism, And Theory.* Bloomington: Indiana University Press, c1995.

Morrison, Toni. *Playing in the Dark: Whiteness and the Literary Imagination.* New York: Vintage, 1992.

Nielsen, Aldon L. *Writing Between the Lines: Race and Intertextuality.* Athens: University of Georgia Press, c1994.

Andrews, William L. *The Oxford Companion To African American Literature.* Frances Smith Foster, Trudier Harris, eds.; foreword by Henry Louis Gates, Jr. New York: Oxford University Press, 1997.

Rampersad, Arnold. *The Life of Langston Hughes; Volume I: 1902–1941 and Volume II: 1941-1967: I Dream a World.* New York: Oxford University Press, 1988, 2 vols.

Redding, J. Saunders. *To Make a Poet Black.* Introduction by Henry Louis Gates, Jr. Ithaca, NY: Cornell University Press, 1988, c1939.

Redmond, Eugene B. *Drumvoices: The Mission of Afro-American Poetry.* Garden City, NY: Anchor, 1976.

Ruoff, A. LaVonne Brown, and Jerry W. Ward, Jr. eds. *Redefining American Literary History.* New York: The Modern Language Association of America, 1990.

Sundquist, Eric J. *To Wake the Nations: Race in the Making of American Literature.* Cambridge MA: Harvard University Press, 1993.

Wagner, Jean. *Black Poets of the United States; From Paul Laurence Dunbar to Langston Hughes.* Translated by Kenneth Douglas. Urbana: University of Illinois P, 1973.

Weixman, Joe and Houston A. Baker Jr, eds. *Black Feminist Criticism and Critical Theory.* Greenwood, FL: Penkevill, c1988.

Yellin, Jean Fagen. *Women and Sisters: The Anti-Slavery Feminists in American Culture.* New Haven, CT: Yale University Press, 1989.

Drama Studies

Abramson, Doris. *Negro Playwrights in the American Theater, 1925–1959.* New York: Columbia University Press, 1969.

Archer, Leonard C. *Black Images in American Theater.* Nashville, TN: Pageant Press, 1973.

Brown, Janet. *Feminist Drama: Definition and Critical Analysis*. Englewood Cliffs, NJ: Scarecrow Press, 1979.

Brown-Guillory, Elizabeth. *Their Place on the Stage*. Danbury, CT: Greenwood press, 1988.

Fabre, Genevieve. *Drumbeats, Masks, and Metaphor: Contemporary Afro-American Theatre*. Cambridge MA: Harvard University Press, 1983.

Fraden, Rena. *Blueprints for a Black Federal Theatre, 1935–1939*. New York: Cambridge University Press, 1994.

Hay, Samuel. *African American Theatre: An Historical and Critical Analysis*. New York: Cambridge University Press, 1994.

Hill, Errol, ed. *The Theatre of Black Americans: A Collection of Critical Essays*. New York: Applause, 1987.

Sanders, Leslie Catherine. *The Development of Black Theater in America: From Shadows to Selves*. Baton Rouge: Lousiana State University Press, 1988.

Sporn, Paul. *Against Itself: The Federal Theater and Writers' Projects in the Midwest*. Detroit, MI: Wayne State University Press, 1995.

Woll, Allen. *Black Musical Theatre: From Coontown to Dreamgirls*. Baton Rouge: Louisiana State University Press, 1989.

Autobiography Studies

Andrews, William. *African American Autobiography*. Englewood Cliffs, NJ: Prentice Hall, 1993.

———. *To Tell a Free Story*. Urbana: University of Illinois Press, 1986.

Butterfield, Stephen. *Black Autobiography in America*. Amherst: University of Massachusetts Press, 1983.

Braxton, Joanne M. *Black Women Writing Autobiography*. Philadelphia: Temple University Press, 1989.

Dudley, David L. *My Father's Shadow: Intergenerational Conflict in African American Men's Autobiography*. Philadelphia: University of Pennsylvania Press, 1991.

Foster, Frances Smith. *Written by Herself: Literary Productions of Early African American Women Writers*. Bloomington: Indiana University Press, 1993.

Lionnett, Francoise. *Autobiographical Voices: Race, Gender, Self-Portraiture*. Ithaca, NY: Cornell University Press, 1989.

Sekora, John and Darwin T. Turner, eds. *The Art of the Slave Narrative*. Macomb: Western Illinois University Press, 1982.

Smith, Valerie. *Self-Discovery and Authority in Afro-American Narrative*. Cambridge, MA: Harvard University Press, 1987.

Starling, Marion W. *The Slave Narrative: Its Place in American History*. Boston: G. K. Hall, 1981.

Stepto, Robert. *From Behind the Veil: A Study of Afro-American Narrative*. Urbana: University of Illinois Press, 1979.

VIII. RESOURCES FOR THINKING ABOUT LANGUAGE

Ewers, Traute. *The Origin of American Black English: Be-forms in the Hoodoo Texts*. New York: Mouton de Gruyter, 1996.

Hecht, Michael L. *African American Communication: Ethnic Identity and Cultural Interpretation*. Newbury Park, CA: Sage Publications, 1993.

Holloway, Joseph E., and Winifred K. Vass. *The African Heritage of American English*. Bloomington: Indiana University Press, 1993.

Kochman, Thomas. *Rappin' and Stylin' Out: Communication in Urban Black America*. Urbana: University of Illinois Press, 1972.

Major, Clarence, ed. *Juba to Jive: The Dictionary of African-American Slang*. New York: Penguin, 1994.

Smitherman, Geneva. *Black Talk: Words and Phrases from the Hood to the Amen Corner*. Boston: Houghton Mifflin, 1994.

———. *Discourse and Discrimination*. Detroit: Wayne State University Press, 1988.

———. *Talkin' and Testifyin': The Language of Black America*. Boston: Houghton Mifflin, 1971.

IX. BLACK POPULAR CULTURE

Baker, Houston A. Jr. *Black Studies, Rap and the Academy*. Chicago: University of Chicago Press, 1993.

Dyson, Michael Eric. *Between God and Gangsta Rap: Bearing Witness to Black Culture*. New York: Oxford University Press, 1996.

Eure, Joseph D., and James G. Spady, eds. *Nation Conscious Rap*. New York: PC International Press, 1991.

George, Nelson. *Buppies, B-Boys, Baps and Bohos: Notes on Post-Soul Black Culture*. New York: HarperCollins, 1992.

Toop, David. *The Rap Attack: African Jive to New York Hip Hop*. Boston: South End press, 1984.

X. RESOURCES FOR TEACHING YOUNGER READERS

Angelou, Maya. *Life Doesn't Frighten Me*. Illustrated by Jean-Michel Basquiat. Ed. by Jane Boyers. New York: Stewart, Tabori & Chang: Distribution in the U. S. by Workman, 1993.

Brooks, Gwendolyn. *Very Young Poets*. Chicago: Brook Press, 1983.

———. *Young Poet's Primer*. Chicago: Brooks press, 1980.

Childress, Alice. *A Hero Ain't Nothin' But a Sandwich*. New York: Avon, 1982.

———. *Rainbow Jordan*. New York: Avon, 1982.

Harris, Violet, J. *Teaching Multicultural Literature: K–8*. Norwood, MA: Christopher Gordon Publisher, 1992.

Giovanni, Nikki. *Ego-tripping: And Other Poems for Young People*. New York: Lawrence Hill, 1973.

———. *Spin a soft Black Song: Poems for Children*. New York: Hill and Wang, 1985.

———. *Vacation Time: Poems for Children*. New York: Morrow, 1980.

MacCann, Donnarae, and Gloria Woodard, eds. *The Black American in Books for Children: Readings in Racism*. Metuchen, NJ: Scarecrow, 1985.

Thomas, Joyce Carol, ed. *A Gathering of Flowers: Stories About Being Young in America*. Harper & Row/Harper Keypoint, 1990.

Sanchez, Sonia. *A Sound Investment: Short Stories for Young Readers*. Chicago: Third World Press, 1985.

———. *It's a New Day: Poems for Young Brothas and Sistuhs*. Detroit: Broadside Press, 1971.

Williams, Helen E. *Books by African-American Authors and Illustrators for Children and Young Adults*. Chicago: American Library Association, 1991.

XI. RESOURCES FOR TEACHING AFRICAN AMERICAN LITERATURE AND CULTURE

Andrews, William. *The Oxford Companion to African American Literature*. New York: Oxford University Press, 1997.

Baraka, Amiri Imanu. *The LeRoi Jones/Amiri Baraka Reader*. Ed. by William J. Harris. New York: Thunder's Mouth Press, 1991.

Blessingame, John W., ed. *New Perspectives on Black Studies*. Urbana: University of Illinois Press, 1971.

Brooks, Gwendolyn. *A Capsule Course in Black Poetry Writing*. 1st ed. Detroit: Broadside Press, 1975.

Dyson, Michael Eric. *Reflecting Black: African American Cultural Criticism*. Minneapolis: University of Minnesota Press, 1993.

DuBois, W.E.B. *The Souls of Black Folk*. New York: Dover, 1994, c1903.

Fisher, Dexter, and Robert B. Stepto, eds. *Afro-American Literature: The Reconstruction of Instruction*. New York: MLA, 1979.

Giroux, Henry A. *Living Dangerously: Multiculturalism and the Politics of Difference*. New York: Peter Lang, 1993.

Golden, Marita and Susan Richards Shreve, ed. *Skin Deep: Black Women and White Women Write About Race*. New York: Nan A. Talese, 1995.

hooks, bell. *Teaching to Transgress: Education as the Practice of Freedom*. New York: Routledge, 1994.

Jarret, Joyce M. *Heritage: African American Readings for Writing*. Upper Saddle River, NJ: Prentice Hall, 1997.

McKay, Nellie Y. and Kathryn Earle, eds. *Approaches to Teaching World Literature: The Novels Of Toni Morrison*. New York: PMLA, 1997.

Miller, James A., ed. *Approaches to Teaching World Literature: Wright's Native Son*. New York: PMLA, 1997.

Parr, Susan Resneck and Pancho Savory, eds. *Approaches To Teaching World Literature: Ellison's Invisible Man*. New York: PMLA, 1989.

Perry, Theresa. *Teaching Malcolm X*. New York: Routledge, 1996.

———, and James Fraser. *Freedom's Plow: Teaching in the Multicultural Classroom*. New York: Routledge, 1993.

239

Reed, Ishmael, ed. *MultiAmerica: Essays on Cultural Wars and Cultural Peace*. New York: Viking, 1997.

Roses, Elaine E. and Ruth E. Randolph. *Harlem Renaissance and Beyond: Literary Biographies of 100 Black Women Writers, 1900-1945*. Cambridge MA: Harvard U P, 1990.

Scafe, Suzanne. *Teaching Black Literature*. London: Virago, 1989.

Stanford, Barbara Dodds, and Karima Amin. *Black Literature for High School Students*. Urbana, IL: National Council of Teachers of English, 1978.

Turner, Darwin T., and Barbara Dodds Stanford. *Theory and Practice in the Teaching of Literature by Afro-Americans*. Urbana, IL: National Council of Teachers of English, 1971.

Walker, Margaret. *On Being Female, Black, and Free: Essays by Margaret Walker, 1942-1992*. Ed. by Maryemma Graham. Knoxville: University of Tennessee Press, c1997.

⊟⦂ ABOUT THE CONTRIBUTORS ⦂⊟

Maryemma Graham has been a reader, teacher, writer, and scholar of African American literature for twenty-five years. She is founder and director of the Project on the History of Black Writing (1983) and taught at Chicago State University and the University of Mississippi before coming to Northeastern University. Author of five scholarly books, four curriculum guides and textbooks and more than twenty-five articles on African American literature, Graham is currently working on the biography of Margaret Walker. She is also the recipient of many state and federal grants focusing on the professional development of teachers. Graham lives with her family in Cambridge, Massachusetts.

Sharon Pineault-Burke completed her Masters degree at Northeastern University with an emphasis upon the teaching of writing and African American literature. She was co-director of the highly successful 1993 and 1994 NEH summer institutes, "African American Literature: From Phillis Wheatley to Toni Morrison" which resulted in the publication of this volume. Pineault-Burke is currently a professional development specialist in the Boston area, with a joint affiliation with Northeastern University's Center for Innovation in Urban Education and the Department of African American Studies. She lives with her husband Danny in Lynn, Massachusetts.

Marianna White Davis has taught English at all levels for thirty-six years and has lectured in the fields of English, linguistics, and African American literature across the United States and in Europe. Her ten-book collection, *Contributions of Black Women to America* stands as the first detailed historical research covering the years 1630 to 1980. A

241

former president of the Conference on College Composition and Communications, she is also a 35-year member of the National Council of Teachers of English and Life Member of the College Language Association. Her academic degrees in English were awarded by South Carolina State University, New York University, and Boston University where she was a Crusade Scholar. Currently, Davis is Special Assistant to the President at Benedict College in Columbia, South Carolina, and she is the newly elected Chair of the Jacob Javits Fellowship Board of the United States Department of Education.

William L. Andrews is E. Maynard Adams Professor of English at the University of North Carolina at Chapel Hill. He is the author of *The Literary Career of Charles W. Chesnutt* (1980) and *To Tell a Free Story: The First Century of Afro-American Autobiography, 1760–1865* (1986). He is one of the editors of the *Norton Anthology of African American Literature* (1997) and *The Oxford Companion to African American Literature* (1997) and has edited many texts in African American literature.

Bernard W. Bell is the author of the critically acclaimed *The Afro-American Novel and Its Tradition* (1987), a standard for scholarly study in the field. Bell has lectured around the world, including at Harvard University, the Sorbonne, at teacher-training institutions in Germany and Portugal, and at the Second World Black and African Festival of Arts and Culture in Nigeria. A former Visiting Professor at the University of Freiburg in Germany, a Senior Fulbright-Hays Scholar at the University of Coimbra in Portugal, and Professor of English at University of Massachusetts at Amherst, Bell is currently Professor of English at Pennsylvania State University.

Constance Borab's first teaching experience was in the eighth grade when she was asked by the principal to stay with the first graders, whose teacher one morning had to be rushed to the hospital for an emergency appendectomy. When the principal returned with a substitute several hours later, she found Connie and the class totally involved in an arithmetic game that enlivened lessons on adding and subtracting. From this serendipitous beginning in the adult profession,

Connie has had a variety of teaching experiences ranging from co-creating adult programs for the self-exploration of one's beliefs and philosophies to her mainstay job of teaching literature, speech, theater, and film criticism in an inner city, girls' high school. Her post graduate education includes several teacher institutes sponsored by the National Endowment for the Humanities and the innovative Masters degree program in Critical and Creative Thinking at the University of Massachusetts at Boston. Currently on leave from her job, Connie is splitting her time between her family and a commitment to helping create an innovative pilot high school in the inner city.

Katharine Driscoll Coon is in her tenth year at Noble and Greenough School in Dedham, Massachusetts, where she teaches upper school English courses and co-directs the College Counseling Office. She is also a faculty advisor for the Multicultural Students Association and the Community Service Program. She graduated from Yale University in 1973 with a B.A. in English and received her M.Ed. from Lesley College through the Teacher Training Course at Shady Hill School in Cambridge, Massachusetts, where she specialized in African American literature and African studies. Kate taught English for five years at St. Ann's School in Brooklyn, New York, where she also served as the department chair. In the summer of 1997, she taught writing at the Kokrobitey School, a collaborative venture in education for Ghanaian and American students and teachers in Ghana.

Thadious M. Davis is the Gertrude Conaway Vanderbilt Professor of English at Vanderbilt University. Her recent publications include *Nella Larsen, Novelist of the Harlem Renaissance: A Woman's Life Unveiled* (1994); editions of Jessie Fauset's *The Chinaberry Tree* and *Comedy: American Style* in the G. K. Hall series on African American women writers (1995); an edition of Taylor Gordon's autobiography, *Born to Be* in Nebraska's Blacks in the West series (1995); and a Penguin Classics edition of *Passing* by Nella Larsen (1997).

Trudier Harris is J. Carlyle Sitterson Professor of English at the Uni-

243

versity of North Carolina at Chapel Hill. She is author of several volumes, including *Exorcising Blackness: Historical and Literary Lynching and Burning Rituals* (1984), and *Black Women in the Fiction of James Baldwin* (1985), for which she won the 1987 College Language Association Creative Scholarship Award. Among her numerous edited volumes are six in the *Dictionary of Literary Biography* series, and *New Essays on Baldwin's Go Tell It on the Mountain* (1996). She is also one of the editors of *The Oxford Companion to African American Literature* (1997), *Call and Response: The Riverside Anthology of Southern Literature* (1997), and *The Norton Anthology of Southern Literature* (1997). Her most recent scholarly studies are *Fiction and Folklore: The Novels of Toni Morrison* (1991) and *The Power of the Porch: The Storyteller's Craft in Zora Neale Hurston, Gloria Naylor, and Randall Kenan* (1996).

AnnLouise Keating is Associate Professor of English and Director of Freshman Composition at Eastern New Mexico University where she teaches multicultural U.S. literature, critical theory, women's studies, and composition. Author of *Women Reading Women Writing: Self-Invention in Paula Gunn Allen, Gloria Anzaldua, and Audre Lorde* (1996), she has published articles on a number of nineteenth- and twentieth-century U.S. writers.

Jennifer R. Novak, a recent graduate of Northeastern University, coordinated two programs at Northeastern University: the development of a full-text CD-ROM prototype containing The Project on the History of Black Writing, an archival repository of African American novels from 1853 to 1990 and a teacher institute on Medgar Evers and the Mississippi Civil Rights Movement funded by the National Endowment for the Humanities. She is currently the Communications Coordinator for the Institute for Responsive Education in Boston, MA. Jennifer plans to pursue her interest in African American literature and culture through the study of documentary filmmaking.

Leslie Catherine Sanders is Associate Professor in the Humanities Department at Atkinson College, York University, in Toronto, Canada. Author of *The Development of Black Theatre in America: From Shadows to*

Selves, she has published essays on African American and African Canadian writers and is currently editing the plays of Langston Hughes.

Jane Skelton received her B.A. in Theatre Education from Emerson College in Boston, Massachusetts, and a Masters in Education Administration from Antioch College/Institute of Open Education in Cambridge, Massachusetts. In 1995 she earned a Certificate of Advanced Educational Studies (CAES) in Reading Education from Boston College. She has been teaching in Boston since 1978, most recently at the Muriel S. Snowden International School where until 1997 she taught theater arts, English, and developmental reading courses and where from 1996 to 1997, she chaired the Department of Language Arts/Arts. Currently, Jane is the Senior Coordinator of English Language Arts for Grades 6–12 for the Boston Public Schools.

Elizabeth Swanson Goldberg is a Dissertation Fellow at Miami University of Ohio. She has presented her work in the areas of Women's Studies, American Literature, and Postcolonialism at conferences such as the U.S./China Joint International Conference on Women's Issues in Beijing, China; the Midwest Modern Language Association; the Furious Flower Conference on African American Poetry; and the conference on 20th Century Literature. She currently teaches literature and writing at Fisher College.

Jerry W. Ward, Jr., Lawrence Durgin Professor of Literature at Tougaloo College, is a literary critic and poet whose works have appeared in a number of journals and anthologies. He received the 1997 Humanities Scholar Award from the Mississippi Humanities Council. Co-editor of the *Richard Wright Newsletter,* his most recent work is *Trouble the Water: 250 Years of African American Poetry* (Mentor 1997). His works-in-progress include *Hollis Watkins: An Oral Autobiography* and *Reading Race, Reading America,* a collection of social and literary essays.

⊟: INDEX :⊟